*D*ear Friends of MAGNIFICAT,

One priest subscriber writes, "The best I ever got for $39.95 is MAGNIFICAT. It is superb, and I use it daily. But where do you get all the saints and blesseds unknown to me, at least? I enjoy these so much."

This is a question we hear often – "Where do you find all these saints?" MAGNIFICAT is blessed to have the help of a young man named James Monti. James is an expert researcher and a scholar in Church history. He has published highly regarded books on the life of Saint Thomas More, The King's Good Servant But God's First (Ignatius Press, 1997) and on the history and traditions of Holy Week, The Week of Salvation (Our Sunday Visitor, 1993). And more are on the way!

Each month, James painstakingly pores over ancient Church documents in their original Latin in search of new stories of the saints. He then translates his findings, and works that research into his exquisite prose that comes to you in Saints of Today and Yesterday. *Many readers comment on how much they enjoy the saints of MAGNIFICAT, and how inspiring the saints' lives are for their own lives of faith. Now you know who to thank!*

Happy Fourth of July and a blessed summertime!

God bless you,

Father Peter John Cameron, O.P.

2

EDITORIAL

Peter John Cameron, O.P.

A S THE MOTHER OF THE MOTHER OF GOD, Saint Ann was the Grandmother of God. It is said that the words "nana" and "nanny" are derived from the name Ann. In Hebrew, "Anna" means "God has given a grace." Saint John Damascene exclaims: "O Mother of God, blessed the arms which carried you and the lips that delighted in your innocent kisses, the lips of your parents." Why in particular did the lips of Saint Ann delight in the kisses of her little girl? It was not simply because Mary's kisses were innocent, but because they were Immaculate.

The Byzantine Liturgy prays: "O, Ann divinely wise, you carried in your womb the Mother of God, the Immaculate One who gave life to Life." Saint Ann was the first person to experience the grace of the Immaculate Conception: the grace by which God begins to reverse the curse of sin that condemns us to unrelenting, unspeakable anguish. One classic prayer expresses it this way: "Saint Ann, you were worthy to receive from God the supreme grace of giving life to the treasure-house of all graces, the most holy Virgin Mary." Mary is the Immaculate Conception, and the more we love and rely on Saint Ann, the more we benefit from the treasure-house of graces that she experienced in the gift of her daughter.

Saint Bridget of Sweden once wrote: "Oh! How radiantly the rising sun shone in Ann's womb when Mary's body there was brought to life by the coming of the soul." Pope John Paul II says that Mary learned how to be a mother from Saint Ann. We in turn learn how to be spiritual children by devoting ourselves to Mary and Ann's maternal care.

The great writer and preacher Ronald Knox once said, "It was winter still in all the world around, but in the quiet home where Saint Ann gave birth to her daughter, spring had begun." In our devotion to Saint Ann, spring begins again – no matter how dark and bleak and cold and lifeless our lives may seem – through our closeness to Mary, the Immaculate Conception.

Many people, besides those named Ann, Anna, Nancy, Ann Marie, etc., claim Saint Ann as their holy patroness. Tradition has it that, after Saint Ann's death, Mary Magdalene and Lazarus arranged to have Saint Ann's remains transported to France in the first century. Once they arrived, a bishop buried the remains in a cave at the town of Apt beneath a church dedicated to the Blessed Virgin. The area had all but been forgotten when the church was destroyed by invaders and left in ruins. Six hundred years later, miners working in the area uncovered the cave and discovered the long-lost relics. As a result, Saint Ann is honored as the patron saint of miners.

A hundred years ago, many parts of Europe celebrated Saint Ann's Day by holding a festival "of all Anns." Girls would get decked out and parade through the streets with their escorts. The celebration would culminate with a gala ball. The famous composer of waltzes, Johann Strauss, wrote "Ann Polkas" for the saint's festival, and Johann Sebastian Bach composed a fugue dedicated to Saint Ann that today remains a popular hymn tune.

Also, for some reason, traditionally Saint Ann is the patron saint of rain. There is a popular saying in Italy that "rain is Saint Ann's gift." In Germany, July rain was called "Saint Ann's dowry." It is alleged that when Martin Luther was caught in the infamous thunderstorm that put the fear of God in him, he prayed to Saint Ann for protection. Saint Ann is also the patron saint of married women and the patron of special aid to childless couples in obtaining children. Even more, Saint Ann is the patron saint of unmarried women looking for a husband. One ancient rhyming petition to Saint Ann goes: "I beg you, holy mother Ann,/ send me a good and loving man." But I prefer this equally old, unrhyming version: "Pray, Saint Ann, get me a man… and any old thing won't do."

There is a famous saying of past centuries: "All Anns are beautiful." Saint Ann, woman of faith, Mother of Mary, may we love your beauty and may your beauty make us truly loving.

Matrimony: Sacrament of Human Communion

Cardinal Bernard Law
Archbishop of Boston

The Second Vatican Council reminds us that "the well-being of the individual person and of both human and Christian society is closely bound up with the healthy state of conjugal and family life" (Pastoral Constitution on the Church in the Modern World. *Gaudium et spes*, 47 § 1, as cited in the Catechism of the Catholic Church, 1603). Our Blessed Lord himself teaches this truth among other places when he chose to assist at a wedding celebration in Cana of Galilee. There he changed water into wine. It was his first public miracle. Why would Jesus turn something "natural" like marriage into something "supernatural?" The answer lies in the importance of marriage and family for the well-being of the human race, and the fact that without the help of divine grace it would be difficult for men and women to sustain the kind of human communion that marriage requires.

What kind of human communion does marriage require? It is best explained in the short definition found in the Code of Canon Law. There we read what the Catholic Church believes about marriage: "The matrimonial covenant, by which a man and a woman establish between themselves a partnership of the whole of life, is by its nature ordered toward the good of the spouses and the procreation and education of offspring this covenant between baptized persons has been rais by Christ the Lord to the dignity of a sacrament" (Canon 1055 § 1, which is cited in CCC 1601). If we think for a moment of all that permanently sustaining "a partnership of the whole of life" entails, we better understand Christ's divine purpose in making the marriage of a man and woman one of his seven sacraments of salvation.

Fidelity to the covenant

What is different about marriage as a result of Christ raising it to the dignity of a sacrament? I can think of three things: First, Christian spouses receive new help in remaining faithful to the matrimonial covenant. What effectively binds husband and wife together are the sacred promises that they have exchanged. By these promises, the man and woman express before witnesses that they give themselves freely to each other, and the Church considers that this consent makes the marriage. The subject of consent brings us to a crucial element of the Church's teaching on matrimony: once made, if they are duly made, the promises constitute a mutual personal commitment that remains independent of subsequent changes in either partner's feelings about it. The suggestion that the Church could change what Christ himself teaches about the indissolubility of the sacrament of marriage and accept the judgment of civil divorce fails to appreciate the intention of the Creator that marriage forms a life-long covenant. When spouses remain faithful to each other, they fulfill both the vocation and the commandment embodied in the sacrament of marriage, and demonstrate a generous obedience to the Lord's holy will: "What therefore God has joined together, let no man put asunder" (Mt 19: 6).

The good of spouses

Second, we learn in a clear and definitive way what makes up the good of spouses. The indissolubility of marriage is not simply a matter of Church discipline, but is required by the very nature of conjugal love. Still, when the Church blesses the love of the spouses, they receive instruction in the full truth about marriage and special sacramental graces to meet their responsibilities to one another and to their children. Pope John Paul II speaks about the nuptial meaning of the body. This phrase brilliantly suggests that the plan of the Creator, not to mention his actual design, commits the affective union of the spouses, by which they constitute a communion of persons, to the service of procreation. God ordained that sexual pleasure should knit together no other kind of friendship than the chaste love that unites husband and wife. "It is not good that the man should be alone" (Gn 2: 18). There is a truth to the old adage that there are three persons who get married: the bride, the groom, and Christ himself! In every Christian marriage, the spouses love each other in Christ, and he becomes as it were the hidden friend to both husband and wife.

The gift of children

Third, the procreation and education of children. "Children are the supreme gift of marriage and contribute greatly to the good of the parents themselves" (*Gaudium et spes*, 50, § 1). Christian marriage brings a sense of being fully human, which is consummated in a special way in parenthood. Children, moreover, are experienced as a gift, since the partners in marriage cannot account for this superabundance of life as coming from themselves. This means that parents are cooperators in God's very own creative power. Only God can create a human person, one who is destined to live with him for ever. This gift comes from the Spirit of life, the creator God who can shape human history because he called the universe and all those who dwell in it out of nothing. Whatever good happens in the Church flows from the working of the Holy Spirit, and married couples receive an outpouring of his sevenfold gifts so that their hearts remain pure and full of love.

What are the ramifications of the sacrament of matrimony for the Christian believer? There are many, but I would like to emphasize one that has been re-affirmed by Pope Paul VI in *Humanae vitae*. Christian spouses should avoid succumbing to a contraceptive mentality. Contraceptive practices effectively serve to sterilize the act of sexual union. Because the inherent unchastity of contraception corrupts the human good of the married couple, it disfigures the love between husband and wife. It erodes their ability to practice conjugal charity and the other virtues indispensable for leading a happy married life. Still, the Church encourages the practice of responsible parenthood. Many married couples have expressed their profound gratitude for instruction about Natural Family Planning, and have offered personal testimony to the benefits that its practice has brought to their mutual love. The Church points the way toward strengthening the civilization of love against whatever may threaten its growth. In speaking with married couples and especially with young persons preparing for marriage, it is helpful to remind them of another phrase from the Second Vatican Council: "Authentic married love is caught up into divine love"(*Gaudium et spes*, 48, § 2 as cited in CCC 1639). Those who wish to comprehend fully the Church's special teaching on marriage will find this truth a good place to start.

The Responsorial Psalm

Sister Mary Timothea Elliot, R.S.M.

The revised *General Instruction on the Roman Missal* notes that "the liturgy of the word *must* be celebrated in such a way as to promote meditation," and to accomplish this end it counsels against any kind of haste which might impede recollection. It further recommends brief moments of silence in which the Word of God may be taken into the heart (56). The responsorial psalm, which forms an integral part of the liturgy of the word, holds a great liturgical and pastoral importance in that it significantly assists the faithful in the prayerful reception of, and meditation upon, the divine word (61). "By their silence and song the people make God's word their own (55)."

Throughout Sacred Scripture, whenever individuals or the community of God's people experience his interventions in their history, they "respond" in prayer. If the intervention is one of salvation, the response is praise, thanksgiving, or joy (Ex 15: 1-18; Jgs 5: 2-13; Is 38: 10-20). Mary offers a superb example of such a prayerful response in her *Magnificat*. If the intervention be one of chastisement or one which causes suffering, the response may be sorrow (Jgs 2: 1-5), a cry for mercy (2 Sm 24: 10-14), or a prayer of confident trust (Mk 10: 46-52). God's words and actions open a dialogue.

God addresses the hearts of his people whenever the Word of God is proclaimed in the assembly of the faithful. Whether the first Scripture reading is from the Old Testament or the New Testament, the words or events proclaimed are *actualized* in their hearing. This saving word, taken into the heart and assimilated in silent, attentive listening, calls forth a response. The responsorial psalm serves several purposes. It assists the faithful to meditate upon the Word of God; it focuses the spiritual message of the first reading in a concise way; and it elicits the appropriate sentiments (faith, hope, love, joy, contrition, trust, etc.) in response.

How is the responsorial psalm chosen?

The Sunday lectionary employs more than 80 psalms (or verses from 80 psalms) and approximately 130 of the 150 psalms appear in the complete lectionary between the first and second reading. The psalm always serves in some capacity as a "response" to the Word of

God; however, there are a variety of ways in which the psalm relates to the other readings. If, for example, the Old Testament reading, the Epistle, or even the Gospel quotes a particular psalm verse, that psalm is generally chosen as the responsorial psalm. It may then "echo" the first or second reading, or anticipate the Gospel. Often, the psalm will pick up and extend the mood of the first reading in thanksgiving, praise, or lamentation. In other cases, certain psalms have been associated with particular feasts through a long tradition: Psalm 47, "God goes up with shouts of joy," for the feast of the Ascension; Psalm 118, "This is the day the Lord has made, let us rejoice and be glad," and "The stone which the builders rejected has become the corner stone," for Easter; Psalm 72, "The kings of Arabia and Seba shall bring tribute. All Kings shall pay him homage, all nations shall serve him," for Epiphany.

How is it structured?

The responsorial psalm is composed of two distinct parts: 1) the antiphon or "responsorial" verse, which is sung or recited by the entire assembly, and 2) verses from a psalm which are sung by a cantor or meditatively read by a lector. The cantor/leader and the assembly alternate in singing or praying sets or groups of psalm verses and the antiphon. The preferred manner is that the psalm and antiphon be sung and that the congregation be seated in order to listen to the psalm as an integral part of the liturgy of the word.

How can the faithful pray the psalm better?

Saint Augustine tells us that, "He who sings prays twice," and Saint John Chrysostom admonishes us, "Let us not sing the refrains out of sheer habit, but rather take them anew every time. Each verse can teach us much wisdom." Reflecting upon the sense of the psalm and refrain in the light of the first reading enables us to experience it in a fresh way each time we hear the familiar words. How often have we had the experience of singing the psalm refrain several times and then finding that both the melody and its message lingers in mind and heart throughout the day! This certainly must have been the experience of Saint John Chrysostom. He writes: "I urge you not to leave here with empty hands, but to gather the refrains like pearls, to keep them forever with you, to meditate upon them, to sing them to all your friends and relatives" (Commentary on Psalm 41). The homilist can also assist the assembly to pray the psalm more richly by pointing out the connections between the psalm and its refrain with the other readings of the liturgy of the word.

Sister Mary Timothea Elliott, R.S.M. *is a Religious Sister of Mercy of Alma, MI, the chair of Scripture at Saint John Vianney Seminary in Denver, CO, and the author of* "The Literary Unity of the Canticle" *and* "The Song of Songs" *in the International Bible Commentary.*

Your Word is a Lamp

────── Monsignor James Turro ──────

Sooner or later suffering comes knocking at one's door but, widespread though it is in the human experience, its meaning remains for many obscure – an unyielding mystery. Yet, as with everything else that transpires in life, there must be a divine purpose that is achieved by it. This may be what the long-standing axiom seeks to express: God writes straight with crooked lines. Saint Paul's reflections on the subject are helpful in throwing light on the Christian's experience of suffering.

Saint Paul and suffering

Paul, as it seems, has given much thought to the phenomenon of suffering. Most likely his own bitter experience of pain gave him a strong incentive to think those thoughts.

Along with the Jewish and early Christian traditions Paul believed that one's sufferings were compensated at the end of the age. Daniel gave eloquent expression to this notion: "at that time your people shall be delivered, even everyone whose name is found written in the book. And many of those who sleep in the land of dust shall awake, some to everlasting life, and others to everlasting reproach and contempt." Suffering as experienced by the just will be vindicated and remunerated. This fact infuses meaning into suffering because, when all is said and done, the agonies of the just will be recompensed.

Paul pinpoints all this for the Thessalonians. He remarks how they received his words with much pain but he goes on to assure them that in the end when the Lord Jesus comes, he will deliver them from the wrath to come. This is to say that their present woes in the end will be avenged. Suffering at the present moment has meaning in view of a future vindication.

Suffering for the Gospel

Paul finds a second explanation of suffering, namely suffering for the Gospel. He details this point of view on suffering (2 Cor 6: 1-6): "As servants of God we commend ourselves in every way through great endurance, in affliction, hardships, calamities, beatings, imprisonment, tumults, labors, watching, hunger…" In other words pain and hardship take on significance when endured for the sake of preaching the Gospel.

Another facet of human suffering Paul finds in its assimilation to the suffering of Jesus. Through suffering, a Christian's life comes to resemble ever more the suffering Christ. Suffering can become a window through which the life of Christ is perceived in the life of the Christian. "We are afflicted in every way… always carrying in the body the death of Jesus so that the life of Jesus may be manifested in our mortal flesh" (2 Cor 4: 7-12).

Transformation

Finally Paul views human suffering as a way in which the Christian can be changed for the better, a transformation, a process of refinement, so to say. Suffering can be the opening through which the transforming power of God enters into a human life to raise it to a higher exponent.

To be sure, none of these insights removes the sting of suffering – nor is it meant to do so but rather it is meant to throw light on the meaning of Christian suffering and indeed on the meaning of one's life as a whole. Adversity introduces a man to himself or as C. S. Lewis has written: "God whispers in our pleasures but shouts in our pains."

Blessings

Blessings to Know and Do God's Will _____

"The world and its enticement are passing away. But whoever does the will of God remains forever." (1 Jn 2: 17)

Place before the Lord all the decisions that must be made and all matters needing discernment.

HYMN
Meter: 84 84 88 84
This hymn can be sung to the tune used for
Day is Done

In the just reward of labor,
God's will be done;
In the help we give our neighbor,
God's will be done;
In the worldwide task of caring
For the hungry and despairing,
In the harvests we are sharing,
God's will be done.

OPENING PRAYER

Leader: Lord, in the garden of Gethsemane the night before you died, you warned your disciples that the spirit is willing, but the flesh is weak. We long to be one with you in your self-sacrifice to the Father. And so we pray for the strength to keep watch with you, to take up our cross, and to renounce our willfulness so that God's will, and not our own, may be done in our life now and at every moment. We ask this in your holy name. Amen.

Sunday:

Word of God   Romans 12: 2

DO NOT CONFORM yourself to this age but be transformed by the renewal of your mind, that you may discern what is the will of God, what is good and pleasing and perfect.

Monday:

Word of God   Ephesians 5: 17

DO NOT CONTINUE in ignorance, but try to understand what is the will of the Lord.

Tuesday:

Word of God   Colossians 1: 9; 4: 12b

THEREFORE, from the day we heard this, we do not cease praying for you and asking that you may be filled with the knowledge of God's will through all spiritual wisdom and understanding... so that you may be perfect and fully assured in all the will of God.

Wednesday:

Word of God   1 Thessalonians 4: 3; 5: 16-18

THIS IS THE WILL OF GOD, your holiness: that you refrain from immorality... Rejoice always. Pray without ceasing. In all circumstances give thanks, for this is the will of God for you in Christ Jesus.

Thursday:

Word of God   Hebrews 10: 36; 13: 20-21

YOU NEED ENDURANCE to do the will of God and receive what he has promised... May the God of peace, who brought up from the dead the great shepherd of the sheep by the blood of the eternal covenant, Jesus our Lord, furnish you with all that is good, that you may do his will. May he carry out in you what is pleasing to him through Jesus Christ, to whom be glory forever [and ever]. Amen.

Friday:

Word of God   1 Peter 4: 1-2, 19

THEREFORE, SINCE CHRIST suffered in the flesh, arm yourselves also with the same attitude (for whoever suffers in the flesh has broken with sin), so as not to spend what remains of one's life in the flesh on human desires, but on the will of God... As a result, those who suffer in accord with God's will hand their souls over to a faithful creator as they do good.

Saturday:

Word of God   1 Peter 2: 13-15; 3: 17

BE SUBJECT to every human institution for the Lord's

sake, whether it be to the king as supreme or to governors as sent by him for the punishment of evildoers and the approval of those who do good. For it is the will of God that by doing good you may silence the ignorance of foolish people... For it is better to suffer for doing good, if that be the will of God, than for doing evil.

LITANY OF RESIGNATION TO THE WILL OF GOD

Lord, have mercy on us.
Christ, have mercy on us.
Lord, have mercy on us. Jesus, hear us.
Jesus, graciously hear us.
God the Father, who has created me,
Holy be your will.
God the Son, who has redeemed me,
Not my will but yours be done.
God the Holy Spirit, who has offered sanctification,
Blessed be the most sweet will of God.

You who know and foresee all things,
Have mercy on us.
You who govern and rule all things,
Have mercy on us.
You who, according to your inscrutable designs,
effect all things in a wonderful manner,
Have mercy on us.
You who permit evil in order then to derive
good for the salvation of the elect,
Have mercy on us.

In all things and in all possible events,
Your holy will be done, O my God.
In all circumstances and disgraces,
Your holy will be done, O my God.

In my state and employment,
Your holy will be done, O my God.
In my affairs and occupations,
etc.
In all my actions,
In my health and strength,
In my body and soul,
In my life and death,
In myself and in those who belong to me,
In all men and angels,
In all creatures,
In all parts of the earth,
At all times,
For all eternity,
Although weak nature complains,
Although it costs much to self-love and sensuality,
Solely and only through love for you and your good
    pleasure,
Because you are my Creator,
Because you are the Supreme Lord of all things,
Because you are infinite perfection, therefore do I say,
    with all the saints in Heaven,

With the Blessed Virgin Mary,
Your holy will be done, O my God.
With Jesus in the Garden of Olives,
Your holy will be done, O my God.

Our Father...

℣ May the just, most amiable will of God be done in
   all things.
℟ *May it be praised and magnified forever! Amen.*

Let us pray:

Grant me your grace, O Father, that perfect resignation to your holy will may be with me, and labor with me, and continue with me to the end. Grant me always to desire and will that which is most acceptable to you and which pleases you best. Let your will be mine, and let my will always follow yours and agree perfectly with it. Let me always will and not will the same with you; let me not be able to will or not will anything except what you will or will not.

℟ Amen.

PRAYER OF ABANDONMENT TO GOD'S WILL

"O God of Love! Take my memory and all its memories, take my intelligence so that it will act only for your greatest glory; take my will entirely, so that it will forever be drowned in your own; never again what I want, O my sweet Jesus, but always what you want; receive me, guide me, sanctify me, direct me; to you I abandon myself… Lord, take and sanctify all my words, all my actions, all my desires. Be for my soul its good and its all. To you I give and abandon it. I accept with love all that you send me: pain, sorrow, joy, consolation, dryness, shame, desertion, scorn, humiliation, work, suffering, trials, everything that comes to me from you, everything that you wish, O Jesus. I submit humbly to the glorious control of your providence in supporting me solely by the help of your immense goodness; I promise you the most sincere fidelity. I implore you to accept all of my offering, and I will then be happy and trusting. In you alone I wish to live so that in you alone I may die."

Marthe Robin

Compiled by Peter John Cameron, O.P.

Blessings for the Table

GRACE BEFORE THE MEAL:

O God, you dispel the darkness of our lives
with the shining glory of the resurrection of your Son.
Bless this food and drink which you provide for us,
that being renewed in body and soul,
we may serve you with holiness of life,
through Christ our Lord.

℟   **Amen.**

GRACE AFTER THE MEAL:

O God, our Father,
we come to you at the close of this meal in thanksgiving,
for you are the provider of our souls and bodies.
Shine in the darkness of our night
and forgive our sins and failings.
Through Christ our Lord.

℟   **Amen.**

℣   Let us bless the Lord.
℟   **Thanks be to God.**

Brother Victor-Antoine d'Avila-Latourrette

Hymn of the month

Jesu dulcis memoria

J E- su dulcis memó-ri- a, Dans ve-ra cor-di gáu-
Nil cá- ni- tur su- á-vi- us, Nil audi- tur ju- cún-

di- a : Sed super mel et ómni- a, E- jus dul- cis præ-
di- us, Nil cogi- tá- tur dúl- ci- us, Quam Je- sus De- i

sénti- a.
Fí- li- us.

Sweet is the memory of Jesus   (Ps 48: 9-10; Is 26: 8-9)
giving true joys to the heart;
but above honey and all things   (Sir 24: 27)
is his sweet presence.

Nothing sweeter is sung,   (Ps 135: 3)
nothing more pleasant is heard,   (Song 2: 14)
nothing more lovely is thought,   (Song 4: 1)
than Jesus, the Son of God.

Iesu spes poenitentibus,
Quam pius es petentibus!
Quam bonus te quaerentibus!
Sed quid invenientibus?

O Jesus, hope of penitents,   (Sir 17: 20)
how kind you are to those who pray.   (Mt 7: 7)
How good to those who seek you.   (Lam 3: 25)
But what to those who find you!   (Prv 8: 35)

> *Nec lingua valet dicere,*
> *Nec littera exprimere:*
> *Expertus potest credere,*
> *Quid sit Iesum diligere.*

No tongue can tell,
nor written word express it;
only one having experienced it,
can imagine what it is to love Jesus.   (1 Cor 2: 9)

> *Sis Iesu nostrum gaudium,*
> *Qui es futurus praemium:*
> *Sit nostra in te gloria,*
> *Per cuncta semper saecula.*

O Jesus be our joy,
you who are to be our reward;   (Gn 15: 1)
in you be our glory
through everlasting ages.

Translated by Thomas Aquinas Byrnes, O.P.

Marian Antiphon

Post partum, * Virgo, inviolata permansisti: Dei Génitrix, intercéde pro nobis.

After giving birth, you remained a virgin inviolate:
O Mother of God, intercede for us.

Prayer at Night

Options for July 2001

Prayer at Night is traditionally a short prayer, with fewer variations than the Prayers for Morning and Evening, so that, if desired, it can be memorized. People have most often prayed it alone immediately before retiring for the night. Families or other groups might also want to pray it together.

Two options are suggested for this month.

[OPTION 1]

God, come to my assistance.
Lord, make haste to help me.

Glory to the Father, and to the Son,
and to the Holy Spirit, as it was in the beginning,
is now, and will be for ever. Amen. Alleluia!

Examination of Conscience/Penitential Rite (optional)

Reflect in silence on the ways in which you have allowed yourself to become over-involved in work or social activities to the detriment of prayer and charity, especially when your pace has made you restless and impatient with others.

If several people are praying together, a penitential rite may be used:

I confess to almighty God,
and to you, my brothers and sisters,
that I have sinned through my own fault
in my thoughts and in my words,
in what I have done, and in what I have failed to do;

and I ask blessed Mary, ever virgin,
all the angels and saints,
and you, my brothers and sisters,
to pray for me to the Lord our God.

May almighty God have mercy on us, forgive us our sins,
and bring us to life everlasting. Amen.

HYMN   Meter: CM
                        This hymn can be sung to the tune of
                              O God, Our Help in Ages Past

O Christ, you are the light and day
Which drives away the night,
The ever shining Sun of God
And pledge of future light.

As now the ev'ning shadows fall
Please grant us, Lord, we pray,
A quiet night to rest in you
Until the break of day.

Regard, O Lord, our helplessness
And come to our defense;
May we be governed by your love,
In true obedience.

PSALM 119   145-152

I came into the world as light, so that everyone who believes in me
might not remain in darkness. (Jn 12: 46)

Nightfall can be the moment at which all the evils of the day, real and
imagined, crowd around and beset us, as the storm beset the disciples on the sea. All we need do is call upon Christ our light, and he
will come and say to us: "Do not be afraid."

I call with all my heart; Lord, hear me,
I will keep your statutes.

I call upon you, save me
and I will do your will.

I rise before dawn and cry for help,
I hope in your word.
My eyes watch through the night
to ponder your promise.

In your love hear my voice, O Lord;
give me life by your decrees.
Those who harm me unjustly draw near:
they are far from your law.

But you, O Lord, are close:
your commands are truth.
Long have I known that your will
is established for ever.

Glory to the Father...

Word of God   Mark 6: 47-48, 50

WHEN IT WAS EVENING, the boat was far out on the sea and he was alone on shore. Then he saw that they were tossed about while rowing, for the wind was against them. But at once he spoke with them, "Take courage, it is I, do not be afraid!"

> *Into your hands I commend my spirit.*
> *It is you who will redeem me, Lord.*
> (Ps 31: 6)

CANTICLE OF SIMEON   (Text, back cover D)
Protect us, Lord, as we stay awake; watch over us as we sleep, that awake, we may keep watch with Christ, and asleep, rest in his peace.

PRAYER

Lord Jesus Christ, light in our darkness, peace in our storms, protection against all that frightens us, calm our hearts that we may rest in peace in your presence through this night, who live and reign with God the Father and the Holy Spirit, one God for ever and ever. Amen.

BLESSING

May the Lord grant a peaceful night and a perfect end to us and to all our absent sisters and brothers. Amen.

MARIAN ANTIPHON   (Text, page 25)

[OPTION 2]

God, come to my assistance.
Lord, make haste to help me.

Glory to the Father, and to the Son,
and to the Holy Spirit, as it was in the beginning,
is now, and will be for ever. Amen. Alleluia!

Examination of Conscience/Penitential Rite (optional)

Reflect in silence on the past day or week. How has God acted in your life? How have you accepted or resisted his help?

If several people are praying together, a penitential rite may be used:

Lamb of God, you take away the sins of the world, have mercy on us.

Lamb of God, you take away the sins of the world, have mercy on us.

Lamb of God, you take away the sins of the world, grant us peace.

May almighty God have mercy on us, forgive us our sins, and bring us to life everlasting. Amen.

HYMN Meter: CM

O God, our help in ages past,
Our hope for years to come,
Our shelter from the stormy blast,
And our eternal home!

Under the shadow of your throne
Your saints have dwelt secure;
Sufficient is your arm alone,
And our defense is sure.

PSALM 121

The hand of the Lord will rest on this mountain. (Is 25: 10)

Our help comes from the Lord Jesus Christ crucified upon Mount Calvary for our salvation. In his shelter, we can face with confidence the approaching night.

I lift up my eyes to the mountains:
from where shall come my help?
My help shall come from the Lord
who made heaven and earth.

May he never allow you to stumble!
Let him sleep not, your guard.
No, he sleeps not nor slumbers,
Israel's guard.

The Lord is your guard and your shade;
at your right side he stands.
By day the sun shall not smite you
nor the moon in the night.

The Lord will guard you from evil,
he will guard your soul.

The Lord will guard your going and coming
both now and for ever.

Glory to the Father…

Word of God   Isaiah 11: 9

THERE SHALL BE no harm nor ruin on all my holy mountain; for the earth shall be filled with knowledge of the Lord, as water covers the sea.

> *Into your hands I commend my spirit.*
> *It is you who will redeem me, Lord.*
> *(Ps 31: 6)*

CANTICLE OF SIMEON   (Text, back cover D)

Protect us, Lord, as we stay awake; watch over us as we sleep, that awake, we may keep watch with Christ, and asleep, rest in his peace.

PRAYER

Lord Jesus Christ, your cross stands upon Mount Calvary as our guard and our shade, our shield and protection. Guard and keep us through this night until morning breaks, for you live and reign with the Father and the Holy Spirit, one God for ever and ever. Amen.

BLESSING

May the Lord grant a peaceful night and a perfect end to us and to all our absent sisters and brothers. Amen.

MARIAN ANTIPHON   (Text, page 25)

Word of God

for a Sunday

Luke 9: 51-62

"**F**oxes have dens..." Jesus warns the would-be disciple of the high cost of discipleship. Animals and birds are more advantageously situated than the disciple of Christ who must live as the Master lives, unhoused and otherwise unprovided for. In point of fact the same high degree of self-sacrifice is asked of the modern day follower of Christ.

Monsignor James Turro

▪ Suggested Prayer of the Faithful ▪

(Each local community should compose its own Universal Prayer, but may find inspiration in the texts proposed here.)

Let us offer our petitions to the Father in union with his Son Jesus Christ our Lord, who has called us to be his followers and to proclaim his kingdom to the world.

That the Church may respond in faith and love to the call of Christ our Lord by carrying the message of the Good News of the kingdom of God to all the nations of the world, especially those who have never heard the truths of the Gospel.

That our Holy Father may be encouraged by the loyal support of his fellow bishops in the work of evangelization.

That our country may celebrate the freedom that Christ won for us, the freedom for excellence that chooses to live by the beatitudes he gave us.

For those who are enslaved by poverty, addictions, or any form of injustice, that they may receive compassionate assistance in their need and attain to the freedom of God's children.

That in the face of all difficulties we may freely choose life and so find fulfillment for ourselves and for all whose lives we touch.

That in this season of vacations we may find rest for body and soul in the beauty of our woods, mountains, lakes, and seacoasts, as we discover anew God's lavish gifts to us.

For the children of our country, that they may grow in grace and joy, experiencing the warmth of God's love for them in the setting of family life.

Heavenly Father, you have given us in Christ your Son the gift of freedom. Grant that we may embrace this gift and freely share it with our brothers and sisters who do not know you. We ask it through the same Christ, our Lord.

SUNDAY, JULY 1
Thirteenth Sunday in Ordinary Time

Prayer for the Morning

Who is like to God, magnificent in holiness?
Come, let us adore!

Glory to the Father, and to the Son,
and to the Holy Spirit, as it was in the beginning,
is now, and will be for ever. Amen. Alleluia!

HYMN   Meter: 87 87 D
This hymn can be sung to the tune used for
Praise the Lord, Ye Heavens Adore Him

Praise the Lord, for he is glorious;
Never shall his promise fail.
God hath made his saints victorious;
Sin and death shall not prevail.
Praise the God of our salvation;
Hosts on high, his power proclaim.
Heaven and earth and all creation,
Laud and magnify his Name.

Worship, honor, glory, blessing,
Lord, we offer unto thee.
Young and old, thy praise expressing,
In glad homage bend the knee.
All the saints in heaven adore thee;
We would bow before thy throne.
As thine angels serve before thee,
So on earth thy will be done.

CANTICLE   Exodus 15: 2, 11a, 13, 17-18

Through the blood of Jesus we have confidence of entrance into the
sanctuary. (Heb 10: 19)

Just as God led the people of Israel through sea and desert to worship in his holy dwelling place, the temple on Mount Zion, so Jesus Christ leads us, his people, through his death and resurrection, to worship in his dwelling place, the Church, in anticipation of the day when we hope to dwell with him for ever in glory.

My strength and my courage is the Lord,
and he has been my savior.
He is my God, I praise him;
the God of my father, I extol him.

Who is like to you among the gods, O Lord?
Who is like to you, magnificent in holiness?

In your mercy you led the people you redeemed;
in your strength you guided them to your holy dwelling.

And you brought them in and planted them on the
    mountain of your inheritance –
the place where you made your seat, O Lord,
the sanctuary, O Lord, which your hands established.
The Lord shall reign forever and ever.

Glory to the Father...

Word of God   Exodus 20: 24

An altar of earth you shall make for me, and upon it you shall sacrifice your holocausts and peace offerings, your sheep and your oxen. In whatever place I choose for the remembrance of my name I will come to you and bless you.

The Lord is our savior;
we shall sing to stringed instruments
in the house of the Lord all the days of our life.
(Is 38: 20)

CANTICLE OF ZECHARIAH   (Text, back cover B)
We who are receiving the unshakable kingdom should have
gratitude, with which we should offer worship pleasing to God in
reverence and awe. (Heb 12: 28)

INTERCESSIONS

On this day made holy by the death and resurrection of
Jesus Christ, let us offer the worship of hearts raised in
confident faith, asking:

℟   Hear your people, Lord!

You led your people from slavery to freedom:
– grant to all believers the freedom to worship you without fear in every nation of the world redeemed by your
love. ℟

You brought your people into your holy dwelling place:
– gather all believers into your presence in prayer and
praise this day. ℟

You are present to your people as we come to worship
you:
– bring into the light of your eternal presence all those
who have died. ℟

Personal intentions

Our Father…

O Lord our God, you have set aside this day of worship
and called it holy. Make holy your people as we gather in
gratitude to offer you our worship through Jesus Christ,
your Son, our Lord, who lives and reigns with you and
the Holy Spirit, one God for ever and ever. Amen.

MASS
Thirteenth Sunday in Ordinary Time

ENTRANCE ANTIPHON

All nations, clap your hands. Shout with a voice of joy to God. (Ps 46: 2)

GLORIA ———————————————————— page 226

OPENING PRAYER

Father,
you call your children
to walk in the light of Christ.
Free us from darkness
and keep us in the radiance of your truth.
We ask this through our Lord Jesus Christ, your Son,
who lives and reigns with you and the Holy Spirit,
one God, for ever and ever.

ALTERNATIVE OPENING PRAYER

Father in heaven,
the light of Jesus
has scattered the darkness of hatred and sin.
Called to that light
we ask for your guidance.
Form our lives in your truth, our hearts in your love.
We ask this through Christ our Lord.

● *Then Elisha left and followed Elijah as his attendant.* ●

A reading from
the first Book of Kings   19: 16b, 19-21

THE LORD SAID TO Elijah: "You shall anoint Elisha, son of Shaphat of Abel-meholah, as prophet to succeed you."

Elijah set out and came upon Elisha, son of Shaphat, as he was plowing with twelve yoke of oxen; he was fol-

lowing the twelfth. Elijah went over to him and threw
his cloak over him. Elisha left the oxen, ran after Elijah,
and said, "Please, let me kiss my father and mother
goodbye, and I will follow you." Elijah answered, "Go
back! Have I done anything to you?" Elisha left him and,
taking the yoke of oxen, slaughtered them; he used the
plowing equipment for fuel to boil their flesh, and gave
it to his people to eat. Then Elisha left and followed
Elijah as his attendant.

The word of the Lord.

───── • PSALM 16 • ─────

℟ (cf. 5a) **You are my inheritance, O Lord.**

Keep me, O God, for in you I take refuge;
    I say to the LORD, "My LORD are you.
O LORD, my allotted portion and my cup,
    you it is who hold fast my lot." ℟

I bless the LORD who counsels me;
    even in the night my heart exhorts me.
I set the LORD ever before me;
    with him at my right hand I shall not be disturbed. ℟

Therefore my heart is glad and my soul rejoices,
    my body, too, abides in confidence
because you will not abandon my soul to the
        netherworld,
    nor will you suffer your faithful one to undergo
        corruption. ℟

You will show me the path to life,
    fullness of joys in your presence,
    the delights at your right hand forever. ℟

● *You were called for freedom.* ●

A reading from
the Letter of Saint Paul to the Galatians   5: 1, 13-18

BROTHERS AND SISTERS: For freedom Christ set us free; so stand firm and do not submit again to the yoke of slavery.

For you were called for freedom, brothers and sisters. But do not use this freedom as an opportunity for the flesh; rather, serve one another through love. For the whole law is fulfilled in one statement, namely, *You shall love your neighbor as yourself.* But if you go on biting and devouring one another, beware that you are not consumed by one another.

I say, then: live by the Spirit and you will certainly not gratify the desire of the flesh. For the flesh has desires against the Spirit, and the Spirit against the flesh; these are opposed to each other, so that you may not do what you want. But if you are guided by the Spirit, you are not under the law.

The word of the Lord.

Alleluia, alleluia. Speak, Lord, your servant is listening; you have the words of everlasting life. Alleluia, alleluia.

● *He resolutely determined to journey to Jerusalem. I will follow you wherever you go.* ●

A reading from
the holy Gospel according to Luke   9: 51-62

WHEN THE DAYS for Jesus' being taken up were fulfilled, he resolutely determined to journey to Jerusalem, and he sent messengers ahead of him. On the way they entered a Samaritan village to prepare for his reception there, but they would not welcome him because the destination of his journey was Jerusalem. When the disciples James and John saw this they asked, "Lord, do you want us to call down fire from heaven to consume them?" Jesus turned and rebuked them, and they journeyed to another village.

As they were proceeding on their journey someone said to him, "I will follow you wherever you go." Jesus answered him, "Foxes have dens and birds of the sky have nests, but the Son of Man has nowhere to rest his head." And to another he said, "Follow me." But he replied, "Lord, let me go first and bury my father." But he answered him, "Let the dead bury their dead. But you, go and proclaim the kingdom of God." And another said, "I will follow you, Lord, but first let me say farewell to my family at home." To him Jesus said, "No one who sets a hand to the plow and looks to what was left behind is fit for the kingdom of God."
The Gospel of the Lord.

CREDO ———————————————————————— page 227

PRAYER OVER THE GIFTS
Lord God,
through your sacraments
you give us the power of your grace.
May this Eucharist
help us to serve you faithfully.
We ask this in the name of Jesus the Lord.

PREFACE OF SUNDAYS IN ORDINARY TIME ————— page 231

COMMUNION ANTIPHON
O, bless the Lord, my soul, and all that is within me bless his holy name. (Ps 102: 1)

Or:

Father, I pray for them: may they be one in us, so that the world may believe it was you who sent me. (Jn 17: 20-21)

PRAYER AFTER COMMUNION

Lord,
may this sacrifice and communion
give us a share in your life
and help us bring your love to the world.
Grant this through Christ our Lord.

D A Y   B Y   D A Y

Putting Our Hand to the Plow

Suffer courageously even to the point of death, and this will be a sign to me that you love me in truth. Nor must you let human respect or troubles make you look back at what you have already plowed. Rather, rejoice in your troubles. The world makes sport of heaping insults upon me, and you will be saddened in the world when you see them insult me. For when they offend me they offend you, and when they offend you they offend me, since I have become one thing with you.

Think of it! I gifted you with my image and likeness. And when you lost the life of grace through sin, to restore it to you I united my nature with you, hiding it in your humanity. I had made you in my image; now I took your image by assuming a human form. So I am one thing with you – except if a soul leaves me through deadly sin. But those who love me live in me and I live in them. This is why the world persecutes them. The world has no likeness to me, so it persecuted my only-begotten Son even to the shameful death of the cross, and so it persecutes you. Because it has no love for me, the world persecutes you and will persecute you even to the point of death; for if the world had loved me, it would love you as well. Yet be glad, because in heaven your joy will be complete.

SAINT CATHERINE OF SIENA

Saint Catherine († 1380) was a Dominican sister, mystic, and papal counselor.

Prayer for the Evening

Let us bless the Lord of life!

*Glory to the Father, and to the Son,
and to the Holy Spirit, as it was in the beginning,
is now, and will be for ever. Amen. Alleluia!*

HYMN
Meter: CM
This hymn can be sung to the tune used for
Let Saints on Earth in Concert Sing

O Christ, our hope, our hearts' desire,
Redemption's only spring:
Creator of the world art thou,
Its Savior and its King.

For now the bonds of death are burst,
The ransom has been paid;
And thou art on thy Father's throne
In glorious robes arrayed.

Christ Jesus, be our present joy,
Our future great reward;
Our only glory may it be
To glory in the Lord.

PSALM 115   1-4, 11-12a, 13, 17-18

Christ in you is the hope for glory! (cf. Col 1: 27)

As evening falls, and the shadow of death grows darker, let us
remember the true God who delivers from death, lest we place our
hope in the empty promises of dead ideas, lifeless messiahs, or easy
escapes, rather than in the death and resurrection of Jesus Christ,
our risen and glorious Lord.

Not to us, Lord, not to us,
but to your name give the glory
for the sake of your love and your truth,
lest the heathen say: "Where is their God?"

But our God is in the heavens;
he does whatever he wills.
Their idols are silver and gold,
the work of human hands.

You who fear him, trust in the Lord;
he is their help and their shield.
He remembers us, and he will bless us.
The Lord will bless those who fear him,
the little no less than the great.

The dead shall not praise the Lord,
nor those who go down into the silence.
But we who live bless the Lord
now and for ever. Amen.

Glory to the Father...

Word of God   2 Corinthians 1: 9-10

WE HAD ACCEPTED within
ourselves the sentence of
death, that we might trust not in ourselves but in God
who raises the dead. He rescued us from such great dan-
ger of death, and he will continue to rescue us; in him
we have put our hope [that] he will also rescue us again.

Rejoice in hope!
(Rom 12: 12)

CANTICLE OF MARY   (Text, back cover A)
This is the promise that he made us: eternal life. (1 Jn 2: 25)

INTERCESSIONS

To the living Christ, who never ceases to make intercession for us, let us make our prayer:

℟   Lord of glory, hear us!

O Christ, light and salvation of the world,
– pour out your Holy Spirit, the breath of life, on all those who confess their faith in your resurrection. ℞

O Christ, pillar of fire in this world's desert,
– illumine all the world with your light. ℞

O Christ, victor over sin and death,
– open to our brothers and sisters the gates of paradise. ℞

Personal intentions

Our Father…

The grace of the Lord Jesus be with us. Amen. (cf. 1 Cor 16: 23)

MARIAN ANTIPHON   (Text, page 25)

MONDAY, JULY 2

Prayer for the Morning

Be still and know the Lord: in peace, let us pray!

Glory to the Father, and to the Son,
and to the Holy Spirit, as it was in the beginning,
is now, and will be for ever. Amen. Alleluia!

HYMN
Meter: 87 87 D
This hymn can be sung to the tune used for
Come, Thou Fount of Ev'ry Blessing

Glorious things of thee are spoken,
Zion, city of our God;
He, whose word cannot be broken,
Formed thee for his own abode.
On the Rock of Ages founded,
What can shake thy sure repose?
With salvation's walls surrounded,
Thou mayst smile at all thy foes.

See, the streams of living waters,
Springing from eternal love,
Well supply thy sons and daughters,
And all fear of want remove.
Who can faint while such a river
Ever flows their thirst to assuage?
Grace which like the Lord, the giver,
Never fails from age to age.

PSALM 46

By waiting and by calm you shall be saved, in quiet and in trust your
strength lies. (Is 30: 15b)

God in his power is refuge and strength; God in his mercy is the river
that refreshes the soul; God in his beauty stills all our useless strug-
gles and gathers us into his peace.

God is for us a refuge and strength,
a helper close at hand, in time of distress:
so we shall not fear though the earth should rock,
though the mountains fall into the depths of the sea,
even though its waters rage and foam,
even though the mountains be shaken by its waves.

R̷ The Lord of hosts is with us:
    the God of Jacob is our stronghold.

The waters of a river give joy to God's city,
the holy place where the Most High dwells.
God is within, it cannot be shaken;
God will help it at the dawning of the day.
Nations are in tumult, kingdoms are shaken:
he lifts his voice, the earth shrinks away. R̷

Come, consider the works of the Lord,
the redoubtable deeds he has done on the earth.
He puts an end to wars over all the earth;
the bow he breaks, the spear he snaps.
He burns the shields with fire.
"Be still and know that I am God,
supreme among the nations, supreme on the earth!" R̷

Glory to the Father...

Word of God   Isaiah 49: 5

THE LORD HAS SPOKEN who
formed me as his servant
from the womb, that Jacob may be brought back to him
and Israel gathered to him; and I am made glorious in
the sight of the Lord, and my God is now my strength!

The kingdom of God is within you!
(cf. Lk 17: 21)

CANTICLE OF ZECHARIAH   (Text, back cover B)
The Lord himself will fight for you; you have only to keep still.
(Ex 14: 14)

INTERCESSIONS

Let us lay all our needs in the merciful hands of God:

℞   Grant peace, O Lord.

You are a helper close at hand in times of distress:
– grant peace of heart to all who are troubled and
afraid. ℞

You are in our midst when life's ills assail us:
– keep our hearts fixed on you amid all disturbances. ℞

Your word is the river of life which gives joy to your
people:
– refresh in prayer all who are burdened. ℞

You put an end to war and to the weapons of war:
– teach us to lay aside all quarrels and attacks on our
neighbors. ℞

Personal intentions

Our Father…

Almighty and ever-living God, your Word is the rock in
which we take refuge against all outward disturbance
and inner turmoil. Pour forth upon your people the
refreshing stream of living water which wells up from
the heart of your Son, that we may dwell together in
inward and outward peace, through the same Jesus
Christ our Lord, who lives and reigns with you and the
Holy Spirit, one God for ever and ever. Amen.

Mass

Monday of the Thirteenth Week of the Year

(The prayers suggested today are those of the Thirteenth Week in Ordinary Time.)

ENTRANCE ANTIPHON

All nations, clap your hands. Shout with a voice of joy to God.
(Ps 46: 2)

OPENING PRAYER

Father,
you call your children
to walk in the light of Christ.
Free us from darkness
and keep us in the radiance of your truth.
We ask this through our Lord Jesus Christ, your Son,
who lives and reigns with you and the Holy Spirit,
one God, for ever and ever.

● *Are you going to destroy the just man with the sinner?* ●

A reading from
the Book of Genesis   18: 16-33

THE MEN SET OUT from the valley of Mamre and looked down toward Sodom; Abraham was walking with them, to see them on their way. The Lord reflected: "Shall I hide from Abraham what I am about to do, now that he is to become a great and populous nation, and all the nations of the earth are to find blessing in him? Indeed, I have singled him out that he may direct his sons and his posterity to keep the way of the Lord by doing what is right and just, so that the Lord may carry into effect for Abraham the promises he made about him." Then the Lord said: "The outcry against Sodom and

Gomorrah is so great, and their sin so grave, that I must go down and see whether or not their actions fully correspond to the cry against them that comes to me. I mean to find out."

While the two men walked on farther toward Sodom, the Lord remained standing before Abraham. Then Abraham drew nearer to him and said: "Will you sweep away the innocent with the guilty? Suppose there were fifty innocent people in the city; would you wipe out the place, rather than spare it for the sake of the fifty innocent people within it? Far be it from you to do such a thing, to make the innocent die with the guilty, so that the innocent and the guilty would be treated alike! Should not the judge of all the world act with justice?" The Lord replied, "If I find fifty innocent people in the city of Sodom, I will spare the whole place for their sake." Abraham spoke up again: "See how I am presuming to speak to my Lord, though I am but dust and ashes! What if there are five less than fifty innocent people? Will you destroy the whole city because of those five?" "I will not destroy it," he answered, "if I find forty-five there." But Abraham persisted, saying, "What if only forty are found there?" He replied, "I will forbear doing it for the sake of the forty." Then he said, "Let not my Lord grow impatient if I go on. What if only thirty are found there?" He replied, "I will forbear doing it if I can find but thirty there." Still he went on, "Since I have thus dared to speak to my Lord, what if there are no more than twenty?" "I will not destroy it," he answered, "for the sake of the twenty." But he still persisted: "Please, let not my Lord grow angry if I speak up this last time. What if there are at least ten there?" "For the sake of those ten," he replied, "I will not destroy it."

The Lord departed as soon as he had finished speaking with Abraham, and Abraham returned home.
The word of the Lord.

• PSALM 103 •

℟ (8) **The Lord is kind and merciful.**

Bless the Lord, O my soul;
 and all my being, bless his holy name.
Bless the Lord, O my soul,
 and forget not all his benefits. ℟

He pardons all your iniquities,
 he heals all your ills.
He redeems your life from destruction,
 he crowns you with kindness and compassion. ℟

Merciful and gracious is the Lord,
 slow to anger and abounding in kindness.
He will not always chide,
 nor does he keep his wrath forever. ℟

Not according to our sins does he deal with us,
 nor does he requite us according to our crimes.
For as the heavens are high above the earth,
 so surpassing is his kindness toward those
  who fear him. ℟

Alleluia. If today you hear his voice, harden not your
hearts. Alleluia.

● *Follow me.* ●

A reading from
the holy Gospel according to Matthew   8: 18-22

JESUS, SEEING THE PEOPLE crowd
around him, gave orders to

cross the lake to the other shore. A scribe approached him and said, "Teacher, wherever you go I will come after you." Jesus said to him, "The foxes have lairs, the birds in the sky have nests, but the Son of Man has nowhere to lay his head." Another, a disciple, said to him, "Lord, let me go and bury my father first." But Jesus told him, "Follow me, and let the dead bury their dead."

The Gospel of the Lord.

PRAYER OVER THE GIFTS
Lord God,
through your sacraments
you give us the power of your grace.
May this Eucharist
help us to serve you faithfully.
We ask this in the name of Jesus the Lord.

COMMUNION ANTIPHON
O, bless the Lord, my soul, and all that is within me bless his holy name. (Ps 102: 1)

PRAYER AFTER COMMUNION
Lord,
may this sacrifice and communion
give us a share in your life
and help us bring your love to the world.
Grant this through Christ our Lord.

MEDITATION OF THE DAY

Letting the Dead Bury the Dead

Human happiness is not at all lessened when you love God more than you love yourself. As a matter of fact those who really love have a more passionate thirst for happiness than egoists. Egoists fatally shrink their heart's desires, gradually sacrificing the joy of living to their own

comfort – growing increasingly negative and petty so as
to end up in a sort of euthanasia: "To sleep, perchance to
dream" (Hamlet). A strange paradox, well confirmed by
experience, has it that only those who give themselves
entirely are able to enjoy and desire, simply because really being alive always involves running risks that no man
could possibly face if he spent all his time protecting himself against invasion by others.

More profoundly, much more profoundly, do the saints
yearn for happiness. However, they love God more than
they thirst for happiness, because they know that the love
of God, far from quenching thirst or beating back desire,
lies at the very root of that thirst and feeds it endlessly.
The intense desire for happiness is harnessed by their
desire to please God in the torment of his glory and the
love of his holy will. Thus their appetite for living draws
from the true source and is increased a thousandfold.
Love of happiness pours from a wellspring of love which
is infinitely greater than happiness itself, for it draws upon
a more vast good and so eventually attains its full meaning, its splendor, and its intensity. Only to the good in ourselves can we give absolute love: the love of ourselves
must come second, for then we liberate the truth underly-
ing all our desires, giving them free rein to express themselves in spontaneity that anticipates the kingdom of
heaven.

FATHER M. D. MOLINIÉ, O.P.

Father Molinié is a French Dominican priest and author.

Prayer for the Evening

Let the peoples praise you, O God;
let all the peoples praise you.

Glory to the Father, and to the Son,
and to the Holy Spirit, as it was in the beginning,
is now, and will be for ever. Amen. Alleluia!

HYMN   Meter: 76 76 D with refrain

We plow the fields, and scatter
The good seed on the land,
But it is fed and watered
By God's almighty hand;
He sends the snow in winter,
The warmth to swell the grain,
The breezes and the sunshine,
And soft refreshing rain.

℟ All good gifts around us
Are sent from heaven above;
Then thank the Lord, O thank the Lord
For all his love.

We thank thee, then, O Father,
For all things bright and good,
The seedtime and the harvest,
Our life, our health, our food:
No gifts have we to offer
For all thy love imparts,
But that which thou desirest,
Our humble, thankful hearts. ℟

PSALM 67

Neither the one who plants nor the one who waters is anything, but only God, who causes the growth. (1 Cor 3: 7)

God's blessing is true light in the mind's darkness, true rain for the soul's earth, true life for the seed of everlasting life that lies buried in the soil of the human heart. With God's blessing, the earth yields a rich harvest of generous thoughts, kind words, and good deeds. For today's harvest, we give thanks and praise.

O God, be gracious and bless us
and let your face shed its light upon us.

So will your ways be known upon earth
and all nations learn your saving help.

℟   Let the peoples praise you, O God;
     let all the peoples praise you.

Let the nations be glad and exult
for you rule the world with justice.
With fairness you rule the peoples,
you guide the nations on earth. ℟

The earth has yielded its fruit
for God, our God, has blessed us.
May God still give us his blessing
till the ends of the earth revere him. ℟

Glory to the Father…

Word of God   Isaiah 18: 4, 7

Thus says the Lord to me:
I will quietly look on from
where I dwell, like the glowing heat of sunshine, like a
cloud of dew at harvest time. Then will gifts be brought
to the Lord of hosts from a people tall and bronzed,
from a people dreaded near and far, a nation strong and
conquering, whose land is washed by rivers – to Mount
Zion where dwells the name of the Lord of hosts.

Some seed fell on rich soil, and produced fruit,
a hundred or sixty or thirtyfold.
(Mt 13: 8)

CANTICLE OF MARY   (Text, back cover A)
The fruit of the Spirit is love, joy, peace, patience, kindness, generosity, faithfulness. (Gal 5: 22)

INTERCESSIONS

Let us pray to the Lord of the harvest:

℟   Gather us together into a harvest of love.

Lord Jesus, you are sower and harvester:
– water in us the seeds of charity that we may grow
beyond all division. ℟

You are seed and harvest:
– raise up in us fruit of the Spirit. ℟

You freed all those possessed by demons:
– uproot from the fields of this world all the weeds sown
by the evil one. ℟

Personal intentions

Our Father...

*May the Lord bless us and keep us! May the Lord let his face
shine upon us, and be gracious to us! May the Lord look
upon us kindly and give us peace! Amen. (cf. Nm 6: 24-26)*

MARIAN ANTIPHON   (Text, page 25)

SAINTS
OF TODAY AND YESTERDAY

With all your might love your Maker.

BLESSED CATHERINE JARRIGE
Virgin (1754-1836)

A native of Doumis, France, Catherine worked as a maid from the age of nine. After her mother's death four years later she found employment as a skilled lace-maker and became a Dominican tertiary. Having taken a private vow of virginity, she shared a small room with her sister, devoting herself to the care of the poor, the sick, and orphans. In the course of her charitable works she would constantly finger her rosary under her apron, fixing her attention upon Christ in everything she did. Although as a girl she had loved to dance, especially the graceful "*bourrée*" dance of her native Auvergne, Catherine denied herself this pleasure in order to remain faithful to her consecrated life. During the 1790's Catherine rose to the challenge of the French Revolution by instituting a network of safe houses where priests persecuted and hunted by the Jacobin regime could find refuge. In addition to supplying priests with food and clothing, Catherine smuggled into the safe houses hosts, altar wine, and vestments so that the priests could say Mass for the people. After the Revolution she continued her life of charity until her death on July 4, 1836.

We should surrender ourselves wholly to the Creator.
                                        Saint Teresa of Avila

TUESDAY, JULY 3
Saint Thomas

Prayer for the Morning

Come, let us praise the God of our salvation!

*Glory to the Father, and to the Son,
and to the Holy Spirit, as it was in the beginning,
is now, and will be for ever. Amen. Alleluia!*

HYMN   Meter: 888 with alleluia
This hymn can be sung to the tune used for
Ye Sons and Daughters

When Thomas first the tidings heard,
How they had seen the risen Lord,
He doubted the disciples' word.
Alleluia.

"My piercèd side, O Thomas, see;
My hands, my feet I show to thee;
Not faithless, but believing be."
Alleluia.

No longer Thomas then denied;
He saw the feet, the hands, the side;
"Thou art my Lord and God," he cried.
Alleluia.

How blest are they who have not seen,
And yet whose faith hath constant been,
For they eternal life shall win.
Alleluia.

PSALM 31   2-8

Jesus said to Thomas, "Put your finger here and see my hands, and
bring your hand and put it into my side, and do not be unbelieving,
but believe." (Jn 20: 27)

Saint Thomas' experience gives meaning to the medieval mystics'
reflections on Christ's glorified wounds as a refuge in which one is
safe from the snares of sin and death. The psalm invites us to entrust
ourselves in faith to the protective care of the Savior's all-powerful
but wounded hands.

In you, O Lord, I take refuge.
Let me never be put to shame.
In your justice, set me free,
hear me and speedily rescue me.

Be a rock of refuge for me,
a mighty stronghold to save me,
for you are my rock, my stronghold.
For your name's sake, lead and guide me.

Release me from the snares they have hidden
for you are my refuge, Lord.
Into your hands I commend my spirit.
It is you who will redeem me, Lord.

O God of truth, you detest
those who worship false and empty gods.
As for me, I trust in the Lord:
let me be glad and rejoice in your love.

Glory to the Father...

Word of God   Romans 5: 1-2

Since we have been justified
by faith, we have peace with
God through our Lord Jesus Christ, through whom we
have gained access [by faith] to this grace in which we
stand, and we boast in hope of the glory of God.

Blessed are they who put their trust in God.
(Ps 2: 11b)

CANTICLE OF ZECHARIAH   (Text, back cover B)
I do believe, help my unbelief! (Mk 9: 24)

INTERCESSIONS

By Christ's wounds, we were healed. In faith, let us pray:

℟   Let us be glad and rejoice in your love!

You sent your apostles to preach the good news to all the world:
– grant the gift of faith to those who hear your word. ℟

You had compassion on Thomas' lack of faith and healed him:
– grant the gift of faith to those who cannot believe without proof. ℟

You called blessed those who would believe without seeing:
– grant the gift of faith to all who seek you without knowing you. ℟

                                           Personal intentions

Our Father…

God of compassion, you sent your only Son to bring the good news of your reign to believer and unbeliever, Jew and Gentile, alike. Open the hearts of all peoples to receive your Word in faith and love, through the same Jesus Christ, your Son, our Lord, who lives and reigns with you and the Holy Spirit, one God, for ever and ever. Amen.

MASS

Feast of Saint Thomas

● *Saint Thomas is remembered for his incredulity concerning Christ's resurrection from the dead. When confronted by the risen Lord, his disbelief gave way to belief and he proclaimed the Easter faith of the Church: "My Lord and my God!" Nothing certain is known of his life except for this evidence in the Gospels. He is said to have subsequently preached the Gospel to the people of India. Since the fourth century the celebration of the transference of his body to Edessa has been commemorated on July 3.* ●

ENTRANCE ANTIPHON

You are my God: I will give you praise, O my God, I will extol you, for you are my savior. (Ps 117: 28)

GLORIA ——————————————————— page 226

OPENING PRAYER

Almighty Father,
as we honor Thomas the apostle,
let us always experience the help of his prayers.
May we have eternal life by believing in Jesus,
whom Thomas acknowledged as Lord,
for he lives and reigns with you and the Holy Spirit,
one God, for ever and ever.

● *You are part of the building built on the foundation of the apostles.* ●

A reading from
the Letter of Paul to the Ephesians   2: 19-22

Y OU ARE STRANGERS and aliens
no longer. No, you are fel-
low citizens of the saints and members of the household
of God. You form a building which rises on the foundation of the apostles and prophets, with Christ Jesus himself as the capstone. Through him the whole structure is
fitted together and takes shape as a holy temple in the
Lord; in him you are being built into this temple, to
become a dwelling place for God in the Spirit.
The word of the Lord.

• PSALM 117 •

℟ (Mk 16: 15) **Go out to all the world, and tell the Good News.**

Praise the Lord, all you nations;
  glorify him, all you peoples! ℟

For steadfast is his kindness toward us,
  and the fidelity of the Lord endures forever. ℟

Alleluia. You believed in me, Thomas, because you have seen me; happy those who have not seen me, but still believe! Alleluia.

● *My Lord and my God.* ●

A reading from
the holy Gospel according to John   20: 24-29

THOMAS (the name means "Twin"), one of the Twelve, was absent when Jesus came into the room. The other disciples kept telling him: "We have seen the Lord!" His answer was, "I'll never believe it without probing the nailprints in his hands, without putting my finger in the nailmarks and my hand into his side."

A week later, the disciples were once more in the room, and this time Thomas was with them. Despite the locked doors, Jesus came and stood before them. "Peace be with you," he said; then, to Thomas: "Take your finger and examine my hands. Put your hand into my side. Do not persist in your unbelief, but believe!" Thomas said in response, "My Lord and my God!" Jesus then said to him:

"You became a believer because you saw me./ Blest are
they who have not seen and have believed."
The Gospel of the Lord.

PRAYER OVER THE GIFTS
   Lord,
   we offer you our service and we pray:
   protect the gifts you have given us
   as we offer this sacrifice of praise
   on the feast of your apostle Thomas.
   We ask this in the name of Jesus the Lord.

PREFACE OF THE APOSTLES I
   Father, all-powerful and ever-living God,
   we do well always and everywhere to give you thanks.

   You are the eternal Shepherd
   who never leaves his flock untended.
   Through the apostles
   you watch over us and protect us always.
   You made them shepherds of the flock
   to share in the work of your Son,
   and from their place in heaven they guide us still.

   And so, with all the choirs of angels in heaven
   we proclaim your glory
   and join in their unending hymn of praise: Holy...

Or:

PREFACE OF THE APOSTLES II
   Father, all-powerful and ever-living God,
   we do well always and everywhere to give you thanks.

   You founded your Church on the apostles
   to stand firm for ever
   as the sign on earth of your infinite holiness
   and as the living Gospel for all men to hear.

   With steadfast love
   we sing your unending praise:
   we join with the hosts of heaven
   in their triumphant song: Holy...

COMMUNION ANTIPHON

Jesus spoke to Thomas: Put your hand here, and see the place of the nails. Doubt no longer, but believe. (See Jn 20: 27)

PRAYER AFTER COMMUNION

Father,
in this sacrament we have received
the body and blood of Christ.
With Saint Thomas we acknowledge him to be our
    Lord and God.
May we show by our lives that our faith is real.
We ask this through Christ our Lord.

MEDITATION OF THE DAY

Doubting Thomas

This blessed temper of mind, which influences religious men in the greater matter of choosing or rejecting the Gospel, extends itself also into their reception of it in all its parts. As faith is content with but a little light to begin its journey by, and makes it much by acting upon it, so also it reads, as it were, by twilight, the message of truth in its various details. It does not stipulate that the text of Scripture should admit of rigid and labored proofs of its doctrines; it has the practical wisdom to consider that the Word of God must have mainly one, and one only sense, and to try, as well as may be, to find out what that sense is, whether the evidence of it being great or little, and not to quarrel with it if it is not overpowering. It keeps steadily in view that Christ speaks in Scripture, and receives his words as if it heard them, as if some superior and friend spoke them, one whom it wished to please; not as if it were engaged upon the dead letter of a document, which admitted of rude handling, of criticism and exception. It looks off from self to Christ, and instead of seeking impatiently for some personal assurance, is set by obedience, saying, "Here am I; send me." And in like manner towards every institution of Christ, his Church, his sacraments, his ministers, it acts not as a disputer of this world, but as the disciple of him who appointed them. Lastly, it rests contented with the revelation made to it; it has "found the Messiah," and that is enough. The very principle of its former restlessness now keeps it from wandering. When "the Son of God is come, and has given us an understanding to know the true God," wavering, fearfulness, superstitious trust in the creature, pursuit of novelties, are signs, not of faith, but of unbelief.

VENERABLE CARDINAL JOHN HENRY NEWMAN

Cardinal Newman († 1890) established the Oratory in Birmingham, England, and was a preacher of great eloquence.

Prayer for the Evening

The Lord is our praise in the great assembly!

Glory to the Father, and to the Son,
and to the Holy Spirit, as it was in the beginning,
is now, and will be for ever. Amen. Alleluia!

HYMN   Meter: CM

We walk by faith, and not by sight;
No gracious words we hear
From him who spoke as none e'er spoke;
But we believe him near.

Help then, O Lord, our unbelief;
And may our faith abound,
To call on you when you are near
And seek where you are found:

That, when our life of faith is done,
In realms of clearer light
We may behold you as you are
With full and endless sight.

PSALM 22 23-32

O you of little faith, why did you doubt? (Mt 14: 31)

Thomas sought the Lord honestly, even in his doubt. In return, the Lord had mercy on Thomas' poverty of faith. His disbelief purified by what he saw and heard, he devoted his life to the task of telling of the Lord to generations far away from his native Palestine.

I will tell of your name to my brethren
and praise you where they are assembled.
"You who fear the Lord give him praise;
all sons of Jacob, give him glory.
Revere him, Israel's sons.

For he has never despised
nor scorned the poverty of the poor.
From him he has not hidden his face,
but he heard the poor man when he cried."

You are my praise in the great assembly.
My vows I will pay before those who fear him.
The poor shall eat and shall have their fill.
They shall praise the Lord, those who seek him.
May their hearts live for ever and ever!

All the earth shall remember and return to the Lord,
all families of the nations worship before him
for the kingdom is the Lord's; he is ruler of the nations.
They shall worship him, all the mighty of the earth;
before him shall bow all who go down to the dust.

And my soul shall live for him, my children serve him.
They shall tell of the Lord to generations yet to come,
declare his faithfulness to peoples yet unborn:
"These things the Lord has done."

Glory to the Father...

Word of God   Matthew 13: 16-17

B LESSED ARE YOUR EYES, because they see, and your ears, because they hear. Amen, I say to you, many prophets and righteous people longed to see what you see but did not see it, and to hear what you hear but did not hear it.

Thomas answered and said to him,
"My Lord and my God!" (Jn 20: 28)

CANTICLE OF MARY   (Text, back cover A)
Amen, I say to you, if you have faith the size of a mustard seed, you will say to this mountain, "Move from here to there," and it will move. Nothing will be impossible for you. (Mt 17: 20)

INTERCESSIONS

Through the intercession of Saint Thomas, we pray:

℟   Strengthen us in faith, O Lord!

Amid doubt, darkness, and despair: ℟

Amid indifference, hostility, and arrogance: ℟

Amid questions and fears: ℟

Personal intentions

Our Father…

May God keep us firm to the end, irreproachable on the
day of our Lord Jesus Christ. Amen. (cf. 1 Cor 1: 8)

MARIAN ANTIPHON   (Text, page 25)

WEDNESDAY, JULY 4
Saint Elizabeth of Portugal
Independence Day

Prayer for the Morning

Sing praise to God, sing praise!

Glory to the Father, and to the Son,
and to the Holy Spirit, as it was in the beginning,
is now, and will be for ever. Amen. Alleluia!

HYMN   Meter: irregular
This hymn can be sung to the tune used for
God's Blessing Sends Us Forth

O Splendor, Glory bright,
Brought forth as Light from Light!
O Day, all days enlightening!
Angels with one accord
Cry "Holy, holy Lord!"
To you, our everlasting King.

Come, raise the anthem high!
Let praises fill the sky!
Sing out a new song unto the Lord:
Let all, with heart and voice,
Before the throne rejoice
Of him whom heav'n and earth adore.

PSALM 47

No servant can serve two masters. (Lk 16: 13)

This psalm has consequences. On this day when we celebrate our independence as a nation, we are challenged to look honestly at the question of freedom. If we say that God is really the ruler of all the earth, and all earthly authorities, we must ask ourselves whom we honor and why, whom we praise and why, whom we obey and why.

All peoples, clap your hands,
cry to God with shouts of joy!
For the Lord, the Most High, we must fear,
great king over all the earth.

He subdues peoples under us
and nations under our feet.
Our inheritance, our glory, is from him,
given to Jacob out of love.

God goes up with shouts of joy;
the Lord goes up with trumpet blast.
Sing praise for God, sing praise,
sing praise to our king, sing praise.

God is king of all the earth.
Sing praise with all your skill.
God is king over the nations;
God reigns on his holy throne.

The princes of the peoples are assembled
with the people of Abraham's God.
The rulers of the earth belong to God,
to God who reigns over all.

Glory to the Father:..

Word of God   1 Corinthians 15: 25-27a, 28

CHRIST MUST REIGN until he
has put all his enemies
under his feet. The last enemy to be destroyed is death,
for "he subjected everything under his feet." When
everything is subjected to him, then the Son himself will
[also] be subjected to the one who subjected everything
to him, so that God may be all in all.

*Wrath and fury to those who selfishly disobey the
truth and obey wickedness. (Rom 2: 8)*

CANTICLE OF ZECHARIAH   (Text, back cover B)

Do you not know that if you present yourselves to someone as obedient slaves, you are slaves of the one you obey, either of sin, which leads to death, or of obedience, which leads to righteousness? (Rom 6: 16)

INTERCESSIONS

To the God of heaven and earth, we pray:

℟   Your kingdom come!

God of power and might, all authority comes from you:
– enlighten with your wisdom all those whom you appoint to positions of authority in Church or state. ℟

All obedience is due to you:
– instill in us a spirit of responsible obedience to all those whom you have entrusted with legitimate authority. ℟

All honor is yours by right:
– grant us a spirit of discernment so that we may honor only those who are truly honorable in your sight. ℟

All freedom is your gift:
– teach us to use our freedom faithfully to serve your glory and our neighbor's good. ℟

Personal intentions

Our Father…

O Lord our God, you alone are God, and there is no other. Grant us an undivided heart, to love and serve you with all our mind and all our strength, through Jesus Christ our Lord. Amen.

MASS

Wednesday of the Thirteenth Week of the Year

(Today, the prayers for Independence Day, given below, could be used.)

ENTRANCE ANTIPHON
Give peace, Lord, to those who wait for you; listen to the prayers of your servants, and guide us in the way of justice. (See Sir 36: 18-19)

The Gloria may be said.

OPENING PRAYER
>All-powerful Father,
>today we rededicate ourselves to your service,
>and to the works of justice and freedom for all.
>As you have called us from many peoples
>to be one nation,
>help us to give witness in our lives
>and in our life as a nation
>to the rich diversity of your gifts.
>We ask this through our Lord Jesus Christ, your Son,
>who lives and reigns with you and the Holy Spirit,
>one God, for ever and ever.

The following scriptural readings are suggested for the eucharistic celebration of Independence Day. Other readings may be selected.

First Reading:	Isaiah 32: 15-20
Psalm:	72: 1-2, 3-4, 7-8, 12-13, 17
Second Reading:	1 Peter 1: 3-9
Alleluia:	John 14: 27
Gospel:	John 14: 23-29

● *The slave girl's son will not share the inheritance with my son Isaac.* ●

A reading from
the Book of Genesis   21: 5, 8-20

ABRAHAM WAS a hundred years old when his son Isaac

was born to him. Isaac grew, and on the day of the child's weaning, Abraham held a great feast.

Sarah noticed the son whom Hagar the Egyptian had borne to Abraham playing with her son Isaac; so she demanded of Abraham: "Drive out that slave and her son! No son of that slave is going to share the inheritance with my son Isaac!" Abraham was greatly distressed, especially on account of his son Ishmael. But God said to Abraham: "Do not be distressed about the boy or about your slave woman. Heed the demands of Sarah, no matter what she is asking of you; for it is through Isaac that descendants shall bear your name. As for the son of the slave woman, I will make a great nation of him also, since he too is your offspring."

Early the next morning Abraham got some bread and a skin of water and gave them to Hagar. Then, placing the child on her back, he sent her away. As she roamed aimlessly in the wilderness of Beer-sheba, the water in the skin was used up. So she put the child down under a shrub, and then went and sat down opposite him, about a bowshot away; for she said to herself, "Let me not watch the child die." As she sat opposite him, he began to cry. God heard the boy's cry, and God's messenger called to Hagar from heaven: "What is the matter, Hagar? Don't be afraid; God has heard the boy's cry in this plight of his. Arise, lift up the boy and hold him by the hand; for I will make of him a great nation." Then God opened her eyes, and she saw a well of water. She went and filled the skin with water, and then let the boy drink.

God was with the boy as he grew up.
The word of the Lord.

• PSALM 34 •

℟ (7) **The Lord hears the cry of the poor.**

When the afflicted man called out, the Lord heard,
and from all his distress he saved him.
The angel of the Lord encamps
around those who fear him, and delivers them. ℟

Fear the Lord, you his holy ones,
for nought is lacking to those who fear him.
The great grow poor and hungry;
but those who seek the Lord want for no good
thing. ℟

Come, children, hear me;
I will teach you the fear of the Lord.
Which of you desires life,
and takes delight in prosperous days? ℟

Alleluia. Our Savior Jesus Christ has done away with
death, and brought us life through his gospel. Alleluia.

● *He came before the appointed time to torture the
demons.* ●

A reading from
the holy Gospel according to Matthew   8: 28-34

AS JESUS APPROACHED the
Gadarene boundary, he
encountered two men coming out of the tombs. They
were possessed by demons and were so savage that no
one could travel along the road. With a sudden shriek
they cried: "Why meddle with us, Son of God? Have you
come to torture us before the appointed time?" Some
distance away a large herd of swine was feeding. The
demons kept appealing to him, "If you expel us, send us

into the herd of swine." He answered, "Out with you!" At that they came forth and entered the swine. The whole herd went rushing down the bluff into the sea and were drowned.

The swineherds took to their heels, and upon their arrival in the town related everything that had happened, including the story about the two possessed men. The upshot was that the entire town came out to meet Jesus. When they caught sight of him, they begged him to leave their neighborhood.

The Gospel of the Lord.

PRAYER OVER THE GIFTS

> God of mercy,
> as we present this bread and wine,
> make all of us a leaven for good,
> to make the good news of Christ present everywhere.
> Draw the hearts of all to yourself,
> and make our country one nation
> dedicated to your service.
> We ask this through Christ our Lord.

PREFACE FOR INDEPENDENCE DAY I

> Father,
> all-powerful and ever-living God,
> we do well to sing your praise for ever,
> and to give you thanks in all we do
> through Jesus Christ our Lord.

> He spoke to men a message of peace
> and taught us to live as brothers.
> His message took form in the vision of our fathers
> as they fashioned a nation
> where men might live as one.
> This message lives on in our midst
> as a task for men today
> and a promise for tomorrow.

> We thank you, Father, for your blessings in the past
> and for all that, with your help, we must yet achieve.

And so, with hearts full of love,
we join the angels today and every day of our lives,
to sing your glory in a hymn of endless praise: Holy...

COMMUNION ANTIPHON
Lord, you are the source of life, and in the light of your glory,
we find happiness. (Ps 36: 10)

PRAYER AFTER COMMUNION
Lord,
in this Eucharist
you show us here on earth
an image and foretaste of the unity and joy
of your people in heaven.
Deepen our unity and increase our joy
that all who believe in you
may work together to build the city of lasting peace.
We ask this through Christ our Lord.

SOLEMN BLESSING
God the Father has called us
to be one family of peoples.
May he fill your hearts with deep longing
for peace and harmony.
Amen.

The Son of God came to share our lives
and make us children of the one Father.
May he enable you to grow in wisdom and grace
before God and the human family.
Amen.

The Holy Spirit is the bond of love
between Father and Son.
May he be the bond of love among you,
in our nation, and among all people.
Amen.

May almighty God bless you,
the Father, and the Son, and the Holy Spirit.
Amen.

MEDITATION OF THE DAY

Demons, Tyrants, and the Son of God

Americans have been powerfully reminded in recent years that you cannot have a democracy without a sufficient number of democrats: without a sufficient critical mass of men and women who have internalized the habits of the heart and the habits of the mind – the virtues, if you will – that are essential to democratic self-governance. Contrary to some of the expectations of the past, American democracy is not "a machine that will run itself." The machine can, for a time, compensate for the inadequacies of the citizenry. But over the long haul, the machine needs mechanics – and mechanics of a certain cast of mind and soul – to make it work such that the machinery serves the ends of human flourishing. The machine needs mechanics who will continue to affirm the superiority of this kind of machine over others, because of how they conceive their own moral worth and that of their neighbors.

Certainly Christian orthodoxy does not constitute the only set of religious and moral warrants capable of turning tyrants, which is what we all are at birth, into democrats. But I think it undeniable that democrats, like Christians, are made, not born. The *ethos* of democracy has to be learned. Christian personalism, and a Christian analysis of the human condition, can powerfully promote attitudes toward "the other" that are essential to the democratic *ethos*, and thus to the proper functioning of the democratic experiment.

GEORGE WEIGEL

George Weigel is president of the Ethics and Public Policy Center in Washington, D.C.

Prayer for the Evening

Let us rejoice and sing psalms to our God!

Glory to the Father, and to the Son,
and to the Holy Spirit, as it was in the beginning,
is now, and will be for ever. Amen. Alleluia!

HYMN   Meter: LM
This hymn can be sung to the tune used for
Praise God from Whom All Blessings Flow

Lord Jesus Christ, abide with us
Now that the sun has run its course;
Let hope not be obscured by night
But may faith's darkness be as light.

Lord Jesus Christ, give us your peace,
And when the trials of earth shall cease,
Grant us the morning light of grace,
The radiant splendor of your face.

Immortal, Holy Threefold Light,
Yours be the kingdom, pow'r and might;
All glory be eternally
To you, life-giving Trinity.

PSALM 75   2-8, 10-11

Whoever exalts himself will be humbled; but whoever humbles himself will be exalted. (Mt 23: 12)

Truly humble people are centers of peace because they fear neither their own failure nor others' success. Lest we be tempted to glory in the freedom we enjoy as if it were our own achievement only, let us pray for the wisdom to judge as God judges: to look at our own and others' achievements from God's perspective.

We give thanks to you, O God,
we give thanks and call upon your name.
We recount your wonderful deeds.

"When I reach the appointed time,
then I will judge with justice.
Though the earth and all who dwell in it may rock,
it is I who uphold its pillars.

To the boastful I say: 'Do not boast,'
to the wicked: 'Do not flaunt your strength,
do not flaunt your strength on high.
Do not speak with insolent pride.'"

For neither from the east nor from the west,
nor from desert or mountains comes judgment,
but God himself is the judge.
One he humbles, another he exalts.

As for me, I will rejoice for ever
and sing psalms to Jacob's God.
He shall break the power of the wicked,
while the strength of the just shall be exalted.

Glory to the Father…

Word of God   Ephesians 4: 1-6

I, THEN, A PRISONER for the Lord, urge you to live in a manner worthy of the call you have received, with all humility and gentleness, with patience, bearing with one another through love, striving to preserve the unity of the spirit through the bond of peace: one body and one Spirit, as you were also called to the one hope of your call; one Lord, one faith, one baptism; one God and Father of all, who is over all and through all and in all.

Humble yourselves before the Lord
and he will exalt you.

(Jas 4: 10)

CANTICLE OF MARY (Text, back cover A)
Whoever boasts, should boast in the Lord. (2 Cor 10: 17)

INTERCESSIONS

Let us pray with confidence to God our strength:

℟ We call upon your name!

Your deeds are wonderful:
– teach us to boast of your love rather than of our accomplishments. ℟

You are the rock upon which the world stands firm:
– grant us faith to depend on you rather than on our own achievements. ℟

You are the true judge of all things:
– open our eyes to see as you see. ℟

You have broken the power of sin and death:
– raise our beloved dead to the true and final freedom which is the gift of redemption. ℟

Personal intentions

Our Father…

May the blessing of almighty God, Father, Son, and Holy Spirit, descend upon us and remain with us always. Amen.

MARIAN ANTIPHON (Text, page 25)

SAINTS
OF TODAY AND YESTERDAY

Blood of Christ, price of our salvation, save us.

SAINT ULRICH
Bishop (893-973)

As bishop of the south German diocese of Augsburg,
Ulrich followed a demanding daily schedule that
began at three in the morning with the communal
recitation of Matins and Lauds from the Divine
Office and continued with other prayers as well as
attendance at two Masses, the second of which he
himself celebrated. He then went to the hospital to
comfort the sick and wash the feet of twelve paupers,
after which he spent the rest of the day preaching and
performing other pastoral duties as well as visiting
the sick. To his frugal evening meal he always invited
the poor. Ulrich is the first bishop known to have
carried out the popular German Holy Week
ceremony of placing the Eucharist in a shrine on
Good Friday commemorating Christ's burial, and
carrying the sacrament in a triumphant procession
on Easter Sunday to celebrate the resurrection. When
Augsburg was threatened with a barbarian invasion,
Ulrich, who had arranged for the construction of a
wall around the city to protect his people, prayed and
led his people in devotions until the attackers fled in
retreat.

*Cancel out our sins today, then, O true God, wash our
souls' face with your only-begotten Son's blood.*
Saint Catherine of Siena

THURSDAY, JULY 5
Saint Anthony Mary Zaccaria

Prayer for the Morning

Come, let us adore the Lord our God!

Glory to the Father, and to the Son,
and to the Holy Spirit, as it was in the beginning,
is now and will be for ever. Amen. Alleluia!

HYMN Meter: 88 88 88
This hymn can be sung to the tune used for
Eternal Father, Strong to Save

Before thy throne, O God, we kneel:
Give us a conscience quick to feel,
A ready mind to understand
The meaning of thy chast'ning hand;
What e'er the pain and shame may be,
Bring us, O Father, nearer thee.

Search out our hearts and make us true;
Help us to give to all their due.
From love of pleasure, lust of gold,
From sins which make the heart grow cold,
Wean us and train us with thy rod.
Teach us to know our faults, O God.

For sins of heedless word and deed,
For pride ambitious to succeed,
From crafty trade and subtle snare
To catch the simple unaware,
For lives bereft of purpose high,
Forgive, forgive, O Lord, we cry.

PSALM 49 2-13

Whoever exalts himself will be humbled. (Mt 23: 12)

Pride sets subtle snares. Whenever we imagine that we are in control of life – our own or someone else's – we have fallen prey to the ancient whisper in the Garden: "You shall be like gods." Mortality is the enduring reminder that we become like God not by our own power but by the power of the cross.

Hear this, all you peoples,
give heed, all who dwell in the world,
men both low and high,
rich and poor alike!

My lips will speak words of wisdom.
My heart is full of insight.
I will turn my mind to a parable,
with the harp I will solve my problem.

Why should I fear in evil days
the malice of the foes who surround me,
men who trust in their wealth,
and boast of the vastness of their riches?

For no man can buy his own ransom,
or pay a price to God for his life.
The ransom of his soul is beyond him.
He cannot buy life without end,
nor avoid coming to the grave.

He knows that wise men and fools must both perish
and leave their wealth to others.
Their graves are their homes for ever,
their dwelling place from age to age,
though their names spread wide through the land.

In his riches, man lacks wisdom:
he is like the beasts that are destroyed.

Glory to the Father...

Word of God
Sirach 10: 7, 12–13a, 15-16

ODIOUS TO THE LORD and to men is arrogance, and the sin of oppression they both hate. The beginning of pride is man's stubbornness in withdrawing his heart from his Maker; for pride is the reservoir of sin, a source which runs over with vice. The roots of the proud God plucks up, to plant the humble in their place: he breaks down their stem to the level of the ground, then digs their roots from the earth.

Blessed are the humble of heart!

CANTICLE OF ZECHARIAH
(Text, back cover B)
Whoever humbles himself will be exalted. (Mt 23: 12)

INTERCESSIONS

In the mystery of the incarnation and still more of the cross, Jesus Christ reveals the true power of self-abasement. Let us pray:

℞   Make us wise, O Lord.

You did not think equality with God something to be clung to:
– release us from the desire for power and prestige, we pray. ℞

You emptied yourself, taking on the nature of a slave:
– free us from all disdain for works of service, we pray. ℞

You became obedient, even unto death, death on the cross:
– deliver us from the lure of self-sufficiency, we pray. ℞

Personal intentions

Our Father...

O Christ, you washed the feet of your disciples, you who are both Lord and Master. Strip us of the garments of pride and free us to do for one another the tasks of love as you have done them for us. In your name we pray, Lord Jesus Christ, who live and reign, one God with the Father and the Holy Spirit for ever and ever. Amen.

MASS

Thursday of the Thirteenth Week of the Year

ANTHONY ZACCARIA   *Optional memorial*

● *Saint Anthony Zaccaria was born in Cremona, Lombardy, in 1502. He studied medicine in Padua. After his ordination to the priesthood, he founded the Society of Clerics of Saint Paul, also known as the Barnabites. The Society did much to reform the morals of the faithful. He died in 1539.* ●

ENTRANCE ANTIPHON

The Spirit of God is upon me; he has anointed me. He sent me to bring good news to the poor, and to heal the broken-hearted. (Lk 4: 18)

OPENING PRAYER

Lord,
enable us to grasp in the spirit of Saint Paul,
the sublime wisdom of Jesus Christ,
the wisdom which inspired Saint Anthony Zaccaria
to preach the message of salvation in your Church.
Grant this through our Lord Jesus Christ, your Son,
who lives and reigns with you and the Holy Spirit,
one God, for ever and ever.

● *The sacrifice of Abraham, our father in faith.* ●

A reading from
the Book of Genesis

GOD PUT ABRAHAM to the test. He called to him, "Abraham!" "Ready!" he replied. Then God said: "Take your son Isaac, your only one, whom you love, and go to the land of Moriah. There you shall offer him up as a holocaust on a height that I will point out to you." Early the next morning Abraham saddled his donkey, took with him his son Isaac, and two of his servants as well, and with the wood that he had cut for the holocaust, set out for the place of which God had told him.

On the third day Abraham got sight of the place from afar. Then he said to his servants: "Both of you stay here with the donkey, while the boy and I go on over yonder. We will worship and then come back to you." Thereupon Abraham took the wood for the holocaust and laid it on his son Isaac's shoulders, while he himself carried the fire and the knife. As the two walked on together, Isaac spoke to his father Abraham. "Father!" he said. "Yes, son," he replied. Isaac continued, "Here are the fire and the wood, but where is the sheep for the holocaust?" "Son," Abraham answered, "God himself will provide the sheep for the holocaust." Then the two continued going forward.

When they came to the place of which God had told him, Abraham built an altar there and arranged the wood on it. Next he tied up his son Isaac, and put him on top of the wood on the altar. Then he reached out and took the knife to slaughter his son. But the Lord's messenger called to him from heaven, "Abraham, Abraham!" "Yes, Lord," he answered. "Do not lay your hand on the boy," said the messenger. "Do not do the least thing to him. I know now how devoted you are to God, since you did not withhold from me your own beloved son." As Abraham looked about, he spied a ram caught by its horns in the thicket. So he went and took the ram and offered it up as a holocaust in place of his son. Abraham named the site Yahweh-yireh; hence people now say, "On the mountain the Lord will see."

Again the Lord's messenger called to Abraham from heaven and said: "I swear by myself, declares the Lord, that because you acted as you did in not withholding from me your beloved son, I will bless you abundantly and make your descendants as countless as the stars of the sky and the sands of the seashore; your descendants shall take possession of the gates of their enemies, and in your descendants all the nations of the earth shall find blessing – all this because you obeyed my command."

Abraham then returned to his servants, and they set out together for Beer-sheba, where Abraham made his home. The word of the Lord.

• PSALM 115 •

R (9) **I will walk in the presence of the Lord,
in the land of the living.**

Or: Alleluia.

Not to us, O Lord, not to us
  but to your name give glory
because of your kindness, because of your truth.
Why should the pagans say,
  "Where is their God?" R

Our God is in heaven;
  whatever he wills, he does.
Their idols are silver and gold,
  the handiwork of men. R

They have mouths but speak not;
  they have eyes but see not;
They have ears but hear not;
  they have noses but smell not. ℟

Their makers shall be like them,
  everyone that trusts in them.
The house of Israel trusts in the Lord;
  he is their help and their shield. ℟

Alleluia. The Lord is faithful in all his words and holy in his deeds. Alleluia.

● *They praised God for giving such power to men.* ●

A reading from
the holy Gospel according to Matthew   9: 1-8

JESUS ENTERED A BOAT, made the crossing, and came back to his own town. There the people at once brought to him a paralyzed man lying on a mat. When Jesus saw their faith he said to the paralytic, "Have courage, son, your sins are forgiven." At that some of the scribes said to themselves, "The man blasphemes." Jesus was aware of what they were thinking and said: "Why do you harbor evil thoughts? Which is less trouble to say, 'Your sins are forgiven' or 'Stand up and walk'? To help you realize that the Son of Man has authority on earth to forgive sins" – he then said to the paralyzed man – "Stand up! Roll up your mat, and go home." The man stood up and went toward his home. At the sight, a feeling of awe came over the crowd, and they praised God for giving such authority to men.
The Gospel of the Lord.

PRAYER OVER THE GIFTS
> Father of mercy,
> we have these gifts to offer in honor of your saints
> who bore witness to your mighty power.
> May the power of the Eucharist
> bring us your salvation.
> Grant this through Christ our Lord.

COMMUNION ANTIPHON
I, the Lord, am with you always, until the end of the world.
(Mt 28: 20)

PRAYER AFTER COMMUNION
> Lord,
> may the mysteries we receive
> prepare us for the eternal joys
> Saint Anthony Zaccaria won by his faithful ministry.
> We ask this in the name of Jesus the Lord.

• ———————————————————————— •

M E D I T A T I O N   O F   T H E   D A Y

• ———————————————————————— •

True Forgiveness

A Jesus who agrees with everyone and everything, a Jesus without his holy anger, without the hardness of truth and genuine love is not the real Jesus as he is depicted in the Scriptures, but a pitiable caricature. A concept of "Gospel" that fails to convey the reality of God's anger has nothing to do with the Gospel of the Bible. True forgiveness is something quite different from weak indulgence. Forgiveness is demanding and requires both parties, the one who forgives and the one who is forgiven, to do so with all their minds and hearts. A Jesus who sanctions everything is a Jesus without the Cross, for such a Jesus would not need the torment of the Cross to save mankind. As a matter of fact, the Cross is being increasingly banished from theology and reinterpreted as just a vexatious mischance or a purely political event. The Cross as reconciliation, as a means of forgiving and saving, is incompatible with a certain modern mode of thought. Only when the relationship between truth and love is rightly comprehended can the Cross be comprehensible in its true theological depth. Forgiveness has to do with truth. That is why it requires the Son's Cross and our conversion. Forgiveness is, in fact, the restoration of truth, the renewal of being, and the vanquishment of the lies that lurk in every sin; sin is by nature a departure from the truth of one's own nature and, by consequence, from the truth of the Creator God.

CARDINAL JOSEPH RATZINGER

Cardinal Ratzinger is the prefect of the Vatican Congregation on the Doctrine of the Faith.

Prayer for the Evening

All God's ways are holy: come, let us adore!

*Glory to the Father, and to the Son,
and to the Holy Spirit, as it was in the beginning,
is now, and will be for ever. Amen. Alleluia!*

HYMN   Meter: 87 87 87
This hymn can be sung to the tune used for
Let All Mortal Flesh Keep Silence

Lord, enthroned in heavenly splendor,
First begotten from the dead,
Thou alone, our strong Defender,
Liftest up thy people's head.
Alleluia! Alleluia!
Jesus, true and living Bread!

Life imparting heavenly Manna,
Smitten Rock with streaming side,
Heaven and earth with loud hosanna
Worship thee, the Lamb who died.

Alleluia! Alleluia!
Risen, ascended, glorified!

PSALM 77   14-21

By faith they crossed the Red Sea as if it were dry land. (Heb 11: 29)

We dwell in wonder before the paradox of God. The all-holy,
all-powerful God of mystery and might came down to be with his
people enslaved in Egypt and to lead them to freedom personally
through the sea. Far more amazing still, this same God came to take
our very flesh to lead us through death to life.

Your ways, O God, are holy.
What god is great as our God?
You are the God who works wonders.
You showed your power among the peoples.
Your strong arm redeemed your people,
the sons of Jacob and Joseph.

The waters saw you, O God,
the waters saw you and trembled;
the depths were moved with terror.
The clouds poured down rain,
the skies sent forth their voice;
your arrows flashed to and fro.

Your thunder rolled round the sky,
your flashes lighted up the world.
The earth was moved and trembled
when your way led through the sea,
your path through the mighty waters
and no one saw your footprints.

You guided your people like a flock
by the hand of Moses and Aaron.

Glory to the Father...

Word of God   Wisdom 19: 7-8

THE CLOUD overshadowed their camp; and out of what had before been water, dry land was seen emerging: out of the Red Sea an unimpeded road, and a grassy plain out of the mighty flood. Over this crossed the whole nation sheltered by your hand, after they beheld stupendous wonders.

What god is great as our God?

CANTICLE OF MARY   (Text, back cover A)
He is a deliverer and savior, working signs and wonders in heaven and on earth. (Dn 6: 28)

INTERCESSIONS

God is our deliverer, our savior. In faith let us pray:

℟   You are the God who works wonders!

You rule the wind and storm:
– rule the restlessness of our hearts and save us from all disturbance. ℟

You led your people through the sea dry-shod:
– lead us and our loved ones through the unseen dangers of a disbelieving world. ℟

You delivered your people from slavery and death:
– deliver us from the subtle destruction of indifference and careless habit. ℟

Personal intentions

Our Father…

May the Lord deliver us from all evil and bring us to life everlasting! Amen.

MARIAN ANTIPHON   (Text, page 25)

SAINTS
OF TODAY AND YESTERDAY

Turn to the Lord.

SAINT PROCOPIUS
Abbot († 1053)

Procopius, a priest of the cathedral of Prague
(Bohemia), desiring a more recollected life, retired to
a cave in the forest where he lived in solitude for
several years. One day a hunted stag took refuge
behind Procopius as he was chopping wood. The
hunter – the duke of Bohemia – was surprised to find
a hermit in this place, and consequently sent
Procopius candidates to live under his spiritual
direction on land provided by the duke. Procopius
later became abbot of a Benedictine abbey in Prague.

BLESSED WILLIAM OF HIRSAU
Abbot († 1091)

As abbot of the southwest German abbey of Hirsau,
William continued the reforming efforts of the
preceding abbot. Using the reformed abbey of Cluny
as his model, William composed a book of
constitutions for Hirsau and meticulously observed
the rule himself, setting an example for the rest of his
community and attracting many new vocations.
He also exerted himself in concern for the
underprivileged position of serfs in medieval society
and advocated the education of the people, as well as
the need for learned bishops. His own learning
covered a wide range of subjects including music,
astronomy, mathematics, and poetry.

Christ belongs to the humble-minded.
Saint Clement of Rome

FRIDAY, JULY 6
Saint Maria Goretti

Prayer for the Morning

Merciful is the Lord: come, let us sing praise!

*Glory to the Father, and to the Son,
and to the Holy Spirit, as it was in the beginning,
is now, and will be for ever. Amen. Alleluia!*

HYMN   Meter: 87 87 D
This hymn can be sung to the tune used for
Come, Thou Fount of Ev'ry Blessing

O my soul, bless God the Father;
All within me bless his name:
Bless the Father, and forget not
All his mercies to proclaim,
Who forgives all your transgressions,
Your diseases all who heals;
Who redeems you from destruction,
Who with you so kindly deals.

Far as east from west is distant,
He has put away our sin;
Like the pity of a father
Has the Lord's compassion been.
As it was without beginning,
So it lasts without an end;
To their children's children ever
Shall his righteousness extend.

PSALM 38   2-11, 22-23

I know well the plans I have in mind for you, says the Lord, plans for
your welfare, not for woe! plans to give you a future full of hope.
(Jer 29: 11)

The penitential psalms very often speak of sin as sickness brought on by the attack of enemies. Their vivid descriptions of the sinner's suffering remind us again and again that the misery of sin is not what God wants for his beloved children.

O Lord, do not rebuke me in your anger;
do not punish me, Lord, in your rage.
Your arrows have sunk deep in me;
your hand has come down upon me.

Through your anger all my body is sick:
through my sin, there is no health in my limbs.
My guilt towers higher than my head;
it is a weight too heavy to bear.

My wounds are foul and festering,
the result of my own folly.
I am bowed and brought to my knees.
I go mourning all the day long.

All my frame burns with fever;
all my body is sick.
Spent and utterly crushed,
I cry aloud in anguish of heart.

O Lord, you know all my longing:
my groans are not hidden from you.
My heart throbs, my strength is spent;
the very light has gone from my eyes.

O Lord, do not forsake me!
My God, do not stay afar off!
Make haste and come to my help,
O Lord, my God, my savior!

Glory to the Father...

Word of God
Isaiah 57: 18-19

I SAW [MY PEOPLE'S] ways, but I will heal them and lead them; I will give full comfort to them and to those who mourn for them, I, the Creator, who gave them life. Peace, peace to the far and the near, says the Lord; and I will heal them.

I will heal their defection, I will love them freely.
(Hos 14: 5)

CANTICLE OF ZECHARIAH   (Text, back cover B)
I will restore you to health; of your wounds I will heal you, says the Lord. (Jer 30: 17)

INTERCESSIONS

Let us pray to the Divine Physician:

R/   Have mercy on us, Lord, for we have sinned.

Hold back the punishment we fear:
– grant us the healing for which we long. R/

Lift from us the burden of our guilt:
– grant us the freedom we have sold for illusions of pleasure or power. R/

Strengthen our longing for goodness:
– remove our foolish preferences for sinful rewards. R/

Through the intercession of Saint Maria Goretti:
– protect young people from abuse and strengthen our appreciation for the value of chastity. R/

Personal intentions

Our Father...

O God, our Healer and our Good, you sent your Son to cure the world's sickness by taking upon himself the burden of its guilt. Heal the diseased vision which causes us to mistake evil for good; heal the sickened mind which causes us to mistake selfishness for love; heal the unhealthy habits which we have made our own, that we may stand before you, whole in body, soul, and spirit, to sing your praise for ever with all the saints, through Jesus Christ our Lord. Amen.

MASS

Friday of the Thirteenth Week of the Year

MARIA GORETTI   *Optional memorial*

● *Saint Maria Goretti was born of a poor family in Corinaldi, Italy, in 1890. Near Nettuno she spent a difficult childhood assisting her mother in domestic duties. She was of a pious nature and often at prayer. In 1902 she was stabbed to death, preferring to die rather than be raped.* ● ·

ENTRANCE ANTIPHON

Here is a wise and faithful virgin who went with lighted lamp to meet her Lord.

OPENING PRAYER

Father,
source of innocence and lover of chastity,
you gave Saint Maria Goretti the privilege
of offering her life in witness to Christ.
As you gave her the crown of martyrdom,
let her prayers keep us faithful to your teaching.
We ask this through our Lord Jesus Christ, your Son,
who lives and reigns with you and the Holy Spirit,
one God, for ever and ever.

● *Isaac loved Rebekah – he made her his wife, and was consoled for the loss of his mother.* ●

A reading from
the Book of Genesis   23: 1-4, 19; 24: 1-8, 62-67

THE SPAN OF SARAH'S LIFE was one hundred and twenty-seven years. She died in Kiriatharba (that is, Hebron) in the land of Canaan, and Abraham performed the customary mourning rites for her. Then he left the side of his dead one and addressed the Hittites: "Although I am a resident alien among you, sell me from your holdings a piece of property for a burial ground, that I may bury my dead wife."

After this transaction, Abraham buried his wife Sarah in the cave of the field of Machpelah, facing Mamre (that is, Hebron) in the land of Canaan.

Abraham had now reached a ripe old age, and the Lord had blessed him in every way. Abraham said to the senior servant of his household, who had charge of all his possessions: "Put your hand under my thigh, and I will make you swear by the Lord, the God of heaven and the God of earth, that you will not procure a wife for my son from the daughters of the Canaanites among whom I live, but that you will go to my own land and to my kindred to get a wife for my son Isaac." The servant asked him: "What if the woman is unwilling to follow me to this land? Should I then take your son back to the land from which you migrated?" "Never take my son back there for any reason," Abraham told him. "The Lord, the God of heaven, who took me from my father's house and the land of my kin, and who confirmed by oath the promise he then made to me, 'I will give this land to your descendants' – he will send his messenger before you, and you will obtain a wife for my son there. If the woman is unwilling to follow you, you will be released from this oath. But never take my son back there!"

[A long time later, Isaac went] to live in the region of the Negeb. One day toward evening he went out… in the field, and as he looked around, he noticed that camels were approaching. Rebekah, too, was looking about, and when she saw him, she alighted from her camel and asked the servant, "Who is the man out there, walking through the fields toward us?" "That is my master," replied the servant. Then she covered herself with her veil.

The servant recounted to Isaac all the things he had done. Then Isaac took Rebekah into his tent; he married her, and thus she became his wife. In his love for her Isaac found solace after the death of his mother Sarah. The word of the Lord.

• PSALM 106 •

℟ (1) **Give thanks to the Lord for he is good.**

Or: **Alleluia.**

Give thanks to the Lord, for he is good,
for his kindness endures forever.
Who can tell the mighty deeds of the Lord,
or proclaim all his praises? ℟

Happy are they who observe what is right,
who do always what is just.
Remember me, O Lord, as you favor your people. ℟

Visit me with your saving help,
that I may see the prosperity of your chosen ones,
Rejoice in the joy of your people,
and glory with your inheritance. ℟

Alleluia. God has called us with the gospel; the people won for him by Jesus Christ our Lord. Alleluia.

● *It is not the healthy who need the doctor; what I want is mercy, not sacrifice.* ●

A reading from the holy Gospel according to Matthew   9: 9-13

AS JESUS MOVED ABOUT, he saw a man named Matthew at his post where taxes were collected. He said to him, "Follow me." Matthew got up and followed him. Now it happened that, while Jesus was at table in Matthew's home, many tax collectors and those known as sinners came to join Jesus and his disciples at dinner. The Pharisees saw this and complained to his disciples, "What reason can the Teacher have for eating with tax collectors and those who disregard the law?" Overhearing the remark, he said: "People who are in good health do not need a doctor; sick people do. Go and learn the meaning of the words, 'It is mercy I desire and not sacrifice.' I have come to call, not the self-righteous, but sinners."
The Gospel of the Lord.

PRAYER OVER THE GIFTS
Lord,
we see the wonder of your love
in the life of the virgin Maria Goretti
and her witness to Christ.
Accept our gifts of praise
and make our offering pleasing to you.
Grant this through Christ our Lord.

COMMUNION ANTIPHON
The bridegroom is here; let us go out to meet Christ the Lord.
(Mt 25: 6)

PRAYER AFTER COMMUNION

Lord God,
may this Eucharist renew our courage and strength.
May we remain close to you, like Saint Maria Goretti,
by accepting in our lives
a share in the suffering of Jesus Christ,
who lives and reigns with you for ever and ever.

MEDITATION OF THE DAY

Come to Call Sinners

Sin is following a stranger, that is, following an attraction that does not lead towards destiny, an answer which is off the path. It is not denying the attraction. Sin is really following an answer that does not correspond to the desire for happiness, the desire for fulfillment that my heart is. It seems something normal, it seems something that can answer that desire, but no sooner do I follow it than I discover that the idol has a mouth and does not speak: it does not keep its promises. The strangerliness is precisely in respect to destiny, to the goal, to happiness: something that is outside, external to our happiness, that cannot accomplish it.

FATHER STEFANO ALBERTO

Father Stefano Alberto is an Italian priest of the Missionary Fraternity of Saint Charles Borromeo who teaches theology at the Catholic University of the Sacred Heart in Milan, Italy.

Prayer for the Evening

*By his wounds, we were healed:
let us give thanks and praise!*

*Glory to the Father, and to the Son,
and to the Holy Spirit, as it was in the beginning,
is now, and will be for ever. Amen. Alleluia!*

HYMN   Meter: 87 87 D
                          This hymn can be sung to the tune used for
                                   There's a Wideness in God's Mercy

Lord, whose love in humble service
Bore the weight of human need,
Who did on the Cross forsaken,
Show us mercy's perfect deed;
We, your servants, bring the worship
Not of voice alone but heart:
Consecrating to your purpose
Ev'ry gift which you impart.

Still your children wander homeless;
Still the hungry cry for bread;
Still the captives long for freedom;
Still in grief we mourn our dead.
As, O Lord, your deep compassion
Healed the sick and freed the soul,
Use the love your Spirit kindles
Still to save and make us whole.

As we worship, grant us vision,
Till your love's revealing light,
Till the height and depth and greatness
Dawns upon our human sight:
Making known the needs and burdens
Your compassion bids us bear,
Stirring us to faithful service,
Your abundant life to share.

PSALM 41   2-6, 8-14

Power went out from Jesus and healed them all. (cf. Lk 6: 19)

Human need of every kind cries out to God for healing. The sharpest
cry is the plea of the human heart betrayed and wounded by the sin
of self and others. The Lord hears every call for help and heals by
taking upon himself the suffering of all who are impoverished and
weakened by failure, sin, and death.

Happy the man who considers the poor and the weak.
The Lord will save him in the day of evil,
will guard him, give him life, make him happy in the land
and will not give him up to the will of his foes.
The Lord will help him on his bed of pain,
he will bring him back from sickness to health.

As for me, I said: "Lord, have mercy on me,
heal my soul for I have sinned against you."
My foes are speaking evil against me.
"How long before he dies and his name be forgotten?"

My enemies whisper together against me.
They all weigh up the evil which is on me:
"Some deadly thing has fastened upon him,
he will not rise again from where he lies."
Thus even my friend, in whom I trusted,
who ate my bread, has turned against me.

But you, O Lord, have mercy on me.
Let me rise once more and I will repay them.
By this I shall know that you are my friend,
if my foes do not shout in triumph over me.
If you uphold me I shall be unharmed
and set in your presence for evermore.

Blessed be the Lord, the God of Israel
from age to age. Amen. Amen.

Glory to the Father...

Word of God

Isaiah 53: 4-5

IT WAS OUR INFIRMITIES that he bore, our sufferings that he endured, while we thought of him as stricken, as one smitten by God and afflicted. But he was pierced for our offenses, crushed for our sins, upon him was the chastisement that makes us whole, by his stripes we were healed.

Lord, have mercy on me,
heal my soul for I have sinned against you.

CANTICLE OF MARY   (Text, back cover A)
The Lord hears the cry of the poor. (cf. Ps 10: 17)

INTERCESSIONS

In the name of all who seek to heal the sufferings of the world, we pray:

℟   Hear us, O Lord.

You lifted upon your own shoulders the burdens of the poor and the weak:
– strengthen those who follow in your footsteps in caring for those in need. ℟

You bore the pain of the disbelief of your relatives and neighbors:
– strengthen those who encounter ridicule in their efforts to live the Gospel. ℟

You shunned no leper and turned away from no sinner:
– strengthen those who seek to grow in love for all who suffer. ℟

You died for all who live under the weight of mortality:
– raise to life all our beloved dead. ℟

Personal intentions

Our Father...

For the kingdom, the power, and the glory are yours, now and for ever! Amen.

MARIAN ANTIPHON   (Text, page 25)

Saints
OF TODAY AND YESTERDAY

> *Blessed are you when men revile you*
> *and persecute you and utter all kinds of evil*
> *against you falsely on my account.*

Saint Tranquillinus
Priest and Martyr († 286)

When the Roman martyr Saint Sebastian miraculously healed a mute woman (Saint Zoe) with the sign of the cross, twenty-one people were converted, including Tranquillinus, the father of the martyrs Saints Marcus and Marcellianus. Upon his baptism Tranquillinus was cured of the gout and later became a priest. It was while praying at the tomb of Saint Paul that he was captured and stoned to death in Rome.

Saint Palladius
Bishop († c. 450)

When the early Christians of Britain, including the Scots, were threatened with the Pelagian heresy that essentially denied the doctrine of original sin, Palladius, a deacon of Rome, urged Pope Celestine to take action by sending Saint Germanus of Auxerre to restore the Catholic faith there. Subsequently the pope sent Palladius himself to the Scots to serve as their first bishop. As many of the Scots were at this time living in Ireland, Palladius' mission encompassed Ireland as well as the region of northern Britain that later became Scotland.

> *Blessed saints of God, pray for the wandering weary*
> *soul who has stayed so far behind – you have reached*
> *the summit – pray for me.*
> Saint Elizabeth Ann Seton

SATURDAY, JULY 7

Prayer for the Morning

In honor of Mary, the Mother of God,
let us give praise and thanks to the Lord!

Glory to the Father, and to the Son,
and to the Holy Spirit, as it was in the beginning,
is now, and will be for ever. Amen. Alleluia!

HYMN   Meter: LM
                        This hymn can be sung to the tune used for
                        The God Whom Earth and Sea and Sky

O Mother of almighty God,
Forever blest in all your ways,
Give us your own tranquility,
And strength and comfort all our days.

You are a strong and lovely tree,
The fruit of which is purest gold,
Whose branches spread to shelter us,
Whose quiet leaves all peace enfold.

Pray for us now and when we die,
That we may live and ever praise
The Father, Son and Spirit blest
In endless light and timeless days.

PSALM 52   10-11

I bud forth delights like the vine, my blossoms become fruit fair and
rich. (Sir 24: 17)

One tradition holds that the tree of life in the garden of Eden was the
olive tree. In the Mediterranean world of the Bible, its fruit provided food, and oil for light, heat, and healing. Mary bore the One who
is the light of the world and the healing of the nations.

I am like a growing olive tree
in the house of God.
I trust in the goodness of God
for ever and ever.

I will thank you for evermore;
for this is your doing.
I will proclaim that your name is good,
in the presence of your friends.

Glory to the Father...

Word of God
Sirach 24: 12-14

I HAVE STRUCK ROOT among the glorious people, in the portion of the Lord, his heritage. Like a cedar on Lebanon I am raised aloft, like a cypress on Mount Hermon, like a palm tree in Engedi, like a rosebush in Jericho, like a fair olive tree in the field, like a plane tree growing beside the water.

Every tree is known by its own fruit.
(Lk 6: 44)

CANTICLE OF ZECHARIAH
(Text, back cover B)

Most blessed are you among women, and blessed is the fruit of your womb. (Lk 1: 42)

INTERCESSIONS

Brought to life by the fruit of Mary's womb, let us pray:

℟   Give life, O Lord!

The Virgin Mary received your Word in faith and brought forth fruit in love:
– through her intercession, may your Church bear fruit that will last. ℟

The Virgin Mary gave birth to your Son, our Savior:
– through her intercession, bring your Church to full
maturity in your kingdom. ℟

The Virgin Mary is honored as the Mother of God:
– through her intercession, gather children from every
land into your family through the proclamation of the
word and the celebration of the sacraments. ℟

Personal intentions

Our Father...

O God, you give life to the world through the life, death,
and resurrection of your Son, our Lord Jesus Christ.
Through the intercession of his mother, grant us the light
and healing he brings, who lives and reigns with you and
the Holy Spirit, one God for ever and ever. Amen.

MASS

Saturday of the Thirteenth Week of the Year

(Today, the prayers of the Votive Mass of the Blessed Virgin
Mary, given below, could be used.)

ENTRANCE ANTIPHON
Hail, holy Mother! The child to whom you gave birth is the
King of heaven and earth for ever. (Sedulius)

OPENING PRAYER
Lord God,
give to your people the joy
of continual health in mind and body.
With the prayers of the Virgin Mary to help us,
guide us through the sorrows of this life
to eternal happiness in the life to come.
Grant this through our Lord Jesus Christ, your Son,
who lives and reigns with you and the Holy Spirit,
one God, for ever and ever.

● *Jacob took his brother's place and by fraud received the blessing.* ●

A reading from
the Book of Genesis   27: 1-5, 15-29

WHEN ISAAC WAS SO OLD that his eyesight had failed him, he called his older son Esau and said to him, "Son!" "Yes, father!" he replied. Isaac then said, "As you can see, I am so old that I may now die at any time. Take your gear, therefore – your quiver and bow – and go out into the country to hunt some game for me. With your catch prepare an appetizing dish for me, such as I like, and bring it to me to eat, so that I may give you my special blessing before I die."

Rebekah had been listening while Isaac was speaking to his son Esau, who went out into the country to carry out his father's orders.

Rebekah then took the best clothes of her older son Esau that she had in the house, and gave them to her younger son Jacob to wear; and with the skins of the kids she covered up his hands and the hairless parts of his neck. Then she handed her son Jacob the appetizing dish and the bread she had prepared.

Bringing them to his father, Jacob said, "Father!" "Yes?" replied Isaac. "Which of my sons are you?" Jacob answered his father: "I am Esau, your first-born. I did as you told me. Please sit up and eat some of my game, so that you may give me your special blessing." But Isaac asked, "How did you succeed so quickly, son?" He answered, "The Lord, your God, let things turn out well with me." Isaac then said to Jacob, "Come closer, son, that I may feel you, to learn whether you really are my son Esau or not." So Jacob moved up closer to his father. When Isaac felt him, he said, "Although the voice is

Jacob's, the hands are Esau's." (He failed to identify him because his hands were hairy, like those of his brother Esau; so in the end he gave him his blessing.) Again he asked him, "Are you really my son Esau?" "Certainly," he replied. Then Isaac said, "Serve me your game, son, that I may eat of it and then give you my blessing." Jacob served it to him, and Isaac ate; he brought him wine, and he drank. Finally his father Isaac said to him, "Come closer, son, and kiss me." As Jacob went up and kissed him, Isaac smelled the fragrance of his clothes. With that, he blessed him, saying,

"Ah, the fragrance of my son/ is like the fragrance of a field/ that the Lord has blessed!

"May God give to you/ of the dew of the heavens/ And of the fertility of the earth/ abundance of grain and wine.

"Let peoples serve you,/ and nations pay you homage;/ Be master of your brothers,/ and may your mother's sons bow down to you./ Cursed be those who curse you,/ and blessed be those who bless you."

The word of the Lord.

• PSALM 135 •

℟ (3) **Praise the Lord for he is good!**

Or: **Alleluia.**

Praise the name of the Lord;
   Praise, you servants of the Lord
Who stand in the house of the Lord,
   in the courts of the house of our God. ℟

Praise the Lord, for the Lord is good;
   sing praise to his name, which we love;
For the Lord has chosen Jacob for himself,
   Israel for his own possession. ℟

For I know that the Lord is great;
   our Lord is greater than all gods.
All that the Lord wills he does
   in heaven and on earth,
   in the seas and in all the deeps. ℟

Alleluia. Teach me the meaning of your law, O Lord, and I will guard it with all my heart. Alleluia.

> ● *The wedding guests would never mourn while the bridegroom is still with them.* ●

A reading from
the holy Gospel according to Matthew   9: 14-17

JOHN'S DISCIPLES CAME TO Jesus with the objection, "Why is it that while we and the Pharisees fast, your disciples do not?" Jesus said to them: "How can wedding guests go in mourning so long as the groom is with them? When the day comes that the groom is taken away, then they will fast. Nobody sews a piece of unshrunken cloth on an old cloak; the very thing he has used to cover the hole will pull, and the rip only get worse. People do not pour new wine into old wineskins. If they do, the skins burst, the wine spills out, and the skins are ruined. No, they pour new wine into new wineskins, and in that way both are preserved."
The Gospel of the Lord.

PRAYER OVER THE GIFTS
   Father,
   the birth of Christ your Son
   deepened the virgin mother's love for you,
   and increased her holiness.
   May the humanity of Christ
   give us courage in our weakness;

may it free us from our sins,
and make our offering acceptable.
We ask this through Christ our Lord.

Communion antiphon

Blessed is the womb of the Virgin Mary; she carried the Son of the eternal Father. (See Lk 11: 27)

Prayer after communion

Lord,
we rejoice in your sacraments and ask your mercy
as we honor the memory of the Virgin Mary.
May her faith and love
inspire us to serve you more faithfully
in the work of salvation.
Grant this in the name of Jesus the Lord.

MEDITATION OF THE DAY

New Wine and Mary's Heart

The Son of God gave us the holy heart of his most cherished Mother, which is none other than his own true heart, so that his children have only one heart with their Father and Mother, and all the members of his family have only the heart of the adorable chief. Let us remember that we constantly serve, love, and adore God with a heart worthy of its infinite grandeur: *Corde magno et animo volenti;* with a heart all pure and holy, singing his divine praises and performing all our actions with saintliness, love, humility, and with all the other holy dispositions characteristic of this beautiful Heart of Mary.

To accomplish this, at the beginning of each action, we must completely renounce our own heart, which means our mind, self-love and will, and we give ourselves to our Lord, to be united with the love of his heart and the heart of his most Blessed Mother. Let us work, then, to become detached from our earthly, wicked, and depraved heart, so that we shall gain a heart truly celestial, holy, and divine...

Our most sweet Jesus has given us the very benign heart of his precious Mother as a fountain of wine, milk, and honey, from which we draw the charity, gentleness, and meekness which we must show to our neighbor. Our Lord has also given us her heart as an oracle to be devoutly consulted in all our doubts and perplexities, so that we may know and follow faithfully his adorable will.

Oh Mother of Fair Love, bind our hearts so closely to yours that they may never be separated! Pray that the hearts of your children may have no other sentiments than those of the most Immaculate Heart of their all-perfect Mother.

SAINT JOHN EUDES

Saint John Eudes († 1680) is largely responsible for initiating and popularizing devotion to the Immaculate Heart of Mary.

Prayer for the Evening

Vigil of the Fourteenth Sunday in Ordinary Time

Let us ring out our joy to God our strength!

Glory to the Father, and to the Son,
and to the Holy Spirit, as it was in the beginning,
is now, and will be for ever. Amen. Alleluia!

HYMN   Meter: CMD
This hymn can be sung to the tune used for
All You Who Seek a Comfort Sure

O come to me, the Master said,
My Father knows your need;
And I shall be, the Master said,
Your bread of life indeed.
By faith in him we live and grow

And share the broken bread
And all his love and goodness know,
For so the Master said.

Abide in me, the Master said,
The true and living vine;
My life shall be, the Master said,
Poured out for you as wine.
His body to the cross he gave,
His blood he freely shed,
Who came in love to seek and save,
For so the Master said.

PSALM 81   2-3, 6c-8, 10-11, 14-17

Come to me, all you who labor and are burdened, and I will give you
rest. Take my yoke upon you and learn from me. (Mt 11: 28-29)

Sunday is a day of many blessings: we celebrate our freedom from
the burden of sin with a day of rest in God, our deliverance from
death by participation in the eucharistic memorial of Christ's
passover, God's fulfillment of the promise to feed us with the finest
wheat in holy communion.

Ring out your joy to God our strength,
shout in triumph to the God of Jacob.
Raise a song and sound the timbrel,
the sweet-sounding harp and the lute.

A voice I did not know said to me:
"I freed your shoulder from the burden;
your hands were freed from the load.
You called in distress and I saved you.

Let there be no foreign god among you,
no worship of an alien god.
I am the Lord your God,
who brought you from the land of Egypt.
Open wide your mouth and I will fill it.

O that my people would heed me,
that Israel would walk in my ways!
At once I would subdue their foes,
turn my hand against their enemies.

The Lord's enemies would cringe at their feet
and their subjection would last for ever.
But Israel I would feed with finest wheat
and fill them with honey from the rock."

Glory to the Father...

Word of God   Ezekiel 20: 5-6

THUS SPEAKS the Lord God:
The day I chose Israel,
I swore to the descendants of the house of Jacob; in the
land of Egypt I revealed myself to them and swore: I am
the Lord, your God. That day I swore to bring them out
of the land of Egypt to the land I had scouted for them,
a land flowing with milk and honey, a jewel among all
lands.

Hear, O Israel, the Lord is our God, the Lord alone.
(Dt 6: 4)

CANTICLE OF MARY   (Text, back cover A)
I am the bread of life; whoever comes to me will never hunger, and
whoever believes in me will never thirst. (Jn 6: 35)

INTERCESSIONS

To Christ, our freedom and our peace, we pray:

℟   Hear us as we pray to you!

You have called us to worship you in joy:
– teach us to keep holy your day. ℟

You have freed us from the burden of our sin:
– grant us grace to take on your gentle yoke in its place. ℟

You have saved us from the gods we have created for ourselves:
– feed us with the bread of freedom and of life. ℟

You have promised us a land from which all shadows are banished:
– lead into your light all our beloved dead. ℟

Personal intentions

Our Father…

May the blessing of almighty God, Father, Son, and Holy Spirit, descend upon us and remain with us for ever. Amen.

MARIAN ANTIPHON   (Text, page 25)

SAINTS
OF TODAY AND YESTERDAY

The hope of the righteous ends in gladness.

BLESSED PAULINE OF THE SUFFERING HEART OF JESUS
Virgin and Religious (1865-1942)

At the age of ten, Amabile Wisenteiner emigrated with her family from the South Tyrol region near the Austrian-Italian border to the Santa Catarina province of southern Brazil. Working in her home and in the fields to help her poor parents, she spent her free time catechizing other girls and visiting the sick with a friend. Encouraged by Jesuit missionaries to consider becoming a religious, Amabile at the age of fifteen, along with her friend, moved to a small cottage near Vigolo's Chapel of Saint George in order to devote themselves to the care of a woman dying of cancer. This initial work of mercy ultimately led Amabile to found a new congregation, the Little Sisters of the Immaculate Conception, which received episcopal approval in 1895; it was at this time that she took her religious vows and received the name Pauline of the Suffering Heart of Jesus. After serving as the congregation's superior for fourteen years, she resigned in 1909 and spent the rest of her life as an ordinary sister, dedicating herself to the care of the elderly poor. She died on July 9, 1942.

Leave your future in his hands,
in the heart of Jesus made man.
Saint Theophane Venard

Word of God

for a Sunday

Luke 10: 1-12, 17-20

"Lord, even the demons are subject to us because of your name." The disciples are exultant over their success whereas Jesus rejoices in the Holy Spirit – a significant contrast. Jesus moves quickly to the more cogent reason the disciples have for rejoicing; it is the fact that their names are written in heaven. Therein lie the best grounds they have for euphoria, namely, their salvation.

J. T.

■ Suggested Prayer of the Faithful ■

(Each local community should compose its own Universal Prayer, but may find inspiration in the texts proposed here.)

Let us offer our petitions in the firm confidence of being heard by our God who cherishes us as his own people.

That the Church may delight in the overflowing blessings of her Lord, who has promised to fill her with abundant peace and consolation for the days in which she has known sorrow and tears.

For the welfare and intentions of our Holy Father, and for strength in his unceasing labors for the Church throughout the world.

That the practice of eucharistic adoration may continue to increase and flourish in the parishes of our country, drawing us together in the heart of Christ.

That the leaders of nations may unite in concern for the poor and underprivileged peoples of the world, and find ways of relieving their distress by a common effort.

That those privileged ones whom God is calling to the priesthood and religious life may respond eagerly in faith and generosity and find support in their families and friends.

That all who suffer from terminal illness may find strength in their oneness with Christ dying on his cross and in the compassionate love of his Mother who stood close to him to the end.

For refugees, immigrants, and all victims of famine, war, and natural disasters, that they may receive sympathy and practical assistance as they try to build a new life in our country.

Heavenly Father, you give us your love to balance the woes that beset us because of our human failings. Grant that we may respond to your love in Christ Jesus, your Son and our Lord.

SUNDAY, JULY 8
Fourteenth Sunday in Ordinary Time

Prayer for the Morning

God indeed is the Lord, and there is no other:
come, let us adore!

Glory to the Father, and to the Son,
and to the Holy Spirit, as it was in the beginning,
is now, and will be for ever. Amen. Alleluia!

HYMN

Meter: SM
This hymn can be sung to the tune used for
'Tis Good, Lord, To Be Here

It is a wondrous thing
To glorify and praise
Our God the everlasting Word,
And Lord of endless days.

The trembling cherubim
Bow low and fold their wings,
And all the heav'nly hosts adore
The mighty King of kings.

We would our off'ring give,
O Christ, to thee we pray,
For thou didst break the bands of death
When dawned the glorious day.

To thee, O Three in One,
Ascends our song divine;
One pow'r, one kingdom without end,
And one dominion thine.

O Christ, the source of light,
With light our souls inspire;
Come, make our hearts the bright abode
Of thy celestial fire.

PSALM 97 1-6, 11-12

He will baptize you with the holy Spirit and fire. (Mt 3: 11)

Fire gives light. May the fire of the Holy Spirit which the risen Christ
has sown in the hearts of all the baptized give light to all the world!

The Lord is king, let earth rejoice,
let all the coastlands be glad.
Cloud and darkness are his raiment;
his throne, justice and right.

A fire prepares his path;
it burns up his foes on every side.
His lightnings light up the world,
the earth trembles at the sight.

The mountains melt like wax
before the Lord of all the earth.
The skies proclaim his justice;
all peoples see his glory.

Light shines forth for the just
and joy for the upright of heart.
Rejoice, you just, in the Lord;
give glory to his holy name.

Glory to the Father...

Word of God Isaiah 26: 19

YOUR DEAD SHALL LIVE, their
corpses shall rise; awake
and sing, you who lie in the dust. For your dew is a dew
of light, and the land of shades gives birth.

I am the light of the world, says the Lord.

CANTICLE OF ZECHARIAH (Text, back cover B)
I have come to set the earth on fire, and how I wish it were already
blazing! (Lk 12: 49)

INTERCESSIONS

With awe-filled confidence, let us lay our needs before God:

℟   Enlighten all people, O Lord.

You spoke from the bush that burned but was not consumed:
– speak to us in the word read in our assemblies today. ℟

You dwelt in the pillar of fire by night and the pillar of cloud by day:
– lead us out of darkness into your glorious light. ℟

You cast upon the earth the transforming fire of the Holy Spirit:
– make us new on this Sunday, first of days. ℟

Personal intentions

Our Father...

O God of fire and light, before whom there can be no other, illumine our hearts by the light of your glory, that we may know and worship you as our one true God, through Jesus Christ, your Son, our Lord, who lives and reigns with you and the Holy Spirit, one God for ever and ever. Amen.

MASS

Fourteenth Sunday in Ordinary Time

ENTRANCE ANTIPHON

Within your temple, we ponder your loving kindness, O God. As your name, so also your praise reaches to the ends of the earth; your right hand is filled with justice. (Ps 47: 10-11)

GLORIA ———————————————— page 226

OPENING PRAYER

Father,
through the obedience of Jesus,
your servant and your Son,
you raised a fallen world.
Free us from sin
and bring us the joy that lasts for ever.
We ask this through our Lord Jesus Christ, your Son,
who lives and reigns with you and the Holy Spirit,
one God, for ever and ever.

ALTERNATIVE OPENING PRAYER

Father,
in the rising of your Son
death gives birth to new life.
The sufferings he endured restored hope
   to a fallen world.
Let sin never ensnare us
with empty promises of passing joy.
Make us one with you always,
so that our joy may be holy,
and our love may give life.
We ask this through Christ our Lord.

● *Behold, I will spread prosperity over her like a river.* ●

A reading from
the Book of the Prophet Isaiah   66: 10-14c

THUS SAYS THE LORD:/ Rejoice
with Jerusalem and be glad
because of her,/ all you who love her;/ exult, exult with
her,/ all you who were mourning over her!/ Oh, that you
may suck fully/ of the milk of her comfort,/ that you
may nurse with delight/ at her abundant breasts!/ For
thus says the LORD:/ Lo, I will spread prosperity over

Jerusalem like a river,/ and the wealth of the nations like an overflowing torrent./ As nurslings, you shall be carried in her arms,/ and fondled in her lap;/ as a mother comforts her child,/ so will I comfort you;/ in Jerusalem you shall find your comfort./

When you see this, your heart shall rejoice/ and your bodies flourish like the grass;/ the LORD's power shall be known to his servants.

The word of the Lord.

──── • PSALM 66 • ────

℟ (1) **Let all the earth cry out to God with joy.**

Shout joyfully to God, all the earth,
    sing praise to the glory of his name;
    proclaim his glorious praise.
Say to God, "How tremendous are your deeds!" ℟

"Let all on earth worship and sing praise to you,
    sing praise to your name!"
Come and see the works of God,
    his tremendous deeds among the children of Adam. ℟

He has changed the sea into dry land;
    through the river they passed on foot;
    therefore let us rejoice in him.
He rules by his might forever. ℟

Hear now, all you who fear God,
    while I declare what he has done for me.
Blessed be God who refused me not
    my prayer or his kindness! ℟

● *I bear the marks of Jesus on my body.* ●

A reading from
the Letter of Saint Paul to the Galatians   6: 14-18

Brothers and sisters: May I never boast except in the cross of our Lord Jesus Christ, through which the world has been crucified to me, and I to the world. For neither does circumcision mean anything, nor does uncircumcision, but only a new creation. Peace and mercy be to all who follow this rule and to the Israel of God.

From now on, let no one make troubles for me; for I bear the marks of Jesus on my body.

The grace of our Lord Jesus Christ be with your spirit, brothers and sisters. Amen.
The word of the Lord.

Alleluia, alleluia. Let the peace of Christ control your hearts; let the word of Christ dwell in you richly. Alleluia, alleluia.

Longer Form

● *Your peace will rest on that person.* ●

A reading from
the holy Gospel according to Luke   10: 1-12, 17-20

At that time the Lord appointed seventy-two others whom he sent ahead of him in pairs to every town and place he intended to visit. He said to them, "The harvest is abundant but the laborers are few; so ask the master of the harvest to send out laborers for his harvest. Go on your way; behold, I am sending you like lambs among wolves. Carry no money bag, no sack, no sandals; and greet no one along the way. Into whatever house you enter, first say, 'Peace to this household.' If a peaceful person lives there, your peace will rest on him; but if not, it will return to you. Stay in the same house and eat and drink what is offered to you, for the laborer deserves his payment. Do not move about from one house to another. Whatever town you enter and they welcome you, eat what is set before you, cure the sick in it and say to them, 'The kingdom of God is at hand for you.' Whatever town you enter and they do not receive you, go out into the streets and say, 'The dust of your town that clings to our feet, even that we shake off against you.' Yet know this: the kingdom of God is at hand. I tell you, it will be more tolerable for Sodom on that day than for that town."

The seventy-two returned rejoicing, and said, "Lord, even the demons are subject to us because of your name." Jesus said, "I have observed Satan fall like lightning from the sky. Behold, I have given you the power to 'tread upon serpents' and scorpions and upon the full force of the enemy and nothing will harm you. Nevertheless, do not rejoice because the spirits are subject to you, but rejoice because your names are written in heaven."

The Gospel of the Lord.

Or:

Shorter Form

● *Your peace will rest on that person.* ●

A reading from
the holy Gospel according to Luke
10: 1-9

A T THAT TIME the Lord appointed seventy-two others whom he sent ahead of him in pairs to every town and place he intended to visit. He said to them, "The har-

vest is abundant but the laborers are few; so ask the master of the harvest to send out laborers for his harvest. Go on your way; behold, I am sending you like lambs among wolves. Carry no money bag, no sack, no sandals; and greet no one along the way. Into whatever house you enter, first say, 'Peace to this household.' If a peaceful person lives there, your peace will rest on him; but if not, it will return to you. Stay in the same house and eat and drink what is offered to you, for the laborer deserves his payment. Do not move about from one house to another. Whatever town you enter and they welcome you, eat what is set before you, cure the sick in it and say to them, 'The kingdom of God is at hand for you.'"
The Gospel of the Lord.

CREDO ——————————————————— page 227

PRAYER OVER THE GIFTS
> Lord,
> let this offering to the glory of your name
> purify us and bring us closer to eternal life.
> We ask this in the name of Jesus the Lord.

PREFACE OF SUNDAYS IN ORDINARY TIME ———— page 231

COMMUNION ANTIPHON
Taste and see the goodness of the Lord; blessed is he who hopes in God. (Ps 33: 9)

Or:

Come to me, all you that labor and are burdened, and I will give you rest, says the Lord. (Mt 11: 28)

PRAYER AFTER COMMUNION
> Lord,
> may we never fail to praise you
> for the fullness of life and salvation
> you give us in this Eucharist.
> We ask this through Christ our Lord.

D A Y   B Y   D A Y

Peace, the Enemy, and the Reign of God

It is a fearful and heinous thing for us, because of our love for things corruptible, deliberately to kill the life that was given to us by God as the gift of the Holy Spirit. Those who have trained themselves to prefer truth to self-love will certainly know this fear.

Let us use peace in the right way: repudiating our evil alliance with the world and its ruler, let us at last break off the war which we wage against God through the passions. Concluding an unbreakable covenant of peace with him by destroying the body of sin within us (cf. Rom 6: 6), let us put an end to our hostility towards him.

Rebelling as we do against God through the passions and agreeing to pay tribute in the form of evil to that cunning tyrant and murderer of souls, the devil, we cannot be reconciled with God until we have first begun to fight against the devil with all our strength. For even though we assume the name of faithful Christians, until we have made ourselves the devil's enemies and fight against him, we continue by deliberate choice to serve the shameful passions. And nothing of profit will come to us from our peace in the world, for our soul is in an evil state, rebelling against its own maker, and unwilling to be subject to his kingdom. It is still sold into bondage to hordes of savage masters, who urge it towards evil and treacherously contrive to make it choose the way which leads to destruction instead of that which brings salvation.

God made us so that we might become "partakers of the divine nature" (2 Pt 1: 4) and sharers in his eternity, and so that we might come to be like him (cf. 1 Jn 3: 2) through deification by grace. It is through deification that all things are reconstituted and achieve their permanence; and it is for its sake that what is not is brought into being and given existence.

SAINT MAXIMOS THE CONFESSOR

Saint Maximos the Confessor († 662) was a monk in a monastery near Constantinople and an ardent defender of the faith who was brutally persecuted for his preaching.

Prayer for the Evening

Let us praise the name of the Lord!

Glory to the Father, and to the Son,
and to the Holy Spirit, as it was in the beginning,
is now, and will be for ever. Amen. Alleluia!

HYMN   Meter: 65 65 D

At the name of Jesus
Ev'ry knee shall bow,
Ev'ry tongue confess him
King of glory now;
'Tis the Father's pleasure
We should call him Lord,
Who from the beginning
Was the mighty Word.

Humbled for a season
To receive a name
From the lips of sinners
Unto whom he came;
Faithfully he bore it
Spotless to the last,
Brought it back victorious
When through death he passed.

CANTICLE   Philippians 2: 6-11

Everyone shall be saved who calls on the name of the Lord. (Acts 2: 21)

In the vocabulary of the Bible, the "name" of the Lord represents the person and presence of the Lord. Truly, then, may we call on the name of the Lord to deliver us from the darkness of death into the glorious day of eternal life.

Though he was in the form of God,
Jesus did not consider equality with God
something to be grasped at.

Rather, he emptied himself
and took the form of a slave,
being born in the likeness of men.

He was known to be of human estate,
and it was thus that he humbled himself,
obediently accepting even death,
death on a cross!

Because of this,
God highly exalted him
and bestowed on him the name
above every other name,

So that at Jesus' name
every knee must bend
in the heavens, on the earth,
and under the earth,
and every tongue proclaim
to the glory of God the Father:
JESUS CHRIST IS LORD!

Word of God
                                                    Acts 4: 11-12

THIS JESUS IS "the stone rejected by the builders which has
become the cornerstone." There is no salvation in anyone else, for there is no other name in the whole world
given to men by which we are to be saved.

Blessed be his holy name!

CANTICLE OF MARY   (Text, back cover A)
You shall conceive and bear a son and give him the name Jesus.
(Lk 1: 31)

INTERCESSIONS

In faith, let us call upon the name of the Lord:

℟   Have mercy on us!

Jesus, Son of the living God,
– fill your people with faith in the power of your name. ℟

Jesus, splendor of the Father,
– illumine the darkness of those who have rejected God. ℟

Jesus, author of life,
– bring to everlasting life all those who have gone before us in faith, and those whose faith is known to you alone. ℟

Personal intentions

Our Father...

May the all-powerful God protect us from all evil and bring us to life everlasting. Amen.

MARIAN ANTIPHON   (Text, page 25)

MONDAY, JULY 9

Prayer for the Morning

The Lord is just:
come, let us adore him!

Glory to the Father... Alleluia!

HYMN
Meter: CM
This hymn can be sung to the tune used for
How Good the Name of Jesus Sounds

Tall stands the Tree beside the stream
Where living waters flow;
Wide-flung the branches, cool the shade,
Where all the weary go.

Fresh green the leaves for healing giv'n,
Bright gold the new-pressed oil
That runs as balm upon the banks
Toward which the weary toil.

Deep-scarred the bark, but sweet the wine
That pours down, last and best,
And rich the table spread below,
Where all the weary rest.

Sing praise to God, the gardener
Whose labors never cease
To make beneath the Tree of Life
For all the weary, peace.

PSALM 1   1-3

A spreading olive tree, goodly to behold, the Lord has named you.
(Jer 11: 16)

One tradition holds that the olive tree was the tree of life planted in
Eden. Christian sentiment thinks of the cross as the tree of life that

awaits us in paradise restored. From it flows the grace of the Spirit that reaches us through God's word and all the sacraments. Those who sink their roots into that stream of grace bear, like the tree, life-giving fruit in prayer and in deeds of kindness, justice, and mercy for all.

Happy indeed is the man
who follows not the counsel of the wicked;
nor lingers in the way of sinners
nor sits in the company of scorners,
but whose delight is the law of the Lord
and who ponders his law day and night.

He is like a tree that is planted
beside the flowing waters,
that yields its fruit in due season
and whose leaves shall never fade;
and all that he does shall prosper.

Glory to the Father...

Word of God
Isaiah 44: 3-4

I WILL POUR OUT WATER upon the thirsty ground, and streams upon the dry land; I will pour out my spirit upon your offspring, and my blessing upon your descendants. They shall spring up amid the verdure like poplars beside the flowing waters.

Go and bear fruit that will remain. (Jn 15: 16)

Canticle of Zechariah
(Text, back cover B)

Planted in the house of the Lord, they will flourish in the courts of our God, still bearing fruit when they are old, still full of sap, still green, to proclaim that the Lord is just. (Ps 92: 14-16a)

Intercessions

To Christ our life, we pray:

℟   Bear fruit in us!

You are the fount of life:
– enliven the listless spirits of believers who have lost their taste for prayer. ℟

You are the tree of life:
– make strong the branches who have been weakened by the storms of daily life. ℟

Your Spirit is the living water flowing from your side:
– deepen the roots of those who have grown restless for more abundant life. ℟

Your Church is the orchard fed and pruned by your love:
– may all who seek peace find rest in its shade. ℟

Personal intentions

Our Father…

God our Father, by the death of your Son, you planted the seed of the tree of life deep in this earth. By his resurrection, you gave it light and warmth. By the gift of the Spirit, you water it with the waters of life that flowed from his side on the cross. May our lives bear its fruit, through the same Christ our Lord. Amen.

Mass

Monday of the Fourteenth Week of the Year

(Today, the prayers in Thanksgiving, given below, could be used.)

Entrance antiphon

Sing and play music in your hearts to the Lord, always giving thanks for everything to God the Father in the name of our Lord Jesus Christ. (Eph 5: 19-20)

OPENING PRAYER

Father of mercy,
you always answer your people in their sufferings.
We thank you for your kindness
and ask you to free us from all evil,
that we may serve you in happiness all our days.
We ask this through our Lord Jesus Christ, your Son,
who lives and reigns with you and the Holy Spirit,
one God, for ever and ever.

● *He saw a ladder standing there, angels of God going
up and coming down, and God speaking.* ●

A reading from
the Book of Genesis   28: 10-22a

JACOB DEPARTED from Beer-sheba and proceeded toward
Haran. When he came upon a certain shrine, as the sun
had already set, he stopped there for the night. Taking
one of the stones at the shrine, he put it under his head
and lay down to sleep at that spot. Then he had a dream:
a stairway rested on the ground, with its top reaching to
the heavens; and God's messengers were going up and
down on it. And there was the Lord standing beside him
and saying:

"I, the Lord, am the God of your forefather Abraham
and the God of Isaac; the land on which you are lying
I will give to you and your descendants. These shall be as
plentiful as the dust of the earth, and through them you
shall spread out east and west, north and south. In you
and your descendants all the nations of the earth shall
find blessing. Know that I am with you; I will protect you
wherever you go, and bring you back to this land. I will
never leave you until I have done what I promised you."

When Jacob awoke from his sleep, he exclaimed, "Truly, the Lord is in this spot, although I did not know it!" In solemn wonder he cried out: "How awesome is this shrine! This is nothing else but an abode of God, and that is the gateway to heaven!" Early the next morning Jacob took the stone that he had put under his head, set it up as a memorial stone, and poured oil on top of it. He called that site Bethel, whereas the former name of the town had been Luz.

Jacob then made this vow: "If God remains with me, to protect me on this journey I am making and to give me enough bread to eat and clothing to wear, and I come back safe to my father's house, the Lord shall be my God. This stone that I have set up as a memorial stone shall be God's abode."

The word of the Lord.

• PSALM 91 •

℟ (2) **In you, my God, I place my trust.**

You who dwell in the shelter of the Most High,
   who abide in the shadow of the Almighty,
Say to the Lord, "My refuge and my fortress,
   my God, in whom I trust." ℟

For he will rescue you from the snare of the fowler,
   from the destroying pestilence.
With his pinions he will cover you,
   and under his wings you shall take refuge. ℟

Because he clings to me, I will deliver him;
   I will set him on high because he acknowledges my
      name.
He shall call upon me, and I will answer him;
   I will be with him in distress. ℟

Alleluia. Our Savior Jesus Christ has done away with death, and brought us life through his gospel. **Alleluia.**

● *My daughter has just died, but come to her and she will live.* ●

A reading from
the holy Gospel according to Matthew   9: 18-26

AS JESUS WAS SPEAKING, a synagogue leader came up, did him reverence and said: "My daughter has just died. Please come and lay your hand on her and she will come back to life." Jesus stood up and followed him, and his disciples did the same. As they were going, a woman who had suffered from hemorrhages for twelve years came up behind him and touched the tassel on his cloak. "If only I can touch his cloak," she thought, "I shall get well." Jesus turned around and saw her and said, "Courage, daughter! Your faith has restored you to health." That very moment the woman got well.

When Jesus arrived at the synagogue leader's house and saw the flute players and the crowd who were making a din, he said, "Leave, all of you! The little girl is not dead. She is asleep." At this they began to ridicule him. When the crowd had been put out he entered and took her by the hand, and the little girl got up. News of this circulated throughout the district.
The Gospel of the Lord.

PRAYER OVER THE GIFTS
Lord,
you gave us your only Son
to free us from death and from every evil.
Mercifully accept this sacrifice
in gratitude for saving us from our distress.
We ask this through Christ our Lord.

COMMUNION ANTIPHON

I will give thanks to you with all my heart, O Lord, for you have answered me. (Ps 137: 1)

PRAYER AFTER COMMUNION

All-powerful God,
by this bread of life
you free your people from the power of sin
and in your love renew their strength.
Help us grow constantly in the hope of eternal glory.
Grant this through Christ our Lord.

M E D I T A T I O N   O F   T H E   D A Y

"Daughter"

In 1975, we welcomed Claudia into our l'Arche community in Suyapa, a slum area of Tegucigalpa, Honduras. She was seven years old and had spent practically her whole life in a dismal, overcrowded asylum. Claudia was blind, fearful of relationships, filled with inner pain, and anguish. Technically speaking she was autistic.

Her anguish seemed to increase terribly when she arrived in the community, probably because in leaving the asylum, she lost her reference points, as well as the structured existence that had given her a certain security. Everything and everyone frightened her; she screamed day and night and smeared excrement on the walls. She seemed totally mad; overwhelmed by insecurity, her personality appeared to be disintegrating....

Twenty years after she first arrived at Suyapa, I visited the community and met Claudia again; I found her quite well. She was then a twenty-eight-year-old woman, still blind and autistic but at peace and able to do many things in the community. She still liked being alone but she was clearly not a lonely person. She would often sing to herself and there was a constant smile on her face.

She did get angry at times, when she felt she was not being respected or was put in a situation that provoked feelings of insecurity. One day, I was sitting opposite to her at lunch and said, "Claudia, can I ask you a question?" She replied, "Si, Juan." "Claudia, why are you so happy?" Her answer was simple and direct: "Dios." God. I asked the community leader, Nadine, what the answer meant. Nadine said, "That is Claudia's secret."

It was loneliness and insecurity that had brought Claudia to the chaos of madness. It was community, love, and friendship that finally brought her inner peace. This movement from chaos to inner peace, from self-hate to self-trust, began when Claudia realized that she was loved.

JEAN VANIER

Jean Vanier is the founder of l'Arche, an international network of communities for the mentally disabled.

Prayer for the Evening

God is our shelter and our shield:
come, let us adore!

Glory to the Father, and to the Son,
and to the Holy Spirit, as it was in the beginning,
is now, and will be for ever. Amen. Alleluia!

HYMN
Meter: 87 87 D
This hymn can be sung to the tune used for
Love Divine, All Loves Excelling

Call on God, your one salvation,
Rest beneath the Almighty's shade;
In his hidden habitation
Dwell, and never be dismayed.
God shall charge his angel legions
Over you their care to keep,
Though you walk through hostile regions,
Though in desert wilds you sleep.

Since, with pure and firm affection,
You have set on God your love
With the wings of his protection,
He will shield you from above.
When you call on him in trouble,
He will hearken, he will save;
Here for grief reward you double,
Crown with life beyond the grave.

PSALM 36   6-10

Over all, his glory will be shelter and protection: shade from the parching heat of day, refuge and cover from storm and rain. (Is 4: 6)

Jesus Christ, God's only-begotten Son, is the wealth of his house; the Spirit pouring out upon the world through his death and resurrection is the stream of God's delight and the source of life. These gifts of God's love are the origin of all holiness.

Your love, Lord, reaches to heaven;
your truth to the skies.
Your justice is like God's mountain,
your judgments like the deep.

To both man and beast you give protection.
O Lord, how precious is your love.
My God, the sons of men
find refuge in the shelter of your wings.

They feast on the riches of your house;
they drink from the stream of your delight.
In you is the source of life
and in your light we see light.

Glory to the Father...

Word of God   Revelation 7: 15-16

THEY STAND BEFORE God's
throne and worship him

day and night in his temple. The one who sits on the
throne will shelter them. They will not hunger or thirst
anymore, nor will the sun or any heat strike them.

> *Let me dwell in your tent for ever*
> *and hide in the shelter of your wings.*
> (Ps 61: 5)

CANTICLE OF MARY   (Text, back cover A)
You are a refuge to the poor, a refuge to the needy in distress; shelter
from the rain, shade from the heat. (Is 25: 4)

INTERCESSIONS

God is our promised shelter and our shade. To him we
pray:

℟   Protect us from all harm.

In the midst of life's tribulations,
– strengthen our hope in your promised kingdom. ℟

In the midst of physical ailments,
– grant us trust in your healing power. ℟

In the midst of worry and distress,
– send us peace of heart. ℟

                                            Personal intentions

Our Father…

May the blessing of almighty God, Father, Son, and Holy
Spirit, descend on us and remain with us for ever. Amen.

MARIAN ANTIPHON   (Text, page 25)

Saints
OF TODAY AND YESTERDAY

> *Blood of Christ, stream of mercy, save us.*

BLESSED GIOVANNA (JANE) OF REGGIO
Virgin and Religious (1428-1491)

A native of Reggio Emilia, Italy, Giovanna Scopelli, unable to gain her parents' consent to her desire of becoming a nun, took up the life of a religious in her own home, including the wearing of a habit. Following her parents' deaths Giovanna sought to found a Carmelite convent in Reggio Emilia. A widow with two daughters took her under her own roof that the four might begin the new religious community. The Convent of Our Lady of the People was formally founded four years later with Giovanna as the first prioress. In addition to joining in the nuns' communal recitation of the Divine Office, Giovanna spent an additional five hours each day in private prayer. On one occasion a troubled mother brought her obstinately heretical son Augustine to the prioress in the hope that she might be able to win the boy back to the Church. Giovanna did all she could to persuade the young man by argumentation but her pleas fell on deaf ears; nevertheless after the mother and son had departed she prayed earnestly for Augustine and eventually attained in this way his conversion.

> *O Jesus, as long as you have a heart so merciful,*
> *all my evils have a remedy...*
> Saint Gemma Galgani

TUESDAY, JULY 10

Prayer for the Morning

God gives life to all that lives:
come, let us return thanks and praise!

Glory to the Father, and to the Son,
and to the Holy Spirit, as it was in the beginning,
is now, and will be for ever. Amen. Alleluia!

HYMN
Meter: 87 87 887
This hymn can be sung to the tune used for
Sing Praise to God Who Reigns Above

All living things upon the earth,
Green fertile hills and mountains,
Sing to the God who gave you birth;
Be joyful, springs and fountains.
Lithe water-life, bright air-borne birds,
Wild roving beasts, tame flocks and herds:
Exalt the God who made you.

O men and women everywhere
Lift up a hymn of glory;
All you who know God's steadfast care,
Tell out salvation's story.
No tongue be silent; sing your part,
You humble souls and meek of heart:
Exalt the God who made you.

PSALM 104
1, 14-18, 33-34, 35b

So do not worry and say, "What are we to eat?" or "What are we to
drink?" or "What are we to wear?" (Mt 6: 31)

God did not create the world only to abandon it to its own devices.
He cares day by day for all that he has made, though we do not
always recognize his hand at work.

Bless the Lord, my soul!
Lord God, how great you are!

You make the grass grow for the cattle
and the plants to serve man's needs,
that he may bring forth bread from the earth
and wine to cheer man's heart;
oil, to make him glad
and bread to strengthen man's heart.

The trees of the Lord drink their fill,
the cedars he planted on Lebanon;
there the birds build their nests:
on the tree-top the stork has her home.
The goats find a home on the mountains
and rabbits hide in the rocks.

I will sing to the Lord all my life,
make music to my God while I live.
May my thoughts be pleasing to him.
I find my joy in the Lord.
Bless the Lord, my soul.

Glory to the Father...

Word of God   Matthew 6: 26-30

Look at the birds in the sky;
they do not sow or reap,
they gather nothing into barns, yet your heavenly
Father feeds them. Are not you more important than
they? Can any of you by worrying add a single moment
to your life-span? Why are you anxious about clothes?
Learn from the way the wild flowers grow. They do not
work or spin. But I tell you that not even Solomon in all
his splendor was clothed like one of them. If God so
clothes the grass of the field, which grows today and is

thrown into the oven tomorrow, will he not much more provide for you, O you of little faith?

> *Is not life more than food*
> *and the body more than clothing?*
> (Mt 6: 25)

CANTICLE OF ZECHARIAH (Text, back cover B)
Your heavenly Father knows that you need all these things. (cf. Mt 6: 32)

INTERCESSIONS

With trust in the love our heavenly Father has for us, we pray:

℟   You are our life, O Lord!

You care for all the works of your hands:
– teach us to help and not to hinder your loving providence. ℟

You feed and clothe all your children:
– forgive us the greediness that seeks to deprive others for our own benefit. ℟

You provide for all the earth:
– grant us the wisdom to see and to serve your purposes. ℟

Personal intentions

Our Father…

Loving Father, you desire to feed, clothe, and shelter all your children. Forgive the sin which seeks to feed, to dress, and to live at the expense of those in need; grant the generosity which seeks to care for all that you have given, through Christ our Lord. Amen.

MASS

Tuesday of the Fourteenth Week of the Year

(Today, the prayers for priestly vocations, given below, could
be used.)

ENTRANCE ANTIPHON
Jesus says to his disciples: ask the Lord to send workers into
his harvest. (Mt 9: 38)

OPENING PRAYER
Father,
in your plan for our salvation you provide shepherds
    for your people.
Fill your Church with the spirit of courage and love.
Raise up worthy ministers for your altars
and ardent but gentle servants of the Gospel.
Grant this through our Lord Jesus Christ, your Son,
who lives and reigns with you and the Holy Spirit,
one God, for ever and ever.

● *Your name shall be called Israel, because you have
been strong against God.* ●

A reading from
the Book of Genesis
32: 23-33

IN THE COURSE of the night,
Jacob arose, took his two
wives, with the two maidservants and his eleven children,
and crossed the ford of the Jabbok. After he had taken
them across the stream and had brought over all his possessions, Jacob was left there alone. Then some man wrestled with him until the break of dawn. When the man saw
that he could not prevail over him, he struck Jacob's hip
at its socket, so that the hip socket was wrenched as they
wrestled. The man then said, "Let me go, for it is day-
break." But Jacob said, "I will not let you go until you

bless me." "What is your name?" the man asked. He
answered, "Jacob." Then the man said, "You shall no
longer be spoken of as Jacob, but as Israel, because you
have contended with divine and human beings and have
prevailed." Jacob then asked him, "Do tell me your name,
please." He answered, "Why should you want to know my
name?" With that, he bade him farewell. Jacob named the
place Peniel, "Because I have seen God face to face," he
said, "yet my life has been spared."

At sunrise, as he left Penuel, Jacob limped along
because of his hip. That is why, to this day, the Israelites
do not eat the sciatic muscle that is on the hip socket,
inasmuch as Jacob's hip socket was struck at the sciatic
muscle.

The word of the Lord.

──────── • PSALM 17 • ────────

℟ (15) **In my justice, I shall see your face, O Lord.**

Hear, O Lord, a just suit;
    attend to my outcry;
    hearken to my prayer from lips without deceit. ℟

From you let my judgment come;
    your eyes behold what is right.
Though you test my heart, searching it in the night,
    though you try me with fire, you shall find no malice
        in me. ℟

I call upon you, for you will answer me, O God;
    incline your ear to me; hear my word.
Show your wondrous kindness,
    O savior of those who flee. ℟

Hide me in the shadow of your wings.
    I in justice shall behold your face;
On waking, I shall be content in your presence. ℟

Alleluia. Open our hearts, O Lord, to listen to the words of your Son. Alleluia.

● *The harvest is rich but the laborers are few.* ●

A reading from
the holy Gospel according to Matthew   9: 32-38

SOME PEOPLE BROUGHT JESUS a mute who was possessed by a demon. Once the demon was expelled the mute began to speak, to the great surprise of the crowds. "Nothing like this has ever been seen in Israel!" they exclaimed. But the Pharisees were saying, "He casts out demons through the prince of demons."

Jesus continued his tour of all the towns and villages. He taught in their synagogues, he proclaimed the good news of God's reign, and he cured every sickness and disease. At the sight of the crowds, his heart was moved with pity. They were lying prostrate from exhaustion, like sheep without a shepherd. He said to his disciples: "The harvest is good but laborers are scarce. Beg the harvest master to send out laborers to gather his harvest."
The Gospel of the Lord.

PRAYER OVER THE GIFTS
    Lord,
    accept our prayers and gifts.
    Give the Church more priests
    and keep them faithful in their love and service.
    Grant this in the name of Jesus the Lord.

COMMUNION ANTIPHON
This is how we know what love is: Christ gave up his life for us; and we too must give up our lives for our brothers. (1 Jn 3: 16)

PRAYER AFTER COMMUNION
    Lord,
    hear the prayers of those who are renewed

with the bread of life at your holy table.
By this sacrament of love
bring to maturity
the seeds you have sown
in the field of your Church;
may many of your people choose to serve you
by devoting themselves to the service of their brothers
   and sisters.
We ask this through Christ our Lord.

MEDITATION OF THE DAY

Expelling Demons

Demonic temptation can take place at various levels. The most elementary level is the sharp, one-time entice-ment which eventually passes, either because it is successfully resisted or eventually given in to. At its most profound level, satanic temptation can result in a bondage to sin which exercises a thorough domination over a per-son which seems impossible to overcome. Demonic temptation ranges from simple and everyday occurrences to bizarre thoughts and expressions. It encompasses everything from "little white lies" to murder and adultery.

The main purpose in demonic temptation is to trap people in sin and keep them off guard. Like military com-mandos, evil spirits make quick raids into vulnerable areas of life. They look for opportunities to use men's weaknesses to their own advantage. They know how to present the "right" temptation, tailor-made for each per-son. They gain footholds in people's lives under the cover of the weakness of the flesh. They look for spiritual, phys-ical, emotional, and mental weak points. Keeping close watch on these areas, they look for occasions to strike and inflict whatever damage they can. They will maintain their hold on an area as long as they remain unchal-lenged...

Evil spirits like to get involved in the little things of the day because they can lead to bigger things. Small irritation can escalate into anger and frustration. Disappointment can become envy and self-pity. These sins can often have their roots in the demonic. Through them, evil spirits can keep Christians' lives off balance, stifle their relationships, and move them toward more opportunities to sin.

FATHER MICHAEL SCANLON, T.O.R. AND RANDALL J. CIRNER

Father Michael Scanlon is the past president of the University of Steubenville in Steubenville, OH, and Randall J. Cirner is the former managing editor of New Covenant magazine and is currently engaged in full-time pastoral work.

Prayer for the Evening

God speaks of peace:
come, let us give thanks and praise!

Glory to the Father, and to the Son,
and to the Holy Spirit, as it was in the beginning,
is now, and will be for ever. Amen. Alleluia!

HYMN   Meter: LM

Remember, Lord, thy works of old,
The wonders that our fathers told;
Remember not our sin's dark stain;
Give peace, O God, give peace again!

Whom shall we trust but thee, O Lord?
Where rest but on thy faithful Word?
None ever called on thee in vain,
Give peace, O God, give peace again!

Where saints and angels dwell above
All hearts are knit in holy love;
O bind us in that heavenly chain;
Give peace, O God, give peace again!

PSALM 85 2-4, 7-14

Peace, peace to the far and the near, says the Lord; and I will heal them. (Is 57: 19)

In the Word made flesh in the incarnation, God's mercy and human faithfulness become one Savior, Christ, who is our peace. In him are all people knit together into one Body.

O Lord, you once favored your land
and revived the fortunes of Jacob,
you forgave the guilt of your people
and covered all their sins.
You averted all your rage,
you calmed the heat of your anger.

Will you not restore again our life
that your people may rejoice in you?
Let us see, O Lord, your mercy
and give us your saving help.

I will hear what the Lord God has to say,
a voice that speaks of peace,
peace for his people and his friends
and those who turn to him in their hearts.
His help is near for those who fear him
and his glory will dwell in our land.

Mercy and faithfulness have met;
justice and peace have embraced.
Faithfulness shall spring from the earth
and justice look down from heaven.

The Lord will make us prosper
and our earth shall yield its fruit.
Justice shall march before him
and peace shall follow his steps.

Glory to the Father...

Word of God

Isaiah 45: 8

LET JUSTICE DESCEND, O heavens, like dew from above, like gentle rain let the skies drop it down. Let the earth open and salvation bud forth; let justice also spring up! I, the Lord, have created this.

> *God lowered the heavens and came down.*
> *(Ps 18: 10)*

CANTICLE OF MARY

(Text, back cover A)

It is the seedtime of peace: the vine shall yield its fruit, the land shall bear its crops, and the heavens shall give their dew. (Zec 8: 12)

INTERCESSIONS

Let us pray to the God of our salvation:

℟   Give peace, O Lord.

You forgave the guilt of your people:
– make all one in the love of Christ. ℟

You spoke the final Word of salvation in the incarnation:
– make all holy by the dying and rising of Christ. ℟

You revealed your faithfulness through the longed-for Messiah:
– make us servants of your justice and peace for all who wait for you. ℟

Personal intentions

Our Father...

May grace and peace in Jesus Christ be with all those beloved of God! Amen. (cf. Rom 1: 7)

MARIAN ANTIPHON

(Text, page 25)

SAINTS
OF TODAY AND YESTERDAY

Blood of Christ, courage of martyrs, save us.

THE SEVEN SONS OF SAINT FELICITY
Martyrs (2nd century)

The acts of these martyrs relate that Felicity, a
Christian widow of Rome, by winning many converts
to the faith through her life of prayer and charity,
aroused the anger of the pagan priests who reported
her to the Emperor Antoninus Pius. After Felicity and
her seven sons were arrested, the prefect urged her to
sacrifice to the Roman gods rather than let her sons
suffer, but she answered, "My children will live
eternally if they are faithful, but must expect eternal
death if they sacrifice to idols." When the next day the
prefect resumed his efforts to make the family
capitulate, Felicity said to her boys, "My sons, look up
to heaven, where Jesus Christ with his saints expects
you. Be faithful in his love, and fight courageously for
your souls." After the mother was beaten, the sons
were separated and sent to separate deaths –
Januarius fell under scourging, Felix and Philip were
clubbed, Silvanus was thrown into the Tiber River,
and Alexander, Vitalis, and Martial were beheaded.
Finally Felicity herself was beheaded. Her feast is
observed separately on November 23.

*The martyrs will enter into heaven in a magnificent
and marvelous procession.*

Saint Thomas More

WEDNESDAY, JULY 11
Saint Benedict

Prayer for the Morning

Come, ring out our joy to the Lord;
hail the rock who saves us!

Glory to the Father, and to the Son,
and to the Holy Spirit, as it was in the beginning,
is now, and will be for ever. Amen. Alleluia!

HYMN   Meter: 78 78 88
This hymn can be sung to the tune used for
Word of God, Come Down on Earth

Blessed Jesus, at your word
We are gathered all to hear you;
Let our hearts and minds be stirred
Now to seek and love and fear you;
By your gospel, pure and holy,
Teach us, Lord to love you solely.

Glorious Lord, yourself impart,
Light of light, from God proceeding;
Open now our ears and hearts,
Help us by your Spirit's pleading;
Hear the cry your church now raises,
Lord, accept our prayers and praises.

PSALM 95   1-9

Listen carefully, my son, to the master's instructions, and attend to
them with the ear of your heart. (Rule of Saint Benedict)

Saint Benedict, the father of Western monasticism, built his own life
of prayer and praise on the Word of God. He directed that all those
who would follow in his footsteps, whether as monks or, in more
recent times, as lay oblates, begin their daily prayer with Psalm 95 so
that they might be reminded to keep open the "ear of the heart."

Come, ring out our joy to the Lord;
hail the rock who saves us.
Let us come before him, giving thanks,
with songs let us hail the Lord.

A mighty God is the Lord,
a great king above all gods.
In his hand are the depths of the earth;
the heights of the mountains are his.
To him belongs the sea, for he made it
and the dry land shaped by his hands.

Come in; let us bow and bend low;
let us kneel before the God who made us
for he is our God and we
the people who belong to his pasture,
the flock that is led by his hand.

O that today you would listen to his voice!
"Harden not your hearts as at Meribah,
as on that day at Massah in the desert
when your fathers put me to the test;
when they tried me, though they saw my work."

Glory to the Father…

Word of God Matthew 7: 24-25

Everyone who listens to these words of mine and acts on them will be like a wise man who built his house on rock. The rain fell, the floods came, and the winds blew and buffeted the house. But it did not collapse; it had been set solidly on rock.

My son, to my words be attentive,
to my sayings incline your ear.
(Prv 4: 20)

CANTICLE OF ZECHARIAH   (Text, back cover B)
Come, children, and hear me that I may teach you the fear of the
Lord. (Ps 34: 12)

INTERCESSIONS

With hearts attuned to hear God's word to us today, we
pray:

℟   Speak, Lord, your servants are listening!

You spoke to your people in the desert:
– let us hear your words in the silence of our prayer. ℟

You sent your Son and Word into the world for our salvation:
– open our hearts to the gift of his love. ℟

You teach your people through all the saints:
– instruct us in their wisdom. ℟

                                              Personal intentions

Our Father…

O God, you called Saint Benedict into the wilderness to
dwell with you in solitude and into the heart of a community to dwell with you in service to others. Through
his intercession, lead us by your word to hear and heed
your will for us this day and every day, through Christ
our Lord. Amen.

MASS

Wednesday of the Fourteenth Week of the Year

BENEDICT   *Memorial*

  ● *Saint Benedict was born in Nursia in Umbria about
  the year 480. Educated in Rome, he began the eremitic
  life in Subiaco where he gathered disciples, and then*

departed for Monte Cassino. There he established the famous monastery and composed the Benedictine Rule. Because this rule was subsequently adopted throughout Europe, he received the title of patriarch of Western monasticism. He died on March 21, 547, but since the end of the eighth century, his memory has been observed on this day. ●

ENTRANCE ANTIPHON

The Lord is my inheritance and my cup; he alone will give me my reward. The measuring line has marked a lovely place for me; my inheritance is my great delight. (Ps 15: 5-6)

OPENING PRAYER

God our Father,
you made Saint Benedict an outstanding guide
to teach men how to live in your service.
Grant that by preferring your love to everything else,
we may walk in the way of your commandments.
We ask this through our Lord Jesus Christ, your Son,
who lives and reigns with you and the Holy Spirit,
one God, for ever and ever.

● *We have merited this misery because we have sinned against our brother.* ●

A reading
from the Book of Genesis   41: 55-57; 42: 5-7a, 17-24

WHEN HUNGER CAME to be felt throughout the land of Egypt and the people cried to Pharaoh for bread, Pharaoh directed all the Egyptians to go to Joseph and do whatever he told them. When the famine had spread throughout the land, Joseph opened all the cities that had grain and rationed it to the Egyptians, since the famine had gripped the land of Egypt. In fact, all the world came to Joseph to obtain rations of grain, for famine had gripped the whole world.

The sons of Israel were among those who came to Egypt to procure rations. It was Joseph, as governor of the country, who dispensed the rations to all the people. When Joseph's brothers came and knelt down before him with their faces to the ground, he recognized them as soon as he saw them. But he concealed his own identity from them and spoke sternly to them.

With that, he locked them up in the guardhouse for three days.

On the third day Joseph said to them: "Do this, and you shall live; for I am a God-fearing man. If you have been honest, only one of your brothers need be confined in this prison, while the rest of you may go and take home provisions for your starving families. But you must come back to me with your youngest brother. Your words will thus be verified, and you will not die." To this they agreed.

To one another, however, they said: "Alas, we are being punished because of our brother. We saw the anguish of his heart when he pleaded with us, yet we paid no heed; that is why this anguish has now come upon us." "Didn't I tell you," broke in Reuben, "not to do wrong to the boy? But you wouldn't listen! Now comes the reckoning for his blood." They did not know, of course, that Joseph understood what they said, since he spoke with them through an interpreter. But turning away from them, he wept.
The word of the Lord.

• Psalm 33 •

℟ (22) **Lord, let your mercy be on us,**
as we place our trust in you.

Give thanks to the Lord on the harp;
    with the ten-stringed lyre chant his praises.

Sing to him a new song;
  pluck the strings skillfully, with shouts of gladness. ℟

The Lord brings to nought the plans of nations;
  he foils the designs of peoples.
But the plan of the Lord stands forever;
  the design of his heart, through all generations. ℟

But see, the eyes of the Lord are upon those who fear him,
  upon those who hope for his kindness,
To deliver them from death
  and preserve them in spite of famine. ℟

Alleluia. Shine on the world like bright stars; you are offering it the word of life. Alleluia.

● *Go to the lost sheep of the house of Israel.* ●

A reading from
the holy Gospel according to Matthew   10: 1-7

JESUS SUMMONED his twelve disciples and gave them authority to expel unclean spirits and to cure sickness and disease of every kind.

The names of the twelve apostles are these: first Simon, now known as Peter, and his brother Andrew; James, Zebedee's son, and his brother John; Philip and Bartholomew, Thomas and Matthew the tax collector; James, son of Alphaeus, and Thaddaeus; Simon the Zealot Party member, and Judas Iscariot, who betrayed him. Jesus sent these men on mission as the Twelve, after giving them the following instructions:

"Do not visit pagan territory and do not enter a Samaritan town. Go instead after the lost sheep of the house of Israel. As you go, make this announcement: 'The reign of God is at hand!'"
The Gospel of the Lord.

PRAYER OVER THE GIFTS
>Lord,
>look kindly on these gifts we present
>on the feast of Saint Benedict.
>By following his example in seeking you,
>may we know unity and peace in your service.
>Grant this through Christ our Lord.

COMMUNION ANTIPHON

I solemnly tell you: those who have left everything and followed me will be repaid a hundredfold and will gain eternal life. (See Mt 19: 27-29)

PRAYER AFTER COMMUNION
>Lord,
>hear the prayers of all
>who have received this pledge of eternal life.
>By following the teaching of Saint Benedict,
>may we be faithful in doing your work
>and in loving our brothers and sisters in true charity.
>We ask this in the name of Jesus the Lord.

MEDITATION OF THE DAY

Giving the Gift We Have Received

In his teaching, the abbot should always observe the Apostle's recommendation, in which he says: "Use argument, appeal, reproof." This means that he must vary with circumstances, threatening and coaxing by turns, stern as a taskmaster, devoted and tender as only a father can be. With the undisciplined and restless, he will use firm argument; with the obedient and docile and patient, he will appeal for greater virtue; but as for the negligent and disdainful, we charge him to use reproof and rebuke. He should not gloss over the sins of those who err, but cut them out while he can, as soon as they begin to sprout, remembering the fate of Eli, priest of Shiloh. For upright and perceptive men, his first and second warnings should be verbal; but those who are evil or stubborn, arrogant or disobedient, he can curb only by blows or some other physical punishment at the first offense. It is written, "The fool cannot be corrected with words"; and again, "Strike your son with a rod and you will free his soul from death."

The abbot must always remember what he is and remember what he is called, aware that more will be expected of a man to whom more has been entrusted. He must know what a difficult and demanding burden he has undertaken: directing souls and serving a variety of temperaments, coaxing, reproving, and encouraging them as appropriate. He must so accommodate and adapt himself to each one's character and intelligence that he will not only keep the flock entrusted to his care from dwindling, but will rejoice in the increase of a good flock. Above all, he must not show too great concern for the fleeting and temporal things of this world, neglecting or treating lightly the welfare of those entrusted to him. Rather, he should keep in mind that he has undertaken the care of souls for whom he must give an account.

SAINT BENEDICT

Saint Benedict († 547) founded the Benedictine Order.

Prayer for the Evening

In God we stand firm for ever:
let us give thanks and praise!

Glory to the Father, and to the Son,
and to the Holy Spirit, as it was in the beginning,
is now, and will be for ever. Amen. Alleluia!

HYMN   Meter: 10 10 10 10
This hymn can be sung to the tune used for
Tell Out, My Soul, the Greatness of the Lord

Lord God, we give you thanks for all your saints
Who sought the trackless footprints of your feet,

Who took into their own a hand unseen
And heard a voice whose silence was complete.

In every word and deed they spoke of Christ,
And in their life gave glory to his name;
Their love was unconsumed, a burning bush
Of which the Holy Spirit was the flame.

Blest Trinity, may yours be endless praise
For all who lived so humbly in your sight;
Your holy ones who walked dark ways in faith
Now share the joy of your unfailing light.

PSALM 15

If we wish to dwell in the tent of [God's] kingdom, we will never arrive
unless we run there by doing good deeds. (Rule of Saint Benedict)

Saint Benedict wrote a Rule which has remained since the sixth century a guide to the "good deeds" required of all those, religious and
lay people, who hope to dwell in God's "tent," the temple of the new
Jerusalem.

Lord, who shall be admitted to your tent
and dwell on your holy mountain?

He who walks without fault;
he who acts with justice
and speaks the truth from his heart;
he who does not slander with his tongue;

he who does no wrong to his brother,
who casts no slur on his neighbor,
who holds the godless in disdain,
but honors those who fear the Lord;

he who keeps his pledge, come what may;
who takes no interest on a loan
and accepts no bribes against the innocent.
Such a man will stand firm for ever.

Glory to the Father...

Word of God   Hebrews 10: 23-25

L ET US HOLD unwaveringly to
our confession that gives us
hope, for he who made the promise is trustworthy. We
must consider how to rouse one another to love and
good works. We should not stay away from our assembly, as is the custom of some, but encourage one another, and this all the more as you see the day drawing near.

*Clothed then with faith and the performance of good
works, let us set out on this way, with the Gospel for
our guide, that we may deserve to see him who has
called us to his kingdom. (Rule of Saint Benedict)*

CANTICLE OF MARY   (Text, back cover A)
We are God's handiwork, created in Christ Jesus for the good works
that God has prepared in advance, that we should live in them.
(cf. Eph 2: 10)

INTERCESSIONS

Through the intercession of Saint Benedict, we pray:

℟   Guide us in your ways, O Lord.

Through the example and intercessions of the saints
– you call your people to holiness: ℟

Through the wisdom of those who lived in full fidelity
to the Gospel
– you show us the way to salvation: ℟

Through the love of those who surrendered their lives
joyfully into your hands
– you show us the hope that awaits us: ℟

                                     Personal intentions
Our Father…

*May we be blessed by the Lord, the maker of heaven and
earth. Amen. (cf. Ps 115: 15)*

MARIAN ANTIPHON   (Text, page 25)

Saints
OF TODAY AND YESTERDAY

The prayer of the humble pierces the clouds.

Saint James of Nisibis
Bishop († 350)

A native of Nisibis in Mesopotamia, James went into the mountains to take up a life of prayer and penance in a cave during the winter and in the woods the rest of the year. During this period he embarked on a journey into Persia to encourage the Christians being persecuted there, sharing in their sufferings while bringing about many conversions. Afterwards he was made bishop of Nisibis where in addition to addressing the needs of the poor he also saw to the construction of a majestic church to which a contemporary, Saint Miles, contributed a large quantity of silk for its adornment. The prayers of James twice saved the city from attacks by invading Persian forces.

Saint Olga
Widow († 969)

The Russian Queen Olga, along with her grandson Saint Vladimir, was converted from a life of pagan barbarism and tyrannical cruelty to the Christian faith, with Olga baptized in Constantinople around 957. Shortly thereafter she invited the Holy Roman Emperor Otto I to send missionaries to her country. Although there were other Russian converts before her, Olga is popularly regarded in her native land as the first Russian to be baptized.

O my God, with all my heart I offer you myself.
Saint Francis de Sales

THURSDAY, JULY 12

Prayer for the Morning

Faithful is God, faithful and true:
let us give thanks and praise! (cf. Is 25: 1)

Glory to the Father, and to the Son,
and to the Holy Spirit, as it was in the beginning,
is now, and will be for ever. Amen. Alleluia!

HYMN   Meter: 87 87 877

Guide me, O thou great Redeemer,
Pilgrim through this barren land.
I am weak, but thou art mighty;
Hold me with thy powerful hand.
Bread of heaven, bread of heaven,
Feed me till I want no more;
Feed me till I want no more.

Open now the crystal fountain,
Whence the healing stream doth flow;
Let the fire and cloudy pillar,
Lead me all my journey through.
Strong Deliverer, strong Deliverer,
Be thou still my Strength and Shield;
Be thou still my Strength and Shield.

PSALM 78   13-19, 23-25

You nourished your people with food of angels and furnished them
bread from heaven, ready to hand, untoiled-for, endowed with all
delights and conforming to every taste. (Wis 16: 20)

The ancient Israelites in the desert failed in trust because they
underestimated God's love for them. It is astonishing how we too can
doubt God's love for us even in the teeth of the most dramatic

evidence. Yet he does not withdraw his gifts in anger but continues to care for us in our need.

God divided the sea and led them through
and made the waters stand up like a wall.
By day he led them with a cloud:
by night, with a light of fire.

He split the rocks in the desert.
He gave them plentiful drink as from the deep.
He made streams flow out from the rock
and made waters run down like rivers.

Yet still they sinned against him;
they defied the Most High in the desert.
In their heart they put God to the test
by demanding the food they craved.

They even spoke against God.
They said: "Is it possible for God
to prepare a table in the desert?"

Yet he commanded the clouds above
and opened the gates of heaven.
He rained down manna for their food,
and gave them bread from heaven.

Mere men ate the bread of angels.
He sent them abundance of food.

Glory to the Father…

Word of God Isaiah 48: 20-21

WITH SHOUTS of joy pro-
claim this, make it
known; publish it to the ends of the earth, and say, "The
Lord has redeemed his servant Jacob. They did not
thirst when he led them through dry lands; water from

the rock he set flowing for them; he cleft the rock, and waters welled forth."

Strong is God's love for us!
(Ps 117: 2)

CANTICLE OF ZECHARIAH   (Text, back cover B)
He feeds you with the finest wheat. (Ps 147: 14)

INTERCESSIONS

What father would give his children a stone when they asked for bread? How much more, then, will our heavenly Father give good things to those who ask him? Let us pray:

℟   We put our trust in you!

You led your people through the sea dry-shod:
– let us put our trust in you as you lead us through this day's challenges. ℟

You fed them in the desert:
– let us hear your word of life amid the noise of our busy lives today. ℟

You gave them water from the rock:
– let us drink from the fountain of life and not from bitter and polluted waters. ℟

Personal intentions

Our Father...

O Lord our God, you sent into the midst of faithless humanity the living Bread, your Son, our Lord Jesus Christ, to nourish and strengthen us on the road. Through the mystery of the cross, you poured forth upon us the Spirit, the water of life. Have mercy on our lack of trust, and lead us in your ways today, through the same Christ our Lord. Amen.

MASS

Thursday of the Fourteenth Week of the Year

(The prayers suggested today are those of the Fourteenth Week in Ordinary Time.)

ENTRANCE ANTIPHON

Within your temple, we ponder your loving kindness, O God. As your name, so also your praise reaches to the ends of the earth; your right hand is filled with justice. (Ps 47: 10-11)

OPENING PRAYER

Father,
through the obedience of Jesus,
your servant and your Son,
you raised a fallen world.
Free us from sin
and bring us the joy that lasts for ever.
We ask this through our Lord Jesus Christ, your Son,
who lives and reigns with you and the Holy Spirit,
one God, for ever and ever.

● *God sent me before you into Egypt to preserve your lives.* ●

A reading
from the Book of Genesis   44: 18-21, 23b-29; 45: 1-5

JUDAH APPROACHED JOSEPH and said: "I beg you, my lord, let your servant speak earnestly to my lord, and do not become angry with your servant, for you are the equal of Pharaoh. My lord asked your servants, 'Have you a father, or another brother?' So we said to my lord, 'We have an aged father, and a young brother, the child of his old age. This one's full brother is dead, and since he is the only one by that mother who is left, his father dotes on him.' Then you told your servants, 'Bring him down to me that my eyes may look on him. Unless your youngest brother comes back with you, you shall not come into my presence again.' When we returned to your servant our father, we reported to him the words of my lord.

"Later, our father told us to come back and buy some food for the family. So we reminded him, 'We cannot go down there; only if our youngest brother is with us can we go, for we may not see the man if our youngest brother is not with us.' Then your servant our father said to us, 'As you know, my wife bore me two sons. One of them, however, disappeared, and I had to conclude that he must have been torn to pieces by wild beasts; I have not seen him since. If you now take this one away from me too, and some disaster befalls him, you will send my white head down to the nether world in grief.'"

Joseph could no longer control himself in the presence of all his attendants, so he cried out, "Have everyone withdraw from me!" Thus no one else was about when he made himself known to his brothers. But his sobs were so loud that the Egyptians heard him, and so the news reached Pharaoh's palace. "I am Joseph," he said to his brothers. "Is my father still in good health?" But his brothers could give him no answer, so dumbfounded were they at him.

"Come closer to me," he told his brothers. When they had done so, he said: "I am your brother Joseph, whom you once sold into Egypt. But now do not be distressed, and do not reproach yourselves for having sold me here. It was really for the sake of saving lives that God sent me here ahead of you."

The word of the Lord.

• PSALM 105 •

℟ (5) **Remember the marvels the Lord has done.**

Or: **Alleluia.**

When he called down a famine on the land
    and ruined the crop that sustained them,
He sent a man before them,
    Joseph, sold as a slave. ℟

They had weighed him down with fetters,
    and he was bound with chains,
Till his prediction came to pass
    and the word of the Lord proved him true. ℟

The king sent and released him,
    the ruler of the peoples set him free.
He made him lord of his house
    and ruler of all his possessions. ℟

Alleluia. O praise the Lord, Jerusalem; he sends out his
word to the earth. Alleluia.

● *You received without charge, give without charge.* ●

**A reading from
the holy Gospel according to Matthew**   10: 7-15

JESUS SAID TO HIS DISCIPLES: "As
    you go, make this announce-
ment: 'The reign of God is at hand!' Cure the sick, raise
the dead, heal the leprous, expel demons. The gift you
have received, give as a gift. Provide yourselves with
neither gold nor silver nor copper in your belts; no
traveling bag, no change of shirt, no sandals, no walking
staff. The workman, after all, is worth his keep.

"Look for a worthy citizen in every town or village you come to and stay with him until you leave. As you enter his home bless it. If the home is deserving, your blessing will descend on it. If it is not, your blessing will return to you. If anyone does not receive you or listen to what you have to say, leave that house or town, and once outside it shake its dust from your feet. I assure you, it will go easier for the region of Sodom and Gomorrah on the day of judgment than it will for that town."
The Gospel of the Lord.

PRAYER OVER THE GIFTS

Lord,
let this offering to the glory of your name
purify us and bring us closer to eternal life.
We ask this in the name of Jesus the Lord.

COMMUNION ANTIPHON

Taste and see the goodness of the Lord; blessed is he who hopes in God. (Ps 33: 9)

PRAYER AFTER COMMUNION

Lord,
may we never fail to praise you
for the fullness of life and salvation
you give us in this Eucharist.
We ask this through Christ our Lord.

MEDITATION OF THE DAY

The Gift We Have Received

The morality which is ultimately self-centered is of necessity individualist also – even the service of others can be a form of selfishness; but the morality which is God-centered, though it necessarily involves the perfection of the self, looks directly to the purposes of God. So when we think of the moral life from God's side, in terms of the giving of his power and life through the sacramental system, we cannot forget that this power is given not for ourselves alone. The Church's office is to bring the truth and the life of God to the world, to restore it; sometimes this power is given to individuals entirely for the sake of others; you read in the New Testament of the gifts of "tongues" and prophecy and the rest, which served and empowered the Church as a whole; you read especially of the gift of healing, the healing of body and soul alike by prayer and the laying on of hands; and still today the Church's office and privilege is to bless and to heal – to bless the earth and the fruits of the earth, to bless the animals, to bless mankind, and to heal the sick in body and mind, to heal by prayer and blessing, to heal through the liturgy which has such power to restore and integrate the unconscious, to heal through the touch of the waters at Lourdes where faith makes whole. But that is not all. The life and power that are given to the individual for the individual are given to the man in his environment, are given to the man as taking part in the cosmic struggle, and so are given in their turn for the blessing and healing of all things.

FATHER GERALD VANN, O.P.

Father Vann († 1963) was an English Dominican and a popular preacher, lecturer, and author.

Prayer for the Evening

*Let us bless the Lord
in the communion of the saints!*

**Glory to the Father, and to the Son,
and to the Holy Spirit, as it was in the beginning,
is now, and will be for ever. Amen. Alleluia!**

HYMN   Meter: CMD
This hymn can be sung to the tune used for
I Heard the Voice of Jesus Say

We sing for all the unsung saints,
That countless, nameless throng,
Who kept the faith and passed it on
With hope steadfast and strong
Through all the daily griefs and joys
No chronicles record,
Forgetful of their lack of fame
But mindful of their Lord.

Though uninscribed with date or place,
With title, rank, or name,
As living stones their stories join
To form a hallowed frame
Around the myst'ry in their midst:
The Lamb once sacrificed,
The Love that wrested life from death,
The wounded, risen Christ.

So we take heart from unknown saints
Bereft of earthly fame,
Those faithful ones who have received
A more enduring name:
For they reveal true blessing comes
When we our pride efface
And offer back our lives to be
The vessels of God's grace.

PSALM 26

May my thoughts be pleasing to him. (Ps 104: 34)

Most of us would feel like the hypocrites and liars of the third stanza if we were to pray this psalm on our own merits, but Christ prays them in and with us, his Body, as he works to bring us to full maturity in him, together with all his saints, known and unknown. Let us strive to take our place with them, relying on their prayer as we journey toward their great assembly.

Give judgment for me, O Lord:
for I walk the path of perfection.
I trust in the Lord; I have not wavered.

Examine me, Lord, and try me;
O test my heart and my mind,
for your love is before my eyes
and I walk according to your truth.

I never take my place with liars
and with hypocrites I shall not go.
I hate the evil-doer's company:
I will not take my place with the wicked.

To prove my innocence I wash my hands
and take my place around your altar,
singing a song of thanksgiving,
proclaiming all your wonders.

O Lord, I love the house where you dwell,
the place where your glory abides.

Do not sweep me away with sinners,
nor my life with bloodthirsty men
in whose hands are evil plots,
whose right hands are filled with gold.

As for me, I walk the path of perfection.
Redeem me and show me your mercy.
My foot stands on level ground:
I will bless the Lord in the assembly.

Glory to the Father...

Word of God

Ephesians 4: 7, 12-13

G RACE WAS GIVEN to each of us according to the measure of Christ's gift for building up the body of Christ, until we all attain to the unity of faith and knowledge of the Son of God, to mature manhood, to the extent of the full stature of Christ.

In him we live and move and have our being.
(*Acts 17: 28*)

CANTICLE OF MARY (Text, back cover A)
Since we have [God's] promises, beloved, let us cleanse ourselves from every defilement of flesh and spirit, making holiness perfect in the fear of God. (2 Cor 7: 1)

INTERCESSIONS

The Lord has chosen us to be holy and blameless in his sight. Let us pray:

℟ Abide with us, O Lord!

Make us walk according to your truth, O Lord: ℟

Let us not go with hypocrites, O Lord: ℟

Keep us from the company of evil-doers, O Lord: ℟

Redeem us and show us your mercy, O Lord: ℟

Personal intentions

Our Father…

May grace and peace from God our Father descend upon all the faithful who desire to be holy. Amen. (cf. Col 1: 2)

MARIAN ANTIPHON (Text, page 25)

SAINTS
OF TODAY AND YESTERDAY

I will help you, says the Lord.

SAINT JOHN THE IBERIAN
Monk († c. 1002)

Leaving his life in the world, John, a native of the Asian region of Georgia, entered a Greek monastery on Mount Olympus and later moved to the more secluded monastery of Saint Athanasius on Mount Athos. Subsequently he along with his son and his brother-in-law established a separate religious community on Mount Athos for Georgian monks – Ivirion. In his final years he was confined to bed by illness; before dying he exhorted his fellow monks, "Let no one distract you from our holy work and from the love of God."

SAINT JOHN JONES/BUCKLEY
Priest, Religious, and Martyr († 1598)

John Jones, from Caernarvonshire, Wales, having become a Franciscan priest in Rome, sought and obtained permission in 1592 to serve the persecuted Catholics of England, where after four years he was arrested, imprisoned, and tortured. At his trial, charged with treason because of his priesthood, he answered, "If this be a crime I must own myself guilty; for I am a priest, and came to England to gain as many souls as I could to Christ." He was executed on July 12, 1598.

Never fail to receive guests well and share with the poor, according as you are able, those things which God in his goodness has given to you.
Saint John the Iberian

FRIDAY, JULY 13
Saint Henry

Prayer for the Morning

God is in our midst, a mighty savior:
come, let us adore!

Glory to the Father, and to the Son,
and to the Holy Spirit, as it was in the beginning,
is now, and will be for ever. Amen. Alleluia!

HYMN   Meter: 8 7 8 7 D
This hymn can be sung to the tune used for
Those Who Love and Those Who Labor

All who seek to know and serve God,
See the past and understand:
None who hoped were disappointed;
Rich the blessings from his hand!
None who waited were forsaken;
None who trusted were deceived.
All who asked his gracious pardon,
Gentle mercy have received.

If our God does not condemn us,
Who against us then will stand?
Will the Lord who died for sinners,
Who is now at God's right hand?
What could take us from Christ Jesus?
Neither hunger, sword, nor pain!
Neither life nor death shall part us
From the Lamb for us once slain.

PSALM 39   9-14

At the time, all discipline seems a cause not for joy but for pain, yet
later it brings the peaceful fruit of righteousness to those who are
trained by it. (Heb 12: 11)

Our sins can weigh us down with discouragement. Saint Ignatius of Loyola tells us that discouragement is never from God because it clouds faith and hope. God's love does not deal in punishment as human vengeance does. God's love disciplines us in order to free and purify us – sometimes a painful process – so that we may not die but live in Christ.

Set me free from all my sins,
do not make me the taunt of the fool.
I was silent, not opening my lips,
because this was all your doing.

Take away your scourge from me.
I am crushed by the blows of your hand.
You punish man's sins and correct him;
like the moth you devour all he treasures.

Mortal man is no more than a breath;
O Lord, hear my prayer.
O Lord, turn your ear to my cry.
Do not be deaf to my tears.

In your house I am a passing guest,
a pilgrim, like all my fathers.
Look away that I may breathe again
before I depart to be no more.

Glory to the Father…

Word of God   Zephaniah 3: 16-18

ON THAT DAY, it shall be said to Jerusalem: Fear not, O Zion, be not discouraged! The Lord, your God, is in your midst, a mighty savior; he will rejoice over you with gladness, and renew you in his love, he will sing joyfully because of you, as one sings at festivals. I will remove disaster from among you, so that none may recount your disgrace.

> *Take courage, it is I; do not be afraid.*
> (Mt 14: 27)

CANTICLE OF ZECHARIAH   (Text, back cover B)
My soul, give thanks to the Lord, all my being, bless his holy name.
(Ps 103: 1)

INTERCESSIONS

Mindful of God's saving love for us, we pray:

℟   Have mercy on your people, Lord.

You are the potter and we the clay:
– shape us in your image according to your will. ℟

You are the shepherd and we the flock:
– seek out those who have strayed from your ways. ℟

You are the host and we the guests at your table:
– feed the hungry of spirit with the bread of your loving forgiveness. ℟

You are the source and model of all true authority:
– inspire all political authorities to use their power for good, through the example and intercession of Saint Henry. ℟

Personal intentions

Our Father...

God of mercy and compassion, you brought about the salvation of the world through the death and resurrection of Jesus Christ. Have mercy on us when we fail to live the new life you have given us; raise us up when our sinfulness sinks us into discouragement; grant us courage to renew our desire to live according to your will, through the same Christ our Lord. Amen.

Mass

Friday of the Fourteenth Week of the Year

Henry   *Optional memorial*

● *Saint Henry was born in Bavaria in 973. He succeeded his father in ruling over a duchy and was later elected emperor. He was most remarkable for his work in Church reform and for fostering missionary activity. He died in 1024 and was enrolled among the saints by Pope Eugene III in 1146.* ●

Entrance antiphon

May all your works praise you, Lord, and your saints bless you; they will tell of the glory of your kingdom and proclaim your power. (Ps 144: 10-11)

Opening prayer

Lord,
you filled Saint Henry with your love
and raised him from the cares of an earthly kingdom
to eternal happiness in heaven.
In the midst of the changes of this world,
may his prayers keep us free from sin
and help us on our way toward you.
Grant this through our Lord Jesus Christ, your Son,
who lives and reigns with you and the Holy Spirit,
one God, for ever and ever.

● *Now I can die, because I have seen you again.* ●

A reading from
the Book of Genesis   46: 1-7, 28-30

I SRAEL SET OUT with all that
was his. When he arrived at

Beer-sheba, he offered sacrifices to the God of his father Isaac. There God, speaking to Israel in a vision by night, called, "Jacob! Jacob!" "Here I am," he answered. Then he said: "I am God, the God of your father. Do not be afraid to go down to Egypt, for there I will make you a great nation. Not only will I go down to Egypt with you; I will also bring you back here, after Joseph has closed your eyes."

So Jacob departed from Beer-sheba, and the sons of Israel put their father and their wives and children on the wagons that Pharaoh had sent for his transport. They took with them their livestock and the possessions they had acquired in the land of Canaan. Thus Jacob and all his descendants migrated to Egypt. His sons and his grandsons, his daughters and his granddaughters – all his descendants – he took with him to Egypt.

Israel had sent Judah ahead to Joseph, so that he might meet him in Goshen. On his arrival in the region of Goshen, Joseph hitched the horses to his chariot and rode to meet his father Israel in Goshen. As soon as he saw him, he flung himself on his neck and wept a long time in his arms. And Israel said to Joseph, "At last I can die, now that I have seen for myself that Joseph is still alive."
The word of the Lord.

—————— • PSALM 37 • ——————

℟ (39) **The salvation of the just comes from the Lord.**

Trust in the Lord and do good,
    that you may dwell in the land and enjoy security.
Take delight in the Lord,
    and he will grant you your heart's requests. ℟

The Lord watches over the lives of the wholehearted;
  their inheritance lasts forever.
They are not put to shame in an evil time;
  in days of famine they have plenty. ℟

Turn from evil and do good,
  that you may abide forever;
For the Lord loves what is right,
  and forsakes not his faithful ones.
Criminals are destroyed,
  and the posterity of the wicked is cut off. ℟

The salvation of the just is from the Lord;
  he is their refuge in time of distress.
And the Lord helps them and delivers them;
  he delivers them from the wicked and saves them,
  because they take refuge in him. ℟

Alleluia. Happy are they who have kept the word with a
generous heart, and yield a harvest through perseverance. Alleluia.

> ● *It is not you who speak, but the Spirit speaking in
> you.* ●

A reading from
the holy Gospel according to Matthew   10: 16-23

JESUS SAID TO HIS DISCIPLES:
"I am sending you out like
sheep among wolves. You must be clever as snakes and
innocent as doves. Be on your guard with respect to others. They will hale you into court, they will flog you in
their synagogues. You will be brought to trial before
rulers and kings, to give witness before them and the
Gentiles on my account. When they hand you over, do
not worry about what you will say or how you will say
it. When the hour comes, you will be given what you are

to say. You yourselves will not be the speakers; the Spirit of your Father will be speaking in you.

"Brother will hand over brother to death, and the father his child; children will turn against parents and have them put to death. You will be hated by all on account of me. But whoever holds out till the end will escape death. When they persecute you in one town, flee to the next. I solemnly assure you, you will not have covered the towns of Israel before the Son of Man comes." The Gospel of the Lord.

PRAYER OVER THE GIFTS
Lord,
in your kindness hear our prayers
and the prayers which the saints offer on our behalf.
Watch over us that we may offer fitting service at your
altar.
Grant this in the name of Jesus the Lord.

COMMUNION ANTIPHON
May the just rejoice as they feast in God's presence, and delight in gladness of heart. (Ps 67: 4)

PRAYER AFTER COMMUNION
Father, our comfort and peace,
we have gathered as your family
to praise your name and honor your saints.
Let the sacrament we have received
be the sign and pledge of our salvation.
We ask this through Christ our Lord.

MEDITATION OF THE DAY

"You will be given what you are to say"

It is difficult to imagine with how much anxiety our faithful in Vietnam – during the years of greatest trial – defying threats of punishment or imprisonment for listening to "foreign and reactionary propaganda," tuned in to Vatican Radio in order to hear the heartbeat of the universal Church and be united with the successor of Peter.

Much later, I encountered similar circumstances.

I was in isolation in Hanoi when one day, a police woman brought a small fish for me to cook. As soon as I saw the wrappings, I immediately felt a start of joy, but I was careful not to show this externally. My happiness was not because of the fish, but because of the pages of newspaper in which it was wrapped: two pages of the *L'Osservatore Romano*. At that time, when the Vatican newspaper arrived at the post office in Hanoi, it was often confiscated and sold at the market as paper. Those two pages had been used to wrap the little fish. Calmly, without bringing attention to myself, I washed those sheets of newspaper to remove the smell, and then dried them in the sun and preserved them as a relic.

For me, in that unbroken regime of isolation, those pages were a sign of communion with Rome, with Peter, with the Church, and an embrace from Rome. I would not have been able to survive without an awareness of being part of the Church.

Today we live in a world that rejects the values of the civilization of life, of love, and of truth; our hope is the Church, *Image of the Trinity*.

CARDINAL FRANCIS XAVIER NGUYÊN VÂN THUÂN

Cardinal Nguyên Vân Thuân was imprisoned by the Vietnamese government for thirteen years. He is the president of the Pontifical Council for Justice and Peace.

Prayer for the Evening

Jesus Christ is the source of life:
come, let us adore him!

Glory to the Father, and to the Son,
and to the Holy Spirit, as it was in the beginning,
is now, and will be for ever. Amen. Alleluia!

HYMN

Meter: 76 76 D
This hymn can be sung to the tune used for
The Church's One Foundation

No weight of gold or silver
Can measure human worth;
No soul secures its ransom
With all the wealth of earth;
No sinner finds his freedom
But by the gift unpriced,
The Lamb of God unblemished,
The precious blood of Christ.

In Christ the past is over,
A new world now begins.
With him we rise to freedom
Who saves us from our sins.
We live by faith in Jesus
To make his glory known:
Behold, the Man of sorrows,
The Lamb upon his throne!

PSALM 49

6-12, 15b-16

Store up treasures in heaven, where neither moth nor decay destroys,
nor thieves break in and steal. For where your treasure is, there also
will your heart be. (Mt 6: 20-21)

Where we invest our trust and our hope, we invest our lives. Let us
choose to invest in the true source of life, Jesus Christ!

Why should I fear in evil days
the malice of the foes who surround me,
men who trust in their wealth,
and boast of the vastness of their riches?

For no man can buy his own ransom,
or pay a price to God for his life.
The ransom of his soul is beyond him.

He cannot buy life without end,
nor avoid coming to the grave.

He knows that wise men and fools must both perish
and leave their wealth to others.
Their graves are their homes for ever,
their dwelling place from age to age,
though their names spread wide through the land.

With the morning their outward show vanishes
and the grave becomes their home.
But God will ransom me from death
and take my soul to himself.

Glory to the Father...

Word of God   1 Peter 1: 17-21

N OW IF YOU INVOKE as Father
him who judges impartial-
ly according to each one's works, conduct yourselves
with reverence during the time of your sojourning, real-
izing that you were ransomed from your futile conduct,
handed on by your ancestors, not with perishable things
like silver or gold but with the precious blood of Christ
as of a spotless unblemished lamb. He was known
before the foundation of the world but revealed in the
final time for you, who through him believe in God who
raised him from the dead and gave him glory, so that
your faith and hope are in God.

> *The Son of Man came to give his life*
> *as a ransom for many. (cf. Mk 10: 45)*

CANTICLE OF MARY   (Text, back cover A)
Peter said, "I have neither silver nor gold, but what I do have I give
you: in the name of Jesus Christ the Nazorean, rise and walk."
(Acts 3: 6)

INTERCESSIONS

To Christ our life we pray:

℟   Ransom us, O Lord.

When we are tempted to compromise Christian principles out of fear of the rich and powerful: ℟

When we are tempted to drain our time, energy, and love from families and friends for the sake of material gain: ℟

When we are tempted to trust in our own resources rather than in you as the source of life: ℟

Personal intentions

Our Father...

In the foreknowledge of God the Father, through sanctification by the Spirit, for obedience and sprinkling with the blood of Jesus Christ: may grace and peace be ours in abundance. Amen. (cf. 1 Pt 1: 2)

MARIAN ANTIPHON   (Text, page 25)

SAINTS
OF TODAY AND YESTERDAY

You are my glory, O Lord.

SAINT EUGENIUS
Bishop († 505)

In 481 Eugenius was made bishop of Carthage in North Africa where despite his own poverty he was lavish in his generosity to the poor. Huneric, king of the Vandal race that had conquered Carthage and an exponent of the Arian heresy that denied Christ's divinity, sought to thwart the bishop by ordering him not to admit into the churches any of the Vandal race who had converted from Arianism to Catholicism. Eugenius met this challenge by replying that the laws of God precluded him from closing the doors of the churches to any who sought to serve God. The king responded with a large-scale persecution of Catholics, with clergy and laity subjected to banishment, torture, and even death. Eugenius was sent into a desert exile where he lived in the custody of an Arian bishop who treated him brutally. A new Vandal king restored the diocese of Carthage to Eugenius in 488, but in another reverse this king's successor saw to the bishop's condemnation to death by beheading. At the last moment the sentence was not carried out. Instead the bishop was exiled to the Languedoc region of France where he founded a monastery.

The joys of heaven incomparably surpass all the joys that can be devised in this wretched world.
Saint John Fisher

SATURDAY, JULY 14
Blessed Kateri Tekakwitha

Prayer for the Morning

Exalt and acclaim God's name!

Glory to the Father, and to the Son,
and to the Holy Spirit, as it was in the beginning,
is now, and will be for ever. Amen. Alleluia!

HYMN   Meter: LM
This hymn can be sung to the tune used for
Praise God from Whom All Blessings Flow

From all that dwell below the skies,
Let the Creator's praise arise;
Let the Redeemer's name be sung,
Through ev'ry land by ev'ry tongue.

Eternal are your mercies, Lord,
Eternal truth attends your word;
Your praise shall sound from shore to shore,
Till suns shall rise and set no more.

CANTICLE OF JUDITH   16: 1-2, 13-15

O praise the Lord, all you nations, acclaim him all you peoples!
(Ps 117: 1)

Delivered from a life of great pain for a life of deep, personal love for
Jesus Christ, Blessed Kateri sang the new hymn of those whose lives
are shaped by the saving sign of the cross.

Strike up the instruments,
a song to my God with timbrels,
chant to the Lord with cymbals.
Sing to him a new song,
exalt and acclaim his name.

For the Lord is God; he crushes warfare,
and sets his encampment among his people;
he snatched me from the hands of my persecutors.

A new hymn I will sing to my God.
O Lord, great are you and glorious,
wonderful in power and unsurpassable.

Let your every creature serve you;
for you spoke, and they were made,
you sent forth your spirit, and they were created;
no one can resist your word.

The mountains to their bases, and the seas, are shaken;
the rocks, like wax, melt before your glance.
But to those who fear you,
you are very merciful.

Glory to the Father...

Word of God   Philippians 3: 7-10

WHATEVER GAINS I HAD, these I have come to consider a loss because of Christ. More than that, I even consider everything as a loss because of the supreme good of knowing Christ Jesus my Lord. For his sake I have accepted the loss of all things and I consider them so much rubbish, that I may gain Christ and be found in him, not having any righteousness of my own based on the law but that which comes through faith in Christ, the righteousness from God, depending on faith to know him and the power of his resurrection and [the] sharing of his sufferings by being conformed to his death.

I love you, Lord, my strength!
(Ps 18: 2)

CANTICLE OF ZECHARIAH (Text, back cover B)
Into your hands I commend my spirit. It is you who will redeem me, Lord. (Ps 31: 6)

INTERCESSIONS

Through the intercession of Blessed Kateri, let us pray:

℟   You are God indeed!

For all who preach the word of God in lands far from home:
– make eloquent their tongues and faithful their lives. ℟

For all who are drawn to accept the Gospel:
– sign them with the sign of the cross and confirm them in faith. ℟

For those who are fearful of conversion because of its price:
– grant them the courage to choose you regardless of the loss. ℟

For those who have chosen a life of virginity for the sake of Christ:
– keep them faithful to their commitment. ℟

Personal intentions

Our Father…

O God of all nations, you called Blessed Kateri to a life of prayer and witness to the intensity of love committed to Jesus Christ. Through her example and intercession, inspire many young men and women to follow your Son even when he leads them away from familiar surroundings by the beauty of the Gospel. We make our prayer in his name, Christ our Lord. Amen.

Mass

Saturday of the Fourteenth Week of the Year

Blessed Kateri Tekakwitha   *Memorial*

● *Kateri was born in 1656 near the town of Auriesville, New York, the daughter of a Mohawk warrior. She was baptized by Jesuit missionary Father Jacques de Lambertville on Easter of 1676 at the age of twenty. She devoted her life to prayer, penitential practices, and the care of the sick and aged in Caughnawaga near Montreal (where her relics are now enshrined). She incurred the hostility of her tribe because of her faith. She was devoted to the Eucharist, and to Jesus Crucified, and was called the "Lily of the Mohawks." She died in 1680 and was beatified June 22, 1980 – the first native American to be declared "Blessed." ●*

Entrance antiphon

Let us rejoice and shout for joy, because the Lord of all things has favored this holy and glorious virgin with his love.

Opening prayer

Lord God,
you called the virgin, Blessed Kateri Tekakwitha,
to shine among the native American people
as an example of innocence of life.
Through her intercession,
may all peoples of every tribe, tongue, and nation,
having been gathered into your Church,
proclaim your greatness
in one song of praise.
We ask this through our Lord Jesus Christ, your Son,
who lives and reigns with you and the Holy Spirit,
one God, for ever and ever.

● *God will visit you and bring about the deliverance of many people.* ●

A reading from
the Book of Genesis   49: 29-33; 50: 15-24

J ACOB GAVE THIS CHARGE to his
sons: "Since I am about to be
taken to my kindred, bury me with my fathers in the cave
that lies in the field of Ephron the Hittite, the cave in the
field of Machpelah, facing on Mamre, in the land of
Canaan, the field that Abraham bought from Ephron the
Hittite for a burial ground. There Abraham and his wife
Sarah are buried, and so are Isaac and his wife Rebekah,
and there, too, I buried Leah – the field and the cave in
it that had been purchased from the Hittites."

When Jacob had finished giving these instructions to
his sons, he drew his feet into the bed, breathed his last,
and was taken to his kindred.

Now that their father was dead, Joseph's brothers
became fearful and thought, "Suppose Joseph has been
nursing a grudge against us and now plans to pay us
back in full for all the wrong we did him!" So they
approached Joseph and said: "Before your father died,
he gave us these instructions: 'You shall say to Joseph,
Jacob begs you to forgive the criminal wrongdoing of
your brothers, who treated you so cruelly.' Please, therefore, forgive the crime that we, the servants of your
father's God, committed." When they spoke these words
to him, Joseph broke into tears. Then his brothers proceeded to fling themselves down before him and said,
"Let us be your slaves!" But Joseph replied to them:
"Have no fear. Can I take the place of God? Even though
you meant harm to me, God meant it for good, to
achieve his present end, the survival of many people.
Therefore have no fear. I will provide for you and for
your children." By thus speaking kindly to them, he
reassured them.

Joseph remained in Egypt, together with his father's family. He lived a hundred and ten years. He saw Ephraim's children to the third generation, and the children of Manasseh's son Machir were also born on Joseph's knees.

Joseph said to his brothers: "I am about to die. God will surely take care of you and lead you out of this land to the land that he promised on oath to Abraham, Isaac and Jacob."

The word of the Lord.

• PSALM 105 •

℟ (33) **Turn to the Lord in your need and you will live.**

Give thanks to the Lord, invoke his name;
    make known among the nations his deeds.
Sing to him, sing his praise,
    proclaim all his wondrous deeds. ℟

Glory in his holy name;
    rejoice, O hearts that seek the Lord!
Look to the Lord in his strength;
    seek to serve him constantly. ℟

You descendants of Abraham, his servants,
    sons of Jacob, his chosen ones!
He, the Lord, is our God;
    throughout the earth his judgments prevail. ℟

Alleluia. Your words, O Lord, give joy to my heart, your teaching is light to my eyes. Alleluia.

● *Do not be afraid of those who can kill the body.* ●

A reading from
the holy Gospel according to Matthew   10: 24-33

JESUS SAID TO HIS APOSTLES: "No pupil outranks his teacher, no slave his master. The pupil should be glad to become like his teacher, the slave like his master. If they call the head of the house Beelzebul, how much more the members of his household! Do not let them intimidate you. Nothing is concealed that will not be revealed, and nothing hidden that will not become known. What I tell you in darkness, speak in the light. What you hear in private, proclaim from housetops.

"Do not fear those who deprive the body of life but cannot destroy the soul. Rather, fear him who can destroy both body and soul in Gehenna. Are not two sparrows sold for next to nothing? Yet not a single sparrow falls to the ground without your Father's consent. As for you, every hair of your head has been counted; so do not be afraid of anything. You are worth more than an entire flock of sparrows. Whoever acknowledges me before men I will acknowledge before my Father in heaven. Whoever disowns me before men I will disown before my Father in heaven."

The Gospel of the Lord.

PRAYER OVER THE GIFTS

Lord,
may the gifts we bring you
help us follow the example of Blessed Kateri Tekakwitha.
Cleanse us from our earthly way of life,
and teach us to live the new life of your kingdom.
We ask this through Christ our Lord.

COMMUNION ANTIPHON

The five sensible virgins took flasks of oil as well as their lamps. At midnight a cry was heard: the bridegroom is here; let us go out to meet Christ the Lord. (Mt 25: 4, 6)

PRAYER AFTER COMMUNION

Lord,
may our reception of the body and blood of your Son keep us from harmful things.
Help us by the example of Blessed Kateri Tekakwitha to grow in your love on earth
that we may rejoice for ever in heaven.
We ask this in the name of Jesus the Lord.

M E D I T A T I O N   O F   T H E   D A Y

"Speak in the light"

I must add another circumstance that happened to a woman of this settlement four days after the death of Katharine. She was one of our oldest and most fervent Christians who had taken the place of Katharine's mother and who had received her in her cabin when she came here from the country of the Iroquois. "One night," says this woman, "after the public prayers, when everyone had gone to bed, I prayed privately for a little while; and then I also went to bed. But scarcely had I fallen asleep when I was awakened by a voice which called me, saying: 'My mother, rise up and look.' I recognized the voice of Katharine. Immediately I sat up and turning toward the side where she was calling me, I saw her standing beside me, her body so surrounded by light that I beheld only her face, which was of an extraordinary beauty. 'My mother,' she added, 'Look well at this cross which I am carrying. Look, look, how beautiful it is. Oh, how I loved it on earth; oh, how I love it still in Paradise! How much I wish that all our cabin should love it and rely upon it as I did!' That is what she said to me, and at that instant she disappeared, leaving me so full of joy, and of such sweet consolation that it has lasted until now. Moreover, the cross she held was so beautiful and gave forth such brilliant light that I have never seen anything so lovely and so charming."

THE POSITIO OF BLESSED KATERI TEKAKWITHA

Prayer for the Evening

Vigil of the Fifteenth Sunday in Ordinary Time

O sing to the Lord, make music to his name!

Glory to the Father, and to the Son,
and to the Holy Spirit, as it was in the beginning,
is now, and will be for ever. Amen. Alleluia!

HYMN
Meter: 87 87 87
This hymn can be sung to the tune used for
Christ is Made the Sure Foundation

I will sing the Lord's high triumph,
Ruling earth and sky and sea;
God my strength, my song, my glory,
My salvation now is he.
Through the waters, through the waters
God has brought us liberty.

By the storm and at the mountain
Grace and judgement both are shown;
All who planned his people's ruin
Power divine has overthrown.
Nations tremble, nations tremble,
God has made his mercy known.

Praise our God who in the thunder
Led a nation through the sea;
Praise the one whose blood released us
From our deeper slavery.
Hallelujah! Hallelujah!
Christ is risen, we are free!

PSALM 68   5-11

We who are receiving the unshakable kingdom should have gratitude, with which we should offer worship pleasing to God in reverence and awe. (Heb 12: 28)

In Christ, the paschal Lamb whose blood poured out on the cross delivered his people from death, we are led from death to life. In our life's journey, we are fed with the bread of life and given the cup of salvation to drink at the eucharistic banquet. At our journey's end lies our heavenly homeland. Let us give thanks and praise!

O sing to the Lord, make music to his name;
make a highway for him who rides on the clouds.
Rejoice in the Lord, exult at his presence.

Father of the orphan, defender of the widow,
such is God in his holy place.
God gives the lonely a home to live in;
he leads the prisoners forth into freedom:
but rebels must dwell in a parched land.

When you went forth, O God, at the head of your people,
when you marched across the desert, the earth trembled:
the heavens melted at the presence of God,
at the presence of God, Israel's God.

You poured down, O God, a generous rain:
when your people were starved you gave them new life.
It was there that your people found a home,
prepared in your goodness, O God, for the poor.

Glory to the Father...

Word of God   Matthew 27: 50-53

J ESUS CRIED OUT again in a loud
voice, and gave up his spirit.
And behold, the veil of the sanctuary was torn in two
from top to bottom. The earth quaked, rocks were split,
tombs were opened, and the bodies of many saints who
had fallen asleep were raised. And coming forth from

their tombs after his resurrection, they entered the holy city and appeared to many.

Now they desire a better homeland, a heavenly one. Therefore, God is not ashamed to be called their God, for he has prepared a city for them. (Heb 11: 16)

CANTICLE OF MARY   (Text, back cover A)
The master then ordered the servant, "Go out to the highways and hedgerows and make people come in that my home may be filled." (Lk 14: 23)

INTERCESSIONS

God has prepared a dwelling place for his people at the end of our journey to freedom in Christ. In joyful hope we pray:

R/   Father, hear your children's prayer!

You sent your Son to dwell in our midst that we may one day dwell with you:
– lead us night and day toward your heavenly city. R/

You give us the bread of life and the cup of salvation to sustain us on our way:
– call faithful men to the priesthood that all peoples everywhere might have this food and drink. R/

You lead us in Christ from slavery to freedom, from desert to homeland, from death to life:
– keep us faithful in his footsteps. R/

Personal intentions

Our Father…

May the God in whose ways our fathers Abraham and Isaac walked, the God who has been our shepherd from our birth to this day, the Angel who has delivered us from all harm, bless us and keep us in peace. Amen. (cf. Gn 48: 15-16)

MARIAN ANTIPHON   (Text, page 25)

SAINTS
OF TODAY AND YESTERDAY

Behold, a great priest,
who in his days pleased God, and was found just.

BLESSED MARIANO DE JESUS EUSE HOYOS
Priest (1845-1926)

Born in Yarumal, Colombia, Mariano worked as a
farmer until the age of sixteen when he revealed to
his devout parents his aspiration to the priesthood.
After receiving spiritual and intellectual formation
under the care of his uncle who was a parish priest,
Mariano entered the seminary of Medellin at the age
of twenty-three and was ordained three years later.
From 1878 until his death on July 13, 1926 he served
as parish priest of Angostura. He assisted the poor,
"Christ's nobles" as he titled them, out of his own
means while exercising his pastoral zeal in exhorting
his people to attend Mass on feast days and to say the
rosary together as families. He advocated devotion to
the Sacred Heart, membership in Catholic
associations, and prayer for vocations. His priestly
ministry was sustained by a life of prayer and
asceticism characterized by devotion to the Eucharist,
the Blessed Mother, the angels, and the saints. In his
final illness he commented, "I have lived long
enough, and my greatest desire is to be united with
my Jesus."

Let the soul therefore long with desire
for its heavenly home.
Saint Gregory the Great

Word of God

for a Sunday

Luke 10: 25-37

When Jesus is asked: "What must I do to inherit eternal life?" the answer is, "You shall love the Lord, your God." When Paul and Silas were asked: "What must I do to be saved?" they replied: "Believe in the Lord Jesus, and you will be saved" (Acts 16: 30-31). Upon reflection it will be seen that Jesus' answer on the one hand and the reply of Paul and Silas on the other, are not contradictory but supplementary, the one to the other.

J. T.

■ Suggested Prayer of the Faithful ■

(Each local community should compose its own Universal Prayer, but may find inspiration in the texts proposed here.)

United with our brothers and sisters throughout the world, let us offer our petitions to God, our common Father, in trust and love.

That the Church may always look to Christ Jesus as her head and founder, the image of the invisible God, in whom all things were created.

That we may give to our Holy Father the Pope the reverence and loyalty due to the Vicar of Christ, whom Saint Catherine of Siena called "the sweet Christ on earth."

For leaders of nations, that they may recognize the law of God as something very near to them, already in their hearts, to be carried out freely and resolutely for the good of all.

That the Person of Christ Jesus may be acknowledged by the media as one to whom all reverence is due as the Son of God and our Redeemer.

That all enmities, wars, and violence may be canceled out and disputing factions reconciled through the Blood of Christ that brings us together as one in his peace.

That we may be alert and alive to the sufferings of our nearest neighbors, pouring the wine and oil of compassion and practical help into their wounds regardless of the cost.

That we may give unstintingly of our time and care to those we may encounter unexpectedly today, and who are in desperate need of our love.

God our Father, teach us to find you and serve you in our neighbor, whom you have given to us for this very reason, as you taught us through your Son, our Lord Jesus Christ.

SUNDAY, JULY 15
Fifteenth Sunday in Ordinary Time

Prayer for the Morning

Sing a new song to the Lord
for he has worked wonders!

Glory to the Father, and to the Son,
and to the Holy Spirit, as it was in the beginning,
is now, and will be for ever. Amen. Alleluia!

HYMN   Meter: 6 6 6 6 88

Rejoice, the Lord is King;
Your Lord and King adore;
Rejoice, give thanks and sing
And triumph evermore:

℟ Lift up your heart, lift up your voice;
Rejoice! Again I say: Rejoice!

Rejoice in glorious hope;
Jesus, the Judge shall come
And take his servants up
To their eternal home: ℟

PSALM 98   3-9

We have seen his glory, the glory of an only Son coming from the
Father. (cf. Jn 1: 14)

The glory of the Lord revealed in Jesus Christ is the transforming
fire of love that purifies and renews the whole earth. In the fire of
God's love, all sin and sorrow, all suffering and death will be consumed as he establishes his kingdom upon earth.

All the ends of the earth have seen
the salvation of our God.
Shout to the Lord all the earth,
ring out your joy.

Sing psalms to the Lord with the harp
with the sound of music.
With trumpets and the sound of the horn
acclaim the King, the Lord.

Let the sea and all within it thunder;
the world, and all its peoples.
Let the rivers clap their hands
and the hills ring out their joy.

Rejoice at the presence of the Lord,
for he comes to rule the earth.
He will rule the world with justice
and the peoples with fairness.

Glory to the Father...

Word of God   Isaiah 29: 18-19

O N THAT DAY THE DEAF shall hear the words of a book; and out of gloom and darkness, the eyes of the blind shall see. The lowly will ever find joy in the Lord, and the poor rejoice in the Holy One of Israel.

*On that day my people shall know my renown,
that it is I who have foretold it. Here I am!* (Is 52: 6)

CANTICLE OF ZECHARIAH   (Text, back cover B)
The Son of Man will come with his angels in his Father's glory, and then he will repay everyone according to his conduct. (Mt 16: 27)

INTERCESSIONS

To the One whose coming we await with joy, let us pray:

℟   Remember your truth and your love.

For your coming in flesh, we give you glory, Lord:
– redeem all your people throughout the world. ℟

For your death on the cross, we give you glory, Lord:
– grant hope to all those who suffer. R⫽

For your resurrection from the dead, we give you glory, Lord:
– raise up all those who have died. R⫽

For your return in majesty, we give you glory, Lord:
– grant us joy in your presence and your promise. R⫽

Personal intentions

Our Father…

O God of our hope, you have promised that your Son will return in glory to bring to completion the work begun in his death and resurrection. May your Church, made new in the waters of baptism, be a living sign of hope for all those who look toward the future, through the same Christ our Lord. Amen.

MASS

Fifteenth Sunday in Ordinary Time

ENTRANCE ANTIPHON
In my justice I shall see your face, O Lord; when your glory appears, my joy will be full. (Ps 16:15)

GLORIA ———————————————— page 226

OPENING PRAYER
God our Father,
your light of truth
guides us to the way of Christ.
May all who follow him
reject what is contrary to the Gospel.
We ask this through our Lord Jesus Christ, your Son,
who lives and reigns with you and the Holy Spirit,
one God, for ever and ever.

ALTERNATIVE OPENING PRAYER

Father,
let the light of your truth
guide us to your kingdom
through a world filled with lights contrary to your own.
Christian is the name and the Gospel we glory in.
May your love make us what you have called us to be.
We ask this through Christ our Lord.

● *The word is very near to you: you have only to carry it out.* ●

A reading from
the Book of Deuteronomy   30: 10-14

MOSES SAID TO the people: "If only you would heed the voice of the LORD, your God, and keep his commandments and statutes that are written in this book of the law, when you return to the LORD, your God, with all your heart and all your soul.

"For this command that I enjoin on you today is not too mysterious and remote for you. It is not up in the sky, that you should say, 'Who will go up in the sky to get it for us and tell us of it, that we may carry it out?' Nor is it across the sea, that you should say, 'Who will cross the sea to get it for us and tell us of it, that we may carry it out?' No, it is something very near to you, already in your mouths and in your hearts; you have only to carry it out." The word of the Lord.

———— • PSALM 69 • ————

℟ (cf. 33) **Turn to the Lord in your need,
and you will live.**

I pray to you, O LORD,
    for the time of your favor, O God!

In your great kindness answer me
 with your constant help.
Answer me, O LORD, for bounteous is your kindness:
 in your great mercy turn toward me. ℟

I am afflicted and in pain;
 let your saving help, O God, protect me.
I will praise the name of God in song,
 and I will glorify him with thanksgiving. ℟

"See, you lowly ones, and be glad;
 you who seek God, may your hearts revive!
For the LORD hears the poor,
 and his own who are in bonds he spurns not." ℟

For God will save Zion
 and rebuild the cities of Judah.
The descendants of his servants shall inherit it,
 and those who love his name shall inhabit it. ℟

Or:

• PSALM 19 •

℟ (9a) **Your words, Lord, are Spirit and life.**

The law of the LORD is perfect,
 refreshing the soul;
the decree of the LORD is trustworthy,
 giving wisdom to the simple. ℟

The precepts of the LORD are right,
 rejoicing the heart;
the command of the LORD is clear,
 enlightening the eye. ℟

The fear of the LORD is pure,
 enduring forever;
the ordinances of the LORD are true,
 all of them just. ℟

They are more precious than gold,
   than a heap of purest gold;
sweeter also than syrup
   or honey from the comb. ℟

● *All things were created through him and for him.* ●

A reading from
the Letter of Saint Paul to the Colossians   1: 15-20

CHRIST JESUS is the image of
the invisible God,/ the first-
born of all creation./ For in him were created all things
in heaven and on earth,/ the visible and the invisible,/
whether thrones or dominions or principalities or powers;/ all things were created through him and for him./
He is before all things,/ and in him all things hold
together./ He is the head of the body, the church./ He is
the beginning, the firstborn from the dead,/ that in all
things he himself might be preeminent./ For in him all
the fullness was pleased to dwell,/ and through him to
reconcile all things for him,/ making peace by the blood
of his cross/ through him, whether those on earth or
those in heaven.
The word of the Lord.

Alleluia, alleluia. Your words, Lord, are Spirit and life;
you have the words of everlasting life. Alleluia, alleluia.

● *Who is my neighbor?* ●

A reading from
the holy Gospel according to Luke   10: 25-37

THERE WAS A SCHOLAR of the
law who stood up to test
Jesus and said, "Teacher, what must I do to inherit eter-

nal life?" Jesus said to him, "What is written in the law? How do you read it?" He said in reply, *You shall love the Lord, your God, with all your heart, with all your being, with all your strength, and with all your mind, and your neighbor as yourself.* He replied to him, "You have answered correctly; do this and you will live."

But because he wished to justify himself, he said to Jesus, "And who is my neighbor?" Jesus replied, "A man fell victim to robbers as he went down from Jerusalem to Jericho. They stripped and beat him and went off leaving him half-dead. A priest happened to be going down that road, but when he saw him, he passed by on the opposite side. Likewise a Levite came to the place, and when he saw him, he passed by on the opposite side. But a Samaritan traveler who came upon him was moved with compassion at the sight. He approached the victim, poured oil and wine over his wounds and bandaged them. Then he lifted him up on his own animal, took him to an inn, and cared for him. The next day he took out two silver coins and gave them to the innkeeper with the instruction, 'Take care of him. If you spend more than what I have given you, I shall repay you on my way back.' Which of these three, in your opinion, was neighbor to the robbers' victim?" He answered, "The one who treated him with mercy." Jesus said to him, "Go and do likewise."
The Gospel of the Lord.

CREDO ———————————————————————— page 227

PRAYER OVER THE GIFTS
>Lord,
>accept the gifts of your Church.
>May this Eucharist
>help us grow in holiness and faith.
>We ask this in the name of Jesus the Lord.

PREFACE OF SUNDAYS IN ORDINARY TIME ———————— page 231

COMMUNION ANTIPHON

The sparrow even finds a home, the swallow finds a nest wherein to place her young, near to your altars, Lord of hosts, my King, my God! How happy they who dwell in your house! For ever they are praising you. (Ps 83: 4-5)

Or:

Whoever eats my flesh and drinks my blood will live in me and I in him, says the Lord. (Jn 6: 57)

PRAYER AFTER COMMUNION

Lord,
by our sharing in the mystery of this Eucharist,
let your saving love grow within us.
Grant this through Christ our Lord.

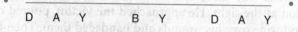

D A Y · B Y · D A Y

Christ the Good Samaritan

This is my beloved, who rose from Judah to become our brother, and became neighbor to him who fell among robbers, healed his wounds with oil, wine, and bandages; then taking him on his own beast, he set him down to rest at an inn, offering two denarii for his stay, and promising that on his return he would repay any service that was discharged over and above his command.

The point of each of these details is surely clear. The man who was an expert in the law wanted to test the Lord and set himself higher than the others, and in his pride had complete contempt for any equality with the rest. And so he said: "And who is my neighbor?" (Lk 10: 29) And then the Word explained, in the form of a story, God's entire economy of salvation. He told of man's descent from heaven, the robbers' ambush, the stripping of the garment of immortality, the wounds of sin, the progress of death over half of man's nature while his soul remained immortal. Then came the passage of law that brought no help – neither the priest nor the Levite tended the wounds of the man who fell among robbers – for it was impossible for the blood of goats and oxen (Heb 9: 13) to remove man's sin. And then he came, clothed in our human nature as the first-fruits of the mass, in which there was a portion of every race, Jewish, Samaritan, Greek – all mankind. With his body he proceeded to the place of man's disaster, healed his wounds and set him upon his own beast. He created for him the inn of his loving providence, in which all those who labor and are burdened can find rest (Mt 11: 28). And those who enter here receive within themselves that which receives them, as the Word himself has said: "He abideth in me, and I in him (Jn 6: 57)."

Man, then, receives within himself the Lord whom nothing can contain, in accordance with his capacity.

SAINT GREGORY OF NYSSA

Saint Gregory of Nyssa († 395) is a Father of the Church who wrote many theological treatises against heresy.

Prayer for the Evening

Worthy is God to receive
our prayer and our praise!

Glory to the Father, and to the Son,
and to the Holy Spirit, as it was in the beginning,
is now, and will be for ever. Amen. Alleluia!

HYMN   Meter: LM
This hymn can be sung to the tune used for
Jesus Shall Reign

Upon the heights, the Lamb stands bright
Against the glorious clouds of light,
Above the city paved in gold
Where death and darkness have no hold.

In bitter sacrifice once slain,
He lives in triumph there to reign
Among the saints clad all in white
In realms where day yields not to night.

To him now let our prayers arise,
In clouds of incense to the skies,
From censer borne by angel hands,
Bright tongues of fire from far-flung lands.

Of all the heavens' praises worth,
He catches up the prayers of earth
In wounded hands, till, countless throng,
The singers come to join the song,

And, "Holy, holy, holy" cry
To you, our Lord and God Most High,
To Father, Son, and Spirit, Three
In One all-holy Mystery.

CANTICLE   Revelation 4: 11; 5: 9-10, 12

Holy, holy, holy is the Lord God almighty, who was, and who is, and
who is to come. (Rv 4: 8)

By the astounding mystery of the resurrection of Christ from the
dead, the cross of shame becomes the throne of glory. He who was
slain now lives for ever. In him, all death has died.

O Lord, our God, you are worthy,
to receive glory and honor and power.

For you have created all things;
by your will they came to be and were made.

Worthy are you, O Lord,
to receive the scroll and break open its seals.

For you were slain;
with your blood you purchased for God

men of every race and tongue,
of every people and nation.

You made of them a kingdom,
and priests to serve our God,
and they shall reign on the earth.

Worthy is the Lamb that was slain
to receive power and riches,
wisdom and strength,
honor and glory and praise.

Word of God   Revelation 5: 13

THEN I HEARD every creature
in heaven and on earth and
under the earth and in the sea, everything in the universe, cry out: "To the one who sits on the throne and to
the Lamb be blessing and honor, glory and might, for
ever and ever."

Praise and honor to you,
Lord Jesus Christ!

CANTICLE OF MARY   (Text, back cover A)
Where, O death, is your victory? Where, O death, is your sting?
(1 Cor 15: 55)

INTERCESSIONS

In Christ, death has died. In wondering love, let us pray:

℟   To you be honor and praise!

You were slain that those slain by sin might rise again
to life:
– redeem those who have given their lives to the works
of darkness and death. ℟

You have marked with the blood of the cross people of every race and nation:
– break down the barriers that human pride and prejudice have erected across the world's boundaries. ℟

You are enthroned in glory:
– raise to life all those who have gone before us in death. ℟

Personal intentions

Our Father...

May God send his truth and his love! Amen. (Ps 57: 4)

MARIAN ANTIPHON   (Text, page 25)

MONDAY, JULY 16
Our Lady of Mount Carmel
Prayer for the Morning

Come, let us go up with joy to the house of the Lord!

Glory to the Father, and to the Son,
and to the Holy Spirit, as it was in the beginning,
is now, and will be for ever. Amen. Alleluia!

HYMN
Meter: 66 84 D
This hymn can be sung to the tune used for
The God of Abraham Praise

The pilgrim church of God,
We mount the narrow way,
We tread the path that Jesus trod,
His call to obey:
To whom God sent his Son,
On whom the Spirit came,
Who in the faith of Christ are one
And in his name.

What though the way we tread
Be dark, or faith be dim?
We look to Christ our risen Head
And walk with him.
So lead your children on
In love and truth and grace,
To come where Christ himself has gone
And see his face.

PSALM 84
2-3, 6-8, 12

I will bring back Israel to her fold, to feed on Carmel till she has her
fill. (cf. Jer 50: 19)

The pilgrim songs of the psalter were sung by God's people on their
annual pilgrimage to Mount Zion, where stood God's temple. Today,
we call to mind another mountain in Israel, Mount Carmel, upon

which dwells the memory of Mary under her title of Our Lady of Mount Carmel. We invoke her help as we make our pilgrim way through life to the eternal dwelling place of God with all humanity.

How lovely is your dwelling place,
Lord, God of hosts.

My soul is longing and yearning,
is yearning for the courts of the Lord.
My heart and my soul ring out their joy
to God, the living God.

They are happy, whose strength is in you,
in whose hearts are the roads to Zion.
As they go through the Bitter Valley
they make it a place of springs,
the autumn rain covers it with blessings.

They walk with ever growing strength,
they will see the God of gods in Zion.
One day within your courts
is better than a thousand elsewhere.

For the Lord God is a rampart, a shield;
he will give us his favor and glory.
The Lord will not refuse any good
to those who walk without blame.

Glory to the Father...

Word of God   Nehemiah 9: 12-13

With a column of cloud you led [your people] by day, and by night with a column of fire, to light the way of their journey, the way in which they must travel. On Mount Sinai you came down, you spoke with them from heaven; you gave them just ordinances, firm laws, good statutes, and commandments.

Come, follow me! (Mk 10: 21)

CANTICLE OF ZECHARIAH   (Text, back cover B)
How beautiful upon the mountains are the feet of the one who
brings glad tidings, announcing peace, bearing good news, announcing salvation, and saying to Zion, "Your God is King!" (cf. Is 52: 7)

INTERCESSIONS

Through the intercession of Our Lady of Mount
Carmel, let us pray with confidence to the God who
calls us to travel toward the kingdom that is to come:

℟   Lead us, O Lord.

We are your people, who walk the desert road to the
Promised Land:
– keep us faithful to the demands of the journey
today. ℟

We are your people, called to follow Jesus, the Lord:
– make us steadfast disciples, freed from all that would
hold us back. ℟

We are your people, destined for the heavenly
Jerusalem:
– give us strength to go on when we grow weary of the
journey. ℟

Personal intentions

Our Father…

O Lord, as we travel through this day of our life, following the example of the Blessed Virgin Mary, our
strength is in you; in our hearts are the roads to our
eternal destination, the place where you dwell for ever
with your people in joy and in peace. Sustain us as we
pass through the bitter valleys of suffering; shield us as
dangers threaten; let us rejoice in the springs of living
water which refresh us on our way. And keep us faithful
until journey's end, through Christ our Lord. Amen.

MASS

Monday of the Fifteenth Week of the Year

OUR LADY OF MOUNT CARMEL   *Optional memorial*

● *Sacred Scripture celebrated the beauty of Carmel where the prophet Elijah defended the purity of Israel's faith in the living God. In the twelfth century, hermits withdrew to that mountain and later founded the Order devoted to the contemplative life under the patronage of Mary, the holy Mother of God.* ●

ENTRANCE ANTIPHON

Hail, holy Mother! The child to whom you gave birth is the king of heaven and earth for ever. (Sedulius)

OPENING PRAYER

Father,
may the prayers of the Virgin Mary protect us
and help us to reach Christ her Son
who lives and reigns with you and the Holy Spirit,
one God, for ever and ever.

● *We must move against Israel lest they become greater in number.* ●

A reading from
the Book of Exodus   1: 8-14, 22

A NEW KING, who knew nothing of Joseph, came to power in Egypt. He said to his subjects, "Look how numerous and powerful the Israelite people are growing, more so than we ourselves! Come, let us deal shrewdly with them to stop their increase; otherwise, in time of war they too may join our enemies to fight against us, and so leave our country."

Accordingly, taskmasters were set over the Israelites to oppress them with forced labor. Thus they had to build for Pharaoh the supply cities of Pithom and Raamses. Yet the more they were oppressed, the more they multiplied and spread. The Egyptians, then, dreaded the Israelites and reduced them to cruel slavery, making life bitter for them with hard work in mortar and brick and all kinds of field work – the whole cruel fate of slaves.

Pharaoh then commanded all his subjects, "Throw into the river every boy that is born to the Hebrews, but you may let all the girls live."

The word of the Lord.

———— • **PSALM 124** • ————

℟ (8) **Our help is in the name of the Lord.**

Had not the Lord been with us –
  let Israel say,
  had not the Lord been with us –
When men rose up against us,
  then would they have swallowed us alive,
When their fury was inflamed against us. ℟

Then would the waters have overwhelmed us;
The torrent would have swept over us;
  over us then would have swept
  the raging waters.
Blessed be the Lord, who did not leave us
  a prey to their teeth. ℟

We were rescued like a bird
  from the fowlers' snare;
Broken was the snare,
  and we were freed.

Our help is in the name of the Lord,
  who made heaven and earth. R/

Alleluia. Receive this message not as the words of man,
but as truly the word of God. Alleluia.

● *I have not come to bring peace, but the sword.* ●

A reading from
the holy Gospel according to Matthew   10: 34–11: 1

JESUS SAID TO HIS APOSTLES: "Do not suppose that my mission on earth is to spread peace. My mission is to spread, not peace, but division. I have come to set a man at odds with his father, a daughter with her mother, a daughter-in-law with her mother-in-law: in short, to make a man's enemies those of his own household. Whoever loves father or mother, son or daughter more than me, is not worthy of me. He who will not take up his cross and come after me is not worthy of me. He who seeks only himself brings himself to ruin, whereas he who brings himself to nought for me discovers who he is.

"He who welcomes you welcomes me, and he who welcomes me welcomes him who sent me. He who welcomes a prophet because he bears the name of prophet receives a prophet's reward; he who welcomes a holy man because he is known as holy receives a holy man's reward. And I promise you that whoever gives a cup of cold water to one of these lowly ones because he is a disciple will not want for his reward."

When Jesus had finished instructing his twelve disciples, he left that locality to teach and preach in their towns.
The Gospel of the Lord.

PRAYER OVER THE GIFTS

> Father,
> the birth of Christ your Son
> deepened the virgin mother's love for you,
> and increased her holiness.
> May the humanity of Christ
> give us courage in our weakness;
> may it free us from our sins,
> and make our offering acceptable.
> We ask this through Christ our Lord.

COMMUNION ANTIPHON

Blessed is the womb of the Virgin Mary; she carried the Son of the eternal Father. (See Lk 11: 27)

PRAYER AFTER COMMUNION

> Lord,
> we rejoice in your sacraments and ask your mercy
> as we honor the memory of the Virgin Mary.
> May her faith and love
> inspire us to serve you more faithfully
> in the work of salvation.
> Grant this in the name of Jesus the Lord.

MEDITATION OF THE DAY

Our Lady of Mount Carmel and Our Gift of Self

Mount Carmel [is] a solitary outcrop of the everlasting hills that stand round about Jerusalem; surrounded as it is by valleys and plains, its very isolation makes it more impressive. Immortal eyes have rested on that sight. "These things do not change," writes a recent traveler, "and Jesus Christ must have known these rocks and these hills. Looking back, the great plain stretching to the sky and the outward thrust spur of Carmel are intensely significant."

And we know that if Carmel is a solitary outcrop of those old hills, our blessed Lady was, in something the same way, a solitary throwback to the innocence of her first parents. Rising suddenly above the groveling level to which Adam's fault had reduced our common human clay, she challenges heaven in the lonely isolation of her purity; all other sanctities must seem petty eminences compared to this. Our tainted nature's solitary boast, she recalls to us, across all those centuries, the first beginning of our race, and the privileges that went with it. When our Lord Jesus Christ looked across the plain from his home in Nazareth, he could see, beyond the plain that lay parched at his feet, the cool heights of Carmel against the sunset. When our Lord Jesus Christ looked at the world his hands had made, and saw, for he could see, all the passions of greed and lust and envy that ruled in the hearts of his fellow men, he could see one heart that was fresh with the freshness of the world's springtime, and that was his blessed Mother's. Her head was like Carmel, towering in its spiritual stature above the world which knew her so little.

MONSIGNOR RONALD A. KNOX

Monsignor Knox († 1957) was a British Catholic apologist and translator of the Bible.

Prayer for the Evening

The Lord will not abandon his people:
let us give thanks and praise!

Glory to the Father, and to the Son,
and to the Holy Spirit, as it was in the beginning,
is now, and will be for ever. Amen. Alleluia!

HYMN   Meter: 10 10 10 10
This hymn can be sung to the tune used for
The Voice of God Goes Out Through All the World

This world, my God, is held within your hand,
Though we forget your love and steadfast might
And in the changing day uncertain stand,
Disturbed by morning, and afraid of night.

From youthful confidence to careful age,
Help us each one to be your loving friend,
Rewarded by the faithful servant's wage,
God in Three Persons, reigning without end.

PSALM 94   9-15, 22

God does not withdraw his mercy, nor permit even one of his
promises to fail. (Sir 47: 22)

Uncertainty is an ever-present reality to the Christian believer. Is
God really there? Is he really interested? Can he really hear prayers?
Does he really act in today's world? Does he keep his promises even
now? The psalmist faced the same questions with a courageous "yes"!

Can he who made the ear, not hear?
Can he who formed the eye, not see?
Will he who trains nations, not punish?
Will he who teaches men, not have knowledge?
The Lord knows the thoughts of men.
He knows they are no more than a breath.

Happy the man whom you teach, O Lord,
whom you train by means of your law:
to him you give peace in evil days
while the pit is being dug for the wicked.

The Lord will not abandon his people
nor forsake those who are his own:
for judgment shall again be just
and all true hearts shall uphold it.
As for me, the Lord will be a stronghold;
my God will be the rock where I take refuge.

Glory to the Father...

Word of God   Luke 12: 27-28

NOTICE HOW THE FLOWERS
grow. They do not toil or

spin. But I tell you, not even Solomon in all his splendor
was dressed like one of them. If God so clothes the grass
in the field that grows today and is thrown into the oven
tomorrow, will he not much more provide for you,
O you of little faith?

> *God is faithful, and by him you were called*
> *to fellowship with his Son, Jesus Christ our Lord.*
> (1 Cor 1: 9)

CANTICLE OF MARY   (Text, back cover A)
The promise is made to you and to your children and to all those far
off, whomever the Lord our God will call. (Acts 2: 39)

INTERCESSIONS

With faith in God who keeps all promises, let us pray:

℟   We place our trust in you!

For those who do not believe in God:
– grant them the gift of faith. ℟

For those who do not believe in Jesus Christ:
– grant them the gift of faith. ℟

For those who do not trust in your love or your
promises:
– grant them the gift of faith. ℟

Personal intentions

Our Father…

May the word of Christ dwell in us richly, and bring us to
life everlasting! Amen. (cf. Col 3: 16)

MARIAN ANTIPHON   (Text, page 25)

SAINTS
OF TODAY AND YESTERDAY

Your saints, O Lord, have followed a wonderful path, keeping your commandments, so as to pass unharmed through mighty waters.

SAINT ATHENOGENES AND COMPANIONS
Bishop and Martyr († c. 305)

The Bishop Athenogenes was martyred in Sebaste, Armenia, under the Roman Emperor Diocletian. Before dying by fire he sang a joyful hymn of his own composition professing the divinity of the Holy Spirit. Ten disciples of the bishop died with him and are honored on this date together with him.

SAINT EUSTACE
Bishop († 338)

After serving as bishop of Beraea, Syria, Eustace was made bishop of the Syrian diocese of Antioch in 324. In response to his active opposition to the heresy of Arianism, the Arians brought false charges against him in order to depose him from his see. Acting on the false charges the Eastern Emperor Constantius II sent Eustace into exile. Before leaving his people, the bishop exhorted them to remain steadfast in the Catholic faith. His words were effective in keeping many faithful to the Church. Eustace was remarkable for his patience in facing both calumny and banishment.

We should, especially on waking in the morning, strive to close the door to any kind of worldly thoughts, and to fill the guest-chamber of our heart with the remembrance of our Lord.
Saint Peter of Alcantara

THE ORDER OF MASS

Greeting

■ In the name of the Father, and of the Son, and of the
   Holy Spirit.
■ Amen.

A _____

■ The grace of our Lord Jesus Christ and the love of God
   and the fellowship of the Holy Spirit be with you all.
■ And also with you.

B _____

■ The grace and peace of God our Father and the Lord
   Jesus Christ be with you.
■ Blessed be God, the Father of our Lord Jesus Christ.

Or:

■ And also with you.

C _____

■ The Lord be with you.
■ And also with you.

Penitential rite

A _____

■ As we prepare to celebrate the mystery of Christ's love,
   let us acknowledge our failures
   and ask the Lord for pardon and strength.

B _____

■ Coming together as God's family,
   with confidence let us ask the Father's forgiveness,
   for he is full of gentleness and compassion.

C _____

■ My brothers and sisters,
   to prepare ourselves to celebrate the sacred mysteries,
   let us call to mind our sins.

A

- I confess to almighty God,
  and to you, my brothers and sisters,
  that I have sinned through my own fault

  (The people strike their breast:)

  in my thoughts and in my words,
  in what I have done,
  and in what I have failed to do;
  and I ask blessed Mary, ever virgin,
  all the angels and saints,
  and you, my brothers and sisters,
  to pray for me to the Lord our God.

B

- Lord, we have sinned against you:
  Lord, have mercy.
- Lord, have mercy.
- Lord, show us your mercy and love.
- And grant us your salvation.

C

*(The priest [or other suitable minister] makes
the following or other invocations:)*

- You were sent to heal the contrite:
  Lord, have mercy.
- Lord, have mercy.
- You came to call sinners:
  Christ, have mercy.
- Christ, have mercy.
- You plead for us at the right hand of the Father:
  Lord, have mercy.
- Lord, have mercy.

- May almighty God have mercy on us,
  forgive us our sins,
  and bring us to everlasting life.
- Amen.

Kyrie

(The Kyrie is omitted if it has already been used in one of the forms of the act of penance.)

- Lord, have mercy.
- Lord, have mercy,
- Christ, have mercy.
- Christ, have mercy.
- Lord, have mercy.
- Lord, have mercy.

Kyrie, eleison.
Kyrie, eleison.
Christe, eleison.
Christe, eleison.
Kyrie, eleison.
Kyrie, eleison.

Gloria

Glory to God in the highest,
  and peace to his people on earth.

Lord God, heavenly King,
almighty God and Father,
  we worship you, we give you thanks,
  we praise you for your glory.

Lord Jesus Christ, only Son of the Father,
Lord God, Lamb of God,
you take away the sin of the world:
  have mercy on us;
you are seated at the right hand of the Father:
  receive our prayer.

For you alone are the Holy One,
you alone are the Lord,
you alone are the Most High,
  Jesus Christ,
  with the Holy Spirit,
  in the glory of God the Father. Amen.

Gloria in excelsis Deo
et in terra pax hominibus bonae voluntatis.
Laudamus te, benedicimus te, adoramus te,
glorificamus te, gratias agimus tibi
propter magnam gloriam tuam,
Domine Deus, Rex caelestis,
Deus Pater omnipotens.
Domine Fili unigenite, Iesu Christe,

Domine Deus, Agnus Dei, Filius Patris,
qui tollis peccata mundi, miserere nobis;
qui tollis peccata mundi,
suscipe deprecationem nostram;
qui sedes ad dexteram Patris, miserere nobis.
Quoniam tu solus Sanctus,
tu solus Dominus,
tu solus Altissimus, Iesu Christe,
cum Sancto Spiritu:
in gloria Dei Patris. Amen.

Opening prayer

LITURGY OF THE WORD

First reading

Responsorial psalm

Second reading

Alleluia or Gospel acclamation

Gospel

The priest [or the deacon] bows before the altar and says inaudibly:
Almighty God, cleanse my heart and my lips that I may worthily
proclaim your Gospel.

- The Lord be with you.
- And also with you.

- A reading from the holy Gospel according to...
  At the end of the Gospel:
- The Gospel of the Lord.
- Praise to you, Lord Jesus Christ.

Then the priest [or the deacon] kisses the book, saying inaudibly:
May the words of the Gospel wipe away our sins.

Homily

Profession of faith

We believe in one God,
the Father, the Almighty,

maker of heaven and earth,
of all that is seen and unseen.

We believe in one Lord, Jesus Christ,
the only Son of God,
eternally begotten of the Father,
God from God, Light from Light,
true God from true God,
begotten, not made, one in Being with the Father.
Through him all things were made.
For us men and for our salvation
he came down from heaven:

All bow during these two lines:

by the power of the Holy Spirit
he was born of the Virgin Mary, and became man.

For our sake he was crucified under Pontius Pilate;
he suffered, died, and was buried.
On the third day he rose again
in fulfillment of the Scriptures;
he ascended into heaven
and is seated at the right hand of the Father.
He will come again in glory to judge the living and the dead,
and his kingdom will have no end.

We believe in the Holy Spirit, the Lord, the giver of life,
who proceeds from the Father and the Son.
With the Father and the Son he is worshiped and glorified.
He has spoken through the Prophets.
We believe in one holy catholic and apostolic Church.
We acknowledge one baptism for the forgiveness of sins.
We look for the resurrection of the dead,
and the life of the world to come. Amen.

The Apostles' Creed

I believe in God, the Father almighty,
creator of heaven and earth.

I believe in Jesus Christ, his only Son, our Lord.
He was conceived by the power of the Holy Spirit
and born of the Virgin Mary.
He suffered under Pontius Pilate,

was crucified, died, and was buried.
He descended to the dead.
On the third day he rose again.
He ascended into heaven,
    and is seated at the right hand of the Father.
He will come again to judge the living and the dead.

I believe in the Holy Spirit,
    the holy catholic Church,
    the communion of saints,
    the forgiveness of sins,
    the resurrection of the body,
    and the life everlasting. Amen.

Credo in unum Deum,
Patrem omnipotentem, factorem caeli et terrae,
visibilium omnium et invisibilium.
Et in unum Dominum Iesum Christum,
Filium Dei unigenitum,
et ex Patre natum ante omnia saecula.
Deum de Deo,
lumen de lumine,
Deum verum de Deo vero,
genitum, non factum, consubstantialem Patri:
per quem omnia facta sunt.
Qui propter nos homines et propter nostram salutem
descendit de caelis.
Et incarnatus est de Spiritu Sancto ex Maria Virgine,
et homo factus est.
Crucifixus etiam pro nobis sub Pontio Pilato,
passus et sepultus est,
et resurrexit tertia die, secundum Scripturas,
et ascendit in caelum, sedet ad dexteram Patris.
Et iterum venturus est cum gloria,
iudicare vivos et mortuos,
cuius regni non erit finis.
Et in Spiritum Sanctum,
Dominum et vivificantem:
qui ex Patre Filioque procedit;
qui cum Patre et Filio,
simul adoratur et conglorificatur:

qui locutus est per prophetas.
Et unam, sanctam, catholicam et apostolicam Ecclesiam.
Confiteor unum baptisma in remissionem peccatorum.
Et exspecto resurrectionem mortuorum,
et vitam venturi saeculi. Amen.

General intercessions

LITURGY OF THE EUCHARIST

Preparation of the altar and the gifts

- Blessed are you, Lord, God of all creation.
  Through your goodness we have this bread to offer,
  which earth has given and human hands have made.
  It will become for us the bread of life.
- **Blessed be God for ever.**

By the mystery of this water and wine may we come
to share in the divinity of Christ, who humbled himself
to share in our humanity.

- Blessed are you, Lord, God of all creation.
  Through your goodness we have this wine to offer,
  fruit of the vine and work of human hands.
  It will become our spiritual drink.
- **Blessed be God for ever.**

Lord God, we ask you to receive us and be pleased with the
sacrifice we offer you with humble and contrite hearts.

Lord, wash away my iniquity; cleanse me from my sin.

- Pray, brethren, that our sacrifice
  may be acceptable to God, the almighty Father.
- **May the Lord accept the sacrifice at your hands
  for the praise and glory of his name,
  for our good, and the good of all his Church.**

Prayer over the gifts

Eucharistic prayer

- The Lord be with you.
- **And also with you.**
- Lift up your hearts.
- **We lift them up to the Lord.**

- Let us give thanks to the Lord our God.
- It is right to give him thanks and praise.

Preface of Sundays in Ordinary Time III

Father, all-powerful and ever-living God,
we do well always and everywhere to give you thanks.

We see your infinite power
in your loving plan of salvation.
You came to our rescue by your power as God,
but you wanted us to be saved by one like us.
Man refused your friendship,
but man himself was to restore it
through Jesus Christ our Lord.

Through him the angels of heaven offer their prayer
    of adoration
as they rejoice in your presence for ever.
May our voices be one with theirs
in their triumphant hymn of praise: Holy…

Preface of Weekdays III

Father, all-powerful and ever-living God,
we do well always and everywhere to give you thanks.

Through your beloved Son
you created our human family.
Through him you restored us to your likeness.

Therefore it is your right
to receive the obedience of all creation,
the praise of the Church on earth,
the thanksgiving of your saints in heaven.

We too rejoice with the angels
as we proclaim your glory for ever:

Holy, holy, holy Lord, God of power and might,
heaven and earth are full of your glory.
    Hosanna in the highest.
Blessed is he who comes in the name of the Lord.
    Hosanna in the highest.

■ **Sanctus, Sanctus, Sanctus**
   Dominus Deus Sabaoth.
   Pleni sunt caeli et terra gloria tua.
   Hosanna in excelsis.
   Benedictus qui venit in nomine Domini.
   Hosanna in excelsis.

Eucharistic prayer I (Roman canon)
(I: below; II: p. 236; III: p. 238; IV: p. 240)

(In the first eucharistic prayer the words in brackets may be omitted.)

We come to you, Father,
with praise and thanksgiving,
through Jesus Christ your Son.
Through him we ask you to accept and bless
these gifts we offer you in sacrifice.
We offer them for your holy catholic Church,
watch over it, Lord, and guide it;
grant it peace and unity throughout the world.
We offer them for … our Pope,
for … our bishop,
and for all who hold and teach the catholic faith
that comes to us from the apostles.

Remember, Lord, your people,
especially those for whom we now pray, … and …
Remember all of us gathered here before you.
You know how firmly we believe in you
and dedicate ourselves to you.
We offer you this sacrifice of praise
for ourselves and those who are dear to us.
We pray to you, our living and true God,
for our well-being and redemption.

In union with the whole Church
we honor Mary,
the ever-virgin mother of Jesus Christ our Lord and God.
We honor Joseph, her husband,
the apostles and martyrs
Peter and Paul, Andrew,
   [James, John, Thomas,

James, Philip,
Bartholomew, Matthew, Simon and Jude;
we honor Linus, Cletus, Clement, Sixtus,
Cornelius, Cyprian, Lawrence, Chrysogonus,
John and Paul, Cosmas and Damian]
and all the saints.
May their merits and prayers
gain us your constant help and protection.
   [Through Christ our Lord. Amen.]

Father, accept this offering
from your whole family.
Grant us your peace in this life,
save us from final damnation.
and count us among those you have chosen.
   [Through Christ our Lord. Amen.]

Bless and approve our offering;
make it acceptable to you,
an offering in spirit and in truth.
Let it become for us
the body and blood of Jesus Christ,
your only Son, our Lord.
   [Through Christ our Lord. Amen.]

The day before he suffered,
he took bread in his sacred hands
and looking up to heaven,
to you, his almighty Father,
he gave you thanks and praise.
He broke the bread,
gave it to his disciples, and said:
Take this, all of you, and eat it:
this is my body which will be given up for you.

When supper was ended,
he took the cup.
Again he gave you thanks and praise,
gave the cup to his disciples, and said:
Take this, all of you, and drink from it:
this is the cup of my blood,
the blood of the new and everlasting covenant.

It will be shed for you and for all
so that sins may be forgiven.
Do this in memory of me.

■ Let us proclaim the mystery of faith:

A ————————————————————————

■ Christ has died,
Christ is risen,
Christ will come again.

B ————————————————————————

■ Dying you destroyed our death,
rising you restored our life.
Lord Jesus, come in glory.

C ————————————————————————

■ When we eat this bread and drink this cup,
we proclaim your death, Lord Jesus,
until you come in glory.

D ————————————————————————

■ Lord, by your cross and resurrection
you have set us free.
You are the Savior of the world.

Father, we celebrate the memory of Christ, your Son.
We, your people and your ministers,
recall his passion,
his resurrection from the dead,
and his ascension into glory;
and from the many gifts you have given us
we offer to you, God of glory and majesty,
this holy and perfect sacrifice:
the bread of life
and the cup of eternal salvation.

Look with favor on these offerings
and accept them as once you accepted
the gifts of your servant Abel,
the sacrifice of Abraham, our father in faith,
and the bread and wine offered by your priest Melchisedech.

Almighty God,
we pray that your angel may take this sacrifice

to your altar in heaven.
Then, as we receive from this altar
the sacred body and blood of your Son,
let us be filled with every grace and blessing.
[Through Christ our Lord. Amen.]

Remember, Lord, those who have died
and have gone before us marked with the sign of faith,
especially those for whom we now pray, ... and ...
May these, and all who sleep in Christ,
find in your presence
light, happiness, and peace.
[Through Christ our Lord. Amen.]

For ourselves, too, we ask
some share in the fellowship of your apostles and martyrs,
with John the Baptist, Stephen, Matthias, Barnabas,
    [Ignatius, Alexander, Marcellinus, Peter,
      Felicity, Perpetua, Agatha, Lucy,
      Agnes, Cecilia, Anastasia]
and all the saints.
Though we are sinners,
we trust in your mercy and love.
Do not consider what we truly deserve,
but grant us your forgiveness.
Through Christ our Lord.

Through him you give us all these gifts.
You fill them with life and goodness,
you bless them and make them holy.

Through him,
with him,
in him,
in the unity of the Holy Spirit,
all glory and honor is yours,
almighty Father,
for ever and ever.

■   Amen.   (Our Father: page 244)

Eucharistic prayer II

Father, it is our duty and our salvation,
always and everywhere
to give you thanks
through your beloved Son, Jesus Christ.

He is the Word through whom you made the universe,
the Savior you sent to redeem us.
By the power of the Holy Spirit
he took flesh and was born of the Virgin Mary.

For our sake he opened his arms on the cross;
he put an end to death
and revealed the resurrection.
In this he fulfilled your will
and won for you a holy people.

And so we join the angels and the saints
in proclaiming your glory
as we say: Holy...

Lord, you are holy indeed,
the fountain of all holiness.
Let your Spirit come upon these gifts to make them holy,
so that they may become for us
the body and blood of our Lord, Jesus Christ.

Before he was given up to death,
a death he freely accepted,
he took bread and gave you thanks.
He broke the bread,
gave it to his disciples, and said:
Take this, all of you, and eat it:
this is my body which will be given up for you.

When supper was ended, he took the cup.
Again he gave you thanks and praise,
gave the cup to his disciples, and said:
Take this, all of you, and drink from it:
this is the cup of my blood,
the blood of the new and everlasting covenant.
It will be shed for you and for all

so that sins may be forgiven.
Do this in memory of me.

■ Let us proclaim the mystery of faith:

A ——————————————————————————

■ Christ has died,
Christ is risen,
Christ will come again.

B ——————————————————————————

■ Dying you destroyed our death,
rising you restored our life.
Lord Jesus, come in glory.

C ——————————————————————————

■ When we eat this bread and drink this cup,
we proclaim your death, Lord Jesus,
until you come in glory.

D ——————————————————————————

■ Lord, by your cross and resurrection
you have set us free.
You are the Savior of the world.

In memory of his death and resurrection,
we offer you, Father, this life-giving bread,
this saving cup.
We thank you for counting us worthy
to stand in your presence and serve you.
May all of us who share in the body and blood of Christ
be brought together in unity by the Holy Spirit.

Lord, remember your Church throughout the world;
make us grow in love,
together with ... our Pope,
... our bishop, and all the clergy.

Remember our brothers and sisters
who have gone to their rest
in the hope of rising again;
bring them and all the departed
into the light of your presence.
Have mercy on us all;
make us worthy to share eternal life

with Mary, the virgin Mother of God,
with the apostles, and with all the saints
who have done your will throughout the ages.
May we praise you in union with them,
and give you glory
through your Son, Jesus Christ.

Through him,
with him,
in him,
in the unity of the Holy Spirit,
all glory and honor is yours,
almighty Father,
for ever and ever.

■ **Amen.**

(Our Father: page 244)

Eucharistic prayer III

Father, you are holy indeed,
and all creation rightly gives you praise.
All life, all holiness comes from you
through your Son, Jesus Christ our Lord,
by the working of the Holy Spirit.
From age to age you gather a people to yourself,
so that from east to west
a perfect offering may be made
to the glory of your name.

And so, Father, we bring you these gifts.
We ask you to make them holy by the power of your Spirit,
that they may become the body and blood
of your Son, our Lord Jesus Christ,
at whose command we celebrate this Eucharist.

On the night he was betrayed,
he took bread and gave you thanks and praise.
He broke the bread, gave it to his disciples, and said:
Take this, all of you, and eat it:
this is my body which will be given up for you.

When supper was ended, he took the cup.
Again he gave you thanks and praise,

gave the cup to his disciples, and said:
Take this, all of you, and drink from it:
this is the cup of my blood,
the blood of the new and everlasting covenant.
It will be shed for you and for all
so that sins may be forgiven.
Do this in memory of me.

■   Let us proclaim the mystery of faith:

A ───────────────────────────────────

■   **Christ has died,**
    Christ is risen,
    Christ will come again.

B ───────────────────────────────────

■   **Dying you destroyed our death,**
    rising you restored our life.
    Lord Jesus, come in glory.

C ───────────────────────────────────

■   **When we eat this bread and drink this cup,**
    we proclaim your death, Lord Jesus,
    until you come in glory.

D ───────────────────────────────────

■   **Lord, by your cross and resurrection**
    you have set us free.
    You are the Savior of the world.

Father, calling to mind the death your Son endured for
    our salvation,
his glorious resurrection and ascension into heaven,
and ready to greet him when he comes again,
we offer you in thanksgiving this holy and living sacrifice.

Look with favor on your Church's offering,
and see the Victim whose death has reconciled us to yourself.
Grant that we, who are nourished by his body and blood,
may be filled with his Holy Spirit,
and become one body, one spirit in Christ.

May he make us an everlasting gift to you
and enable us to share in the inheritance of your saints,
with Mary, the virgin Mother of God;

with the apostles, the martyrs,
(Saint ... the saint of the day or the patron saint)
    and all your saints,
on whose constant intercession we rely for help.

Lord, may this sacrifice,
which has made our peace with you,
advance the peace and salvation of all the world.
Strengthen in faith and love your pilgrim Church on earth;
your servant, Pope ..., our bishop ...,
and all the bishops,
with the clergy and the entire people your Son
    has gained for you.
Father, hear the prayers of the family you have gathered
    here before you.
In mercy and love unite all your children wherever
    they may be.

Welcome into your kingdom our departed brothers and sisters,
and all who have left this world in your friendship.
We hope to enjoy for ever the vision of your glory,
through Christ our Lord, from whom all good things come.

Through him,
with him,
in him,
in the unity of the Holy Spirit,
all glory and honor is yours,
almighty Father,
for ever and ever.

■ **Amen.**

(Our Father: page 244)

Eucharistic prayer IV

Father in heaven,
it is right that we should give you thanks and glory:
you are the one God, living and true.
Through all eternity you live in unapproachable light.
Source of life and goodness, you have created all things,
to fill your creatures with every blessing
and lead all men to the joyful vision of your light.
Countless hosts of angels stand before you to do your will;

they look upon your splendor
and praise you, night and day.
United with them,
and in the name of every creature under heaven,
we too praise your glory as we say: **Holy…**

Father, we acknowledge your greatness:
all your actions show your wisdom and love.
You formed man in your own likeness
and set him over the whole world
to serve you, his creator,
and to rule over all creatures.
Even when he disobeyed you and lost your friendship
you did not abandon him to the power of death,
but helped all men to seek and find you.
Again and again you offered a covenant to man,
and through the prophets taught him to hope for salvation.
Father, you so loved the world
that in the fullness of time you sent your only Son to be
    our Savior.
He was conceived through the power of the Holy Spirit,
and born of the Virgin Mary,
a man like us in all things but sin.
To the poor he proclaimed the good news of salvation,
to prisoners, freedom,
and to those in sorrow, joy.
In fulfillment of your will
he gave himself up to death;
but by rising from the dead,
he destroyed death and restored life.
And that we might live no longer for ourselves but for him,
he sent the Holy Spirit from you, Father,
as his first gift to those who believe,
to complete his work on earth
and bring us the fullness of grace.

Father, may this Holy Spirit sanctify these offerings.
Let them become the body and blood of Jesus Christ our Lord
as we celebrate the great mystery
which he left us as an everlasting covenant.

He always loved those who were his own in the world.
When the time came for him to be glorified by you, his
heavenly Father,
he showed the depth of his love.

While they were at supper,
he took bread, said the blessing, broke the bread,
and gave it to his disciples, saying:
Take this, all of you, and eat it:
this is my body which will be given up for you.

In the same way, he took the cup, filled with wine.
He gave you thanks, and giving the cup to his disciples, said:
Take this, all of you, and drink from it:
this is the cup of my blood,
the blood of the new and everlasting covenant.
It will be shed for you and for all
so that sins may be forgiven.
Do this in memory of me.

- Let us proclaim the mystery of faith:

A

- Christ has died,
  Christ is risen,
  Christ will come again.

B

- Dying you destroyed our death,
  rising you restored our life.
  Lord Jesus, come in glory.

C

- When we eat this bread and drink this cup,
  we proclaim your death, Lord Jesus,
  until you come in glory.

D

- Lord, by your cross and resurrection
  you have set us free.
  You are the Savior of the world.

Father, we now celebrate this memorial of our redemption.
We recall Christ's death, his descent among the dead,
his resurrection, and his ascension to your right hand;
and, looking forward to his coming in glory,
we offer you his body and blood,
the acceptable sacrifice
which brings salvation to the whole world.

Lord, look upon this sacrifice which you have given to
    your Church;
and by your Holy Spirit, gather all who share this one bread
    and one cup
into the one body of Christ, a living sacrifice of praise.

Lord, remember those for whom we offer this sacrifice,
especially … our Pope,
… our bishop, and bishops and clergy everywhere.
Remember those who take part in this offering,
those here present and all your people,
and all who seek you with a sincere heart.
Remember those who have died in the peace of Christ
and all the dead whose faith is known to you alone.
Father, in your mercy grant also to us, your children,
to enter into our heavenly inheritance
in the company of the Virgin Mary, the Mother of God,
and your apostles and saints.
Then, in your kingdom, freed from the corruption of sin
    and death,
we shall sing your glory with every creature through
    Christ our Lord,
through whom you give us everything that is good.

Through him,
with him,
in him,
in the unity of the Holy Spirit,
all glory and honor is yours,
almighty Father,
for ever and ever.
■ Amen.

A

■ Let us pray with confidence to the Father
  in the words our Savior gave us.

B

■ Jesus taught us to call God our Father,
  and so we have the courage to say:

C

■ Let us ask our Father to forgive our sins
  and to bring us to forgive those who sin against us.

D

■ Let us pray for the coming of the kingdom
  as Jesus taught us.

Our Father, who art in heaven,
hallowed be thy name;
thy kingdom come;
thy will be done on earth
as it is in heaven.
Give us this day our daily bread;
and forgive us our trespasses
as we forgive those who trespass against us;
and lead us not into temptation,
but deliver us from evil.

Pater noster, qui es in caelis:
sanctificetur nomen tuum;
adveniat regnum tuum;
fiat voluntas tua,
sicut in caelo, et in terra.
Panem nostrum quotidianum
da nobis hodie;
et dimitte nobis debita nostra,
sicut et nos dimittimus
debitoribus nostris;
et ne nos inducas in tentationem;
sed libera nos a malo.

■ Deliver us, Lord, from every evil,
and grant us peace in our day.
In your mercy keep us free from sin
and protect us from all anxiety
as we wait in joyful hope
for the coming of our Savior,
    Jesus Christ.

■ **For the kingdom, the power, and the glory are yours,
now and for ever.**

Sign of peace

■ Lord Jesus Christ, you said to your apostles:
I leave you peace, my peace I give you.
Look not on our sins, but on the faith of your Church,
and grant us the peace and unity of your kingdom
where you live for ever and ever.

■ **Amen.**

■ The peace of the Lord be with you always.

■ **And also with you.**

(Then the deacon [or the priest] may add:)

Let us offer each other the sign of peace.

Breaking of the bread

■ Lamb of God, you take away the sins of the world:
    have mercy on us.
Lamb of God, you take away the sins of the world:
    have mercy on us.
Lamb of God, you take away the sins of the world:
    grant us peace.

■ Agnus Dei, qui tollis peccata mundi:
    miserere nobis.
Agnus Dei, qui tollis peccata mundi:
    miserere nobis.
Agnus Dei, qui tollis peccata mundi:
    dona nobis pacem.

*(Meanwhile, he takes the host and breaks it over the paten.
He places a small piece in the chalice, saying inaudibly:)*

May this mingling of the body and blood of our Lord Jesus Christ bring eternal life to us who receive it.

Private preparation of the priest
(Then the priest joins his hands and says inaudibly:)

Lord Jesus Christ, Son of the living God, by the will of the Father and the work of the Holy Spirit your death brought life to the world. By your holy body and blood free me from all my sins and from every evil. Keep me faithful to your teaching, and never let me be parted from you.

Or:

Lord Jesus Christ, with faith in your love and mercy I eat your body and drink your blood. Let it not bring me condemnation, but health in mind and body.

Communion

(The priest genuflects. Taking the host, he raises it slightly over the paten and, facing the people, says aloud:)

- This is the Lamb of God
  who takes away the sins of the world.
  Happy are those who are called to his supper.
- Lord, I am not worthy to receive you,
  but only say the word and I shall be healed.

(Facing the altar, the priest says inaudibly:)

May the body of Christ bring me to everlasting life.

*(He reverently consumes the body of Christ.
Then he takes the chalice and says inaudibly:)*

May the blood of Christ bring me to everlasting life.

(He reverently drinks the blood of Christ.)

Communion song
Period of silence or song of praise
Prayer after communion

CONCLUDING RITE

Brief announcements

Greeting

- The Lord be with you.
- And also with you.

Blessing

- May almighty God bless you,
  the Father, and the Son, and the Holy Spirit.
- Amen.

Dismissal

(The deacon [or the priest], with hands joined, sings or says:)

A —————————————————————————————————————

- Go in the peace of Christ.

B —————————————————————————————————————

- The Mass is ended, go in peace.

C —————————————————————————————————————

- Go in peace to love and serve the Lord.

A, B, C —————————————————————————————————

- Thanks be to God.

Eucharistic Exposition
and Benediction

"The worship given to the Trinity of the Father and of the Son and of the Holy Spirit... must fill our churches also outside the timetable of Masses... This worship must be prominent in all our encounters with the Blessed Sacrament... Adoration of Christ in this sacrament of love must also find expression in various forms of Eucharistic devotion: personal prayer before the Blessed Sacrament, hours of adoration, periods of exposition – short, prolonged, and annual (Forty Hours) – Eucharistic benediction, Eucharistic processions, Eucharistic Congresses... Let us be generous with our time in going to meet him in adoration and in contemplation that is full of faith and ready to make reparation for the great faults and crimes of the world. May our adoration never cease."   Pope John Paul II

Exposition

Once the people have assembled, a song such as the following may be sung while the priest or deacon prepares the Holy Eucharist for adoration.

O Saving Victim/O Salutaris

O Saving Victim, op'ning wide
The gate of heav'n to us below!
Our foes press on from ev'ry side:
Your aid supply, your strength bestow.

   O salutáris hóstia,
   Quae caeli pandis óstium:
   Bella premunt hostília,
   Da robur fer auxílium.

To your great name be endless praise,
Immortal Godhead, One in Three;

O grant us endless length of days
When our true native land we see.

Uni trinóque Dómino
Sit sempitérna glória:
Qui vitam sine término
Nobis donet in pátria.

ADORATION

The Liturgy of the Hours may be celebrated during the period of exposition, or there may be prayers, songs, readings from Scripture, and a brief homily to direct the attention of the faithful to the worship of the Lord.

A reading from
the first Letter of Paul to the Corinthians   11: 23-26

FOR I RECEIVED from the Lord what I also handed on to you, that the Lord Jesus, on the night he was handed over, took bread, and after he had given thanks, broke it and said, "This is my body that is for you. Do this in remembrance of me." In the same way also the cup, after supper, saying, "This cup is the new covenant in my blood. Do this, as often as you drink it, in remembrance of me." For as often as you eat this bread and drink the cup, you proclaim the death of the Lord until he comes.
The word of the Lord.
℟ Thanks be to God.

A eucharistic song such as the following may be sung.

Come Adore/Tantum Ergo

Come adore this wondrous presence,
Bow to Christ the source of grace.
Here is kept the ancient promise
Of God's earthly dwelling place.
Sight is blind before God's glory,
Faith alone may see his face.

Tantum ergo Sacraméntum
Venerémur cérnui:
Et antíquum documéntum
Novo cedat rítui:
Praestet fides suppleméntum
Sénsuum deféctui.

Glory be to God the Father,
Praise to his coequal Son,
Adoration to the Spirit,
Bond of love, in Godhead one.
Blest be God by all creation
Joyously while ages run.

Genitóri Genitóque
Laus et jubilátio,
Salus, honor, virtus quoque
Sit et benedíctio:
Procedénti ab utróque
Compar sit laudátio.

BENEDICTION

The priest or deacon may give a blessing. Before the blessing a prayer such as the following may be said.

Minister   You have given them bread from heaven.
R̷   **Containing in itself all delight.**
Minister   Let us pray.

Lord Jesus Christ,
you gave us the Eucharist
as the memorial of your suffering and death.
May our worship of this sacrament of your body and blood
help us to experience the salvation you won for us
and the peace of the kingdom
where you live with the Father and the Holy Spirit,
one God, for ever and ever.
R̷   **Amen.**

After the blessing the minister places the Blessed Sacrament in the tabernacle.

The Divine Praises

Blessed be God.
Blessed be his Holy Name.
Blessed be Jesus Christ, true God and true Man.
Blessed be the Name of Jesus.
Blessed be his most Sacred Heart.
Blessed be his most Precious Blood.
Blessed be Jesus in the most Holy Sacrament of the Altar.
Blessed be the Holy Spirit, the Paraclete.

Blessed be the great Mother of God, Mary most holy.
Blessed be her holy and Immaculate Conception.
Blessed be her glorious Assumption.
Blessed be the name of Mary, Virgin and Mother.
Blessed be Saint Joseph, her most chaste spouse.
Blessed be God in his angels and in his saints.

A closing song such as the following may be sung.

Holy God, We Praise Thy Name

Holy God, we praise thy name!
Lord of all, we bow before thee;
All on earth thy scepter claim,
All in heav'n above adore thee;
Infinite thy vast domain,
Everlasting is thy reign.

Hark! the loud celestial hymn
Angel choirs above are raising;
Cherubim and Seraphim
In unceasing chorus praising,
Fill the heav'ns with sweet accord:
Holy, holy, holy Lord!

Holy Father, Holy Son,
Holy Spirit, Three we name thee,
While in essence only One,
Undivided God we claim thee,
And adoring bend the knee,
While we own the mystery.

Anima Christi

Anima Christi, sanctifica me.
Corpus Christi, salva me.
Sanguis Christi, inebria me.
Aqua lateris Christi, lava me.
Passio Christi, conforta me.
O Bone Iesu, exaudi me.
Intra tua vulnera absconde me.
Ne permittas me separari a te.
Ab hoste maligno defende me.
In hora mortis meae voca me,
et iube me venire ad te,
ut cum Sanctis tuis laudem te
in saecula saeculorum. Amen.

Soul of Christ, sanctify me.
Body of Christ, save me.
Blood of Christ, inebriate me.
Water from the side of Christ, wash me.
Passion of Christ, strengthen me.
O good Jesus, hear me.
Within thy wounds hide me.
Suffer me not to be separated from thee.
From the malicious enemy defend me.
In the hour of my death call me
and bid me come unto thee,
that with thy saints I may praise thee
for ever and ever. Amen.

TUESDAY, JULY 17

Prayer for the Morning

In the morning you hear us, O Lord;
in the morning we offer you our prayer! (cf. Ps 5: 4)

Glory to the Father, and to the Son,
and to the Holy Spirit, as it was in the beginning,
is now, and will be for ever. Amen. Alleluia!

HYMN   Meter: 8 7 8 7 D
                        This hymn can be sung to the tune used for
                        Those Who Love and Those Who Labor

O my soul, bless God the Father;
All within me bless his name:
Bless the Father, and forget not
All his mercies to proclaim,
Who forgiveth thy transgressions,
Thy diseases all who heals;
Who redeems thee from destruction,
Who with thee so kindly deals.

Far as east from west is distant,
He hath put away our sin;
Like the pity of a father
Hath the Lord's compassion been.
As it was without beginning,
So it lasts without an end;
To their children's children ever
Shall his righteousness extend.

PSALM 90   1-6, 14-17

Make us know the shortness of our life that we may gain wisdom of
heart. (Ps 90: 12)

A human life may sometimes look too short to be worth much, but God, who sees the works of his hands from the perspective of enduring love, clothes even the passing wildflowers with splendor. We are only dust – but beloved dust!

O Lord, you have been our refuge
from one generation to the next.
Before the mountains were born
or the earth or the world brought forth,
you are God, without beginning or end.

You turn men back into dust
and say: "Go back, sons of men."
To your eyes a thousand years
are like yesterday, come and gone,
no more than a watch in the night.

You sweep men away like a dream,
like grass which springs up in the morning.
In the morning it springs up and flowers:
by evening it withers and fades.

In the morning, fill us with your love;
we shall exult and rejoice all our days.
Give us joy to balance our affliction
for the years when we knew misfortune.

Show forth your work to your servants;
let your glory shine on their children.
Let the favor of the Lord be upon us:
give success to the work of our hands,
give success to the work of our hands.

Glory to the Father…

Word of God   Ephesians 2: 4-10

GOD, WHO IS RICH in mercy,
because of the great love he

had for us, even when we were dead in our transgressions, brought us to life with Christ (by grace you have been saved), raised us up with him, and seated us with him in the heavens in Christ Jesus, that in the ages to come he might show the immeasurable riches of his grace in his kindness to us in Christ Jesus. For by grace you have been saved through faith, and this is not from you; it is the gift of God; it is not from works, so no one may boast. For we are his handiwork, created in Christ Jesus for the good works that God has prepared in advance, that we should live in them.

You are precious in my eyes.
(Is 43: 4)

CANTICLE OF ZECHARIAH   (Text, back cover B)
The Lord God formed man out of the clay of the ground and blew into his nostrils the breath of life, and so man became a living being. (Gn 2: 7)

INTERCESSIONS

The Lord Jesus Christ took on our fragile flesh and made of it a temple for the living God. With joyful confidence, let us pray:

℞   Let your favor be upon us, O Lord.

O God, we are the works of your hands:
– shape us in the image of Christ our Lord. ℞

O God, we are but a moment in the world's history:
– teach us to store up treasure in heaven by the good we do on earth. ℞

O God, we fear the mortality we cannot cure:
– grant insight and faith to all those who do the work of medical research. ℞

O God, we are saddened by the death of those we love:
– bring them into the everlasting joy of your presence. R/

Personal intentions

Our Father...

O God of wisdom and of love, you have made us as fragile as the flowers of the field, yet you have made us
strong in the hope of life everlasting. Teach us to see this
day as gift enough, that we may live it for your glory and
render it back to you in praise when evening falls,
through Jesus Christ, your Son and our Lord, who lives
and reigns with you and the Holy Spirit, one God for
ever and ever. Amen.

MASS

Tuesday of the Fifteenth Week of the Year

(The prayers suggested today are those of the Fifteenth Week
in Ordinary Time.)

ENTRANCE ANTIPHON
In my justice I shall see your face, O Lord; when your glory
appears, my joy will be full. (Ps 16: 15)

OPENING PRAYER
God our Father,
your light of truth
guides us to the way of Christ.
May all who follow him
reject what is contrary to the Gospel.
We ask this through our Lord Jesus Christ, your Son,
who lives and reigns with you and the Holy Spirit,
one God for ever and ever.

● *He was called by the name Moses because he was taken from the water. Afterwards he grew up to lead his brothers.* ●

A reading from
the Book of Exodus
2: 1-15

A CERTAIN MAN OF THE HOUSE of Levi married a Levite woman, who conceived and bore a son. Seeing that he was a goodly child, she hid him for three months. When she could hide him no longer, she took a papyrus basket, daubed it with bitumen and pitch, and putting the child in it, placed it among the reeds on the river bank. His sister stationed herself at a distance to find out what would happen to him.

Pharaoh's daughter came down to the river to bathe, while her maids walked along the river bank. Noticing the basket among the reeds, she sent her handmaid to fetch it. On opening it, she looked and lo, there was a baby boy, crying! She was moved with pity for him and said, "It is one of the Hebrews' children." Then his sister asked Pharaoh's daughter, "Shall I go and call one of the Hebrew women to nurse the child for you?" "Yes, do so," she answered. So the maiden went and called the child's own mother. Pharaoh's daughter said to her, "Take this child and nurse it for me, and I will repay you." The woman therefore took the child and nursed it. When the child grew, she brought him to Pharaoh's daughter, who adopted him as her son and called him Moses; for she said, "I drew him out of the water."

On one occasion, after Moses had grown up, when he visited his kinsmen and witnessed their forced labor, he saw an Egyptian striking a Hebrew, one of his own kinsmen. Looking about and seeing no one, he slew the

Egyptian and hid him in the sand. The next day he went
out again, and now two Hebrews were fighting! So he
asked the culprit, "Why are you striking your fellow
Hebrew?" But he replied, "Who has appointed you ruler
and judge over us? Are you thinking of killing me as you
killed the Egyptian?" Then Moses became afraid and
thought, "The affair must certainly be known."

Pharaoh, too, heard of the affair and sought to put
him to death. But Moses fled from him and stayed in the
land of Midian.

The word of the Lord.

────── • **PSALM 69** • ──────

℟ (33) **Turn to the Lord in your need, and you will
live.**

I am sunk in the abysmal swamp
    where there is no foothold;
I have reached the watery depths;
    the flood overwhelms me. ℟

But I pray to you, O Lord,
    for the time of your favor, O God!
In your great kindness answer me
    with your constant help. ℟

But I am afflicted and in pain;
    let your saving help, O God, protect me.
I will praise the name of God in song,
    and I will glorify him with thanksgiving; ℟

See, you lowly ones, and be glad;
    you who seek God, may your hearts be merry!
For the Lord hears the poor,
    and his own who are in bonds he spurns not. ℟

Alleluia. If today you hear his voice, harden not your hearts. Alleluia.

> ● *It will not go as hard with Tyre and Sidon and the land of Sodom on Judgment Day as with you.* ●

A reading from
the holy Gospel according to Matthew   11: 20-24

JESUS BEGAN TO REPROACH the towns where most of his miracles had been worked, with their failure to reform: "It will go ill with you, Chorazin! And just as ill with you, Bethsaida! If the miracles worked in you had taken place in Tyre and Sidon, they would have reformed in sackcloth and ashes long ago. I assure you, it will go easier for Tyre and Sidon than for you on the day of judgment. As for you, Capernaum,

'Are you to be exalted to the skies?/ You shall go down to the realm of death!'
If the miracles worked in you had taken place in Sodom, it would be standing today. I assure you, it will go easier for Sodom than for you on the day of judgment."
The Gospel of the Lord.

PRAYER OVER THE GIFTS
Lord,
accept the gifts of your Church.
May this Eucharist
help us grow in holiness and faith.
We ask this in the name of Jesus the Lord.

COMMUNION ANTIPHON
Whoever eats my flesh and drinks my blood will live in me and I in him, says the Lord. (Jn 6: 57)

PRAYER AFTER COMMUNION
Lord,
by our sharing in the mystery of this Eucharist,
let your saving love grow within us.
Grant this through Christ our Lord.

MEDITATION OF THE DAY

The Need to Reform

At the very moment that the sinner receives forgiveness and is caught up by God and restored in grace, at that moment – wonder of wonders! – sin has become the place where God enters into contact with a human being. One even may go further and say that there is no other way to encounter God and to learn to know him than by the way of repentance. Before then God was only a word, a concept, a premonition, a vague longing, the God of philosophers and poets but not yet the God who reveals himself in unfathomable love. For the Lord came to call sinners, to stay with them and to eat with them, not with the righteous; he came to seek that which was lost (Mt 9: 13; Lk 19: 10). Thus God makes himself known by forgiving. And the sinner, by plumbing the depths of his sin, will discover the space of God's mercy at the very moment that the one swallows up the other.

This moment of grace is the primary and most fundamental part of a real encounter with the Gospel. It is the experience of the "little ones," the poor in spirit, and especially of conspicuous sinners, women of the street and publicans, the people who proceed others into the kingdom of God (Mt 21: 31). It is in them and in the likes of them that God decided to meet and to save mankind. There is no other situation in which God so personally presents himself and brings salvation.

FATHER ANDRÉ LOUF, O. CIST.

Father André Louf is abbot of the Cistercian monastery of Katzberg, France.

Prayer for the Evening

O give thanks to the Lord for he is good;
for his love endures for ever.

Glory to the Father, and to the Son,
and to the Holy Spirit, as it was in the beginning,
is now, and will be for ever. Amen. Alleluia!

HYMN   Meter: CM
                              This hymn can be sung to the tune used for
                                                        Arise, O Sleeper

O Son of God, in Galilee
You made the deaf to hear,
The mute to speak, the blind to see;
O blessed Lord, be near.

O listen to the silent prayer
Of your afflicted ones.
O bid them cast on you their care;
Your grace to them make known.

PSALM 107   1, 17-22

I have heard your prayer and seen your tears. I will heal you.
(2 Kgs 20: 5)

Sickness is a harbinger of death. Jesus cured the sick as a countersign:
in the reign of God, there will be neither illness nor dying. By taking
death upon himself on the cross, Jesus cured the one incurable reality that haunts the human race: mortality.

"O give thanks to the Lord for he is good;
for his love endures for ever."

Some were sick on account of their sins
and afflicted on account of their guilt.
They had a loathing for every food;
they came close to the gates of death.

Then they cried to the Lord in their need
and he rescued them from their distress.
He sent forth his word to heal them
and saved their life from the grave.

Let them thank the Lord for his love,
for the wonders he does for men.
Let them offer a sacrifice of thanks
and tell of his deeds with rejoicing.

Glory to the Father...

Word of God   Isaiah 57: 15, 18

ON HIGH I DWELL, and in holiness, and with the crushed and dejected in spirit, to revive the spirits of the dejected, to revive the hearts of the crushed. I saw their ways, but I will heal them and lead them; I will give full comfort to them and to those who mourn for them.

If you will do so, you can cure me.
(Mk 1: 40)

CANTICLE OF MARY   (Text, back cover A)
Heal me, Lord, that I may be healed; save me, that I may be saved, for it is you whom I praise. (Jer 17: 14)

INTERCESSIONS

God dwells with the crushed and dejected in spirit. For them, let us pray:

℟   Lord, hear the cry of the poor.

For those who suffer chronic illness:
– grant them patient endurance. ℟

For those who suffer mental or emotional illness:
– grant them peace of mind. ℟

For those who suffer terminal illness:
– grant them hope as they approach you. ℟

For all who love and care for the sick:
– grant them the reward of your love. ℟

Personal intentions

Our Father…

*May the God of peace himself make us perfect in holiness.
May he preserve us whole and entire, spirit, soul, and
body, irreproachable at the coming of our Lord Jesus
Christ. Amen. (cf. 1 Thes 5: 23)*

MARIAN ANTIPHON (Text, page 25)

Saints
OF TODAY AND YESTERDAY

O Lord, you are our Father; we are the clay, and you are our potter; we are all the work of your hand.

Carmelite Martyrs of Compiègne
Martyrs († 1794)

In June 1794 the anti-Catholic regime of the French Revolution arrested the Carmelite nuns of Compiègne for continuing to observe their religious life despite a government ban on religious orders. Subsequently they were deported to Paris for trial. Other nuns imprisoned with them observed their departure: "We saw them embrace each other before they set off, and they took an affectionate leave of us by the motion of their hands and other friendly gestures." When during their trial the Carmelites were falsely accused of harboring arms, the prioress held up a crucifix and answered, "Here are the only arms that we have ever had in our house." Sentenced to the guillotine for being adherents of what the government characterized as the "fanatical and royalist cult" of devotion to the Sacred Heart of Jesus, the sixteen nuns sang on the way to the place of execution the Latin hymns *Salve Regina* and *Te Deum* and chanted the *Laudate Dominum* (Ps 117) while mounting the scaffold.

We are the victims of the age, and we ought to sacrifice ourselves to obtain its return to God.
Blessed Julia Louisa, Compiègne Martyr

WEDNESDAY, JULY 18
Saint Camillus de Lellis

Prayer for the Morning

Strong is God's love for us; he is faithful for ever:
come, let us give thanks and praise! (cf. Ps 117: 2)

Glory to the Father, and to the Son,
and to the Holy Spirit, as it was in the beginning,
is now, and will be for ever. Amen. Alleluia!

HYMN   Meter: 8 7 8 7 8 8 7

Thanks be to God, O give him praise
And publicize his great name.
Shout out, proclaim aloud his deeds
To ev'ry land and peoples,
Sing songs of beauty to the Lord;
Praise him with spirit jubilant.
Tell over all his marvels!

Glorious is his holy name;
Let ev'ry heart be joyful.
Cleansed they become through fear in faith
Who struggle now with courage.
Look to the Lord and to his strength;
His acts recall, his judgments sound.
Never forget his wonders!

He surely is our God and Lord
Who all the earth rules justly.
His cov'nant he will not forget;
It is his word and promise.
All generations this confirms:
He is unfailing, faithful, true;
His trust is everlasting.

PSALM 89   2-3, 6-9, 14-17

I will extol you and praise your name; for you have fulfilled your
wonderful plans of old, faithful and true. (Is 25: 1)

God is true: he has a long memory for his own promises and a short
memory for our failures to keep ours.

I will sing for ever of your love, O Lord;
through all ages my mouth will proclaim your truth.
Of this I am sure, that your love lasts for ever,
that your truth is firmly established as the heavens.

The heavens proclaim your wonders, O Lord;
the assembly of your holy ones proclaims your truth.
For who in the skies can compare with the Lord
or who is like the Lord among the sons of God?

A God to be feared in the council of the holy ones,
great and dreadful to all around him.
O Lord God of hosts, who is your equal?
You are mighty, O Lord, and truth is your garment.

Yours is a mighty arm, O Lord;
your hand is strong, your right hand ready.
Justice and right are the pillars of your throne,
love and truth walk in your presence.

Happy the people who acclaim such a king,
who walk, O Lord, in the light of your face,
who find their joy every day in your name,
who make your justice the source of their bliss.

Glory to the Father...

Word of God   Isaiah 54: 10

Though the mountains
leave their place and the
hills be shaken, my love shall never leave you nor my

covenant of peace be shaken, says the Lord, who has mercy on you.

> **The Holy One is faithful!** *(cf. Hos 12: 1)*

CANTICLE OF ZECHARIAH (Text, back cover B)
God is faithful, and by him you were called to fellowship with his Son, Jesus Christ our Lord. (1 Cor 1: 9)

INTERCESSIONS

Let us pray with faith to the One who is faithful and true:

℟ Remember your people, O Lord.

You promised that the house of the messianic king would last for ever:
– grant us the grace to put our trust in your fidelity rather than our own short-sightedness. ℟

You have made your promise known in the assembly of the holy ones:
– teach us to hear and to live the words we pray when we are gathered for worship. ℟

You have clothed yourself in truth and beauty:
– make us walk in the ways of truth and beauty today. ℟

You heal the sick and comfort the sorrowing:
– sustain all who care for the sick, through the intercession of Saint Camillus de Lellis. ℟

Personal intentions

Our Father…

O God, you have kept your covenant with every generation. In a world shadowed by the many infidelities of frail humanity, grant us faith in your enduring love, through Christ our Lord. Amen.

MASS

Wednesday of the Fifteenth Week of the Year

CAMILLUS DE LELLIS   *Optional memorial*

● *Saint Camillus de Lellis was born in Chieti in the Abruzzi in 1550. He first entered the military profession, but upon his conversion he devoted himself to the care of the sick. His studies completed, he was ordained to the priesthood and founded a society which established hospitals and cared for the sick. He died in Rome in 1614.* ●

ENTRANCE ANTIPHON
Come, you whom my Father has blessed, says the Lord: I was ill and you comforted me. I tell you, anything you did for one of my brothers, you did for me. (Mt 25: 34, 36, 40)

OPENING PRAYER
Father,
you gave Saint Camillus a special love for the sick.
Through his prayers inspire us with your grace,
so that by serving you in our brothers and sisters
we may come safely to you at the end of our lives.
We ask this through our Lord Jesus Christ, your Son,
who lives and reigns with you and the Holy Spirit,
one God, for ever and ever.

● *The Lord appeared to Moses in the form of fire in the midst of a bush.* ●

A reading from
the Book of Exodus   3: 1-6, 9-12

MOSES WAS TENDING the flock of his father-in-law Jethro, the priest of Midian. Leading the flock across the desert, he came to Horeb, the mountain of God. There an angel of the Lord appeared to him in fire flaming out of a bush. As he looked on, he was surprised to see that the bush, though on fire, was not consumed. So Moses decided, "I must go over to look at this remarkable sight, and see why the bush is not burned."

When the Lord saw him coming over to look at it more closely, God called out to him from the bush, "Moses! Moses!" He answered, "Here I am." God said, "Come no nearer! Remove the sandals from your feet, for the place where you stand is holy ground. I am the God of your father," he continued, "the God of Abraham, the God of Isaac, the God of Jacob." Moses hid his face, for he was afraid to look at God.

The Lord said, "So indeed the cry of the Israelites has reached me, and I have truly noted that the Egyptians are oppressing them. Come, now! I will send you to Pharaoh to lead my people, the Israelites, out of Egypt."

But Moses said to God, "Who am I that I should go to Pharaoh and lead the Israelites out of Egypt?" He answered, "I will be with you; and this shall be your proof that it is I who have sent you: when you bring my people out of Egypt, you will worship God on this very mountain."

The word of the Lord.

———• PSALM 103 •———

℟ (8) **The Lord is kind and merciful.**

Bless the Lord, O my soul;
    and all my being, bless his holy name.
Bless the Lord, O my soul,
    and forget not all his benefits. ℟

He pardons all your iniquities,
    he heals all your ills.
He redeems your life from destruction,
    he crowns you with kindness and compassion. ℟

The Lord secures justice
    and the rights of all the oppressed.
He has made known his ways to Moses,
    and his deeds to the children of Israel. ℟

Alleluia. Blessed are you, Father, Lord of heaven and earth; you have revealed to little ones the mysteries of the kingdom. Alleluia.

● *The Lord hides these things from the wise and reveals them to children.* ●

A reading from
the holy Gospel according to Matthew   11: 25-27

ON ONE OCCASION Jesus spoke thus: "Father, Lord of heaven and earth, to you I offer praise; for what you have hidden from the learned and the clever you have revealed to the merest children. Father, it is true. You have graciously willed it so. Everything has been given over to me by my Father. No one knows the Son but the Father, and no one knows the Father but the Son – and anyone to whom the Son wishes to reveal him."
The Gospel of the Lord.

PRAYER OVER THE GIFTS
    Lord,
    accept the gifts of your people.
    May we who celebrate the love of your Son
    also follow the example of your saints
    and grow in love for you and for one another.
    We ask this through Christ our Lord.

COMMUNION ANTIPHON
By the love you have for one another, says the Lord, everyone
will know that you are my disciples. (Jn 13: 35)

PRAYER AFTER COMMUNION
> Lord,
> we who receive the sacrament of salvation
>   ask your mercy.
> Help us to imitate the love of Saint Camillus
> and give to us a share in his glory.
> We ask this through Christ our Lord.

MEDITATION OF THE DAY

Knowing the Father in the Son

Living spiritually is more than living physically, intellectually, or emotionally. It embraces all that, but it is larger, deeper, and wider. It concerns the core of your humanity. It is possible to lead a very wholesome, emotionally rich, and "sensible" life without being a spiritual person: that is, without knowledge or personal experience of the terrain where the meaning and goal of our human existence are hidden.

The spiritual life has to do with the heart of existence. This is a good word. By heart I do not mean the seat of our feelings as opposed to the seat of our thoughts; I mean the center of our being, that place where we are most ourselves, where we are most human, where we are most real. In that sense the heart is the focus of the spiritual life...

In every phase of my search I've discovered also that Jesus Christ stands at the center of my seeking. If you were to ask me point-blank, "What does it mean to you to live spiritually?" I would have to reply, "Living with Jesus at the center."

Countless questions, problems, discussions, and difficulties always demand one's attention. Despite this, when I look back over the last thirty years of my life, I can say that, for me, the person of Jesus has come to be more and more important. Increasingly, what matters is getting to know Jesus and living in solidarity with him. At one time I was so immersed in problems of Church and society that my whole life had become a sort of drawn-out, wearisome discussion. Jesus had been pushed into the background; he had himself become just another problem. Fortunately, it hasn't stayed that way. Jesus has stepped out in front again and asked me, "And you, who do you say that I am?" It has become clearer to me than ever that my personal relationship with Jesus is the heart of my existence.

FATHER HENRI J. M. NOUWEN

Father Nouwen († 1996) was a Dutch priest who lived a number of years in the United States and Canada and who wrote many best-selling books on spirituality.

Prayer for the Evening

God is our stronghold, the God who shows us love: come, let us give thanks!

Glory to the Father, and to the Son, and to the Holy Spirit, as it was in the beginning, is now, and will be for ever. Amen. Alleluia!

HYMN
Meter: LM
This hymn can be sung to the tune used for
Praise God from Whom All Blessings Flow

O love of God, how strong and true,
Eternal and yet ever new,
Uncomprehended and unbought,
Beyond all knowledge and all thought!

O heav'nly love, how precious still
In days of weariness and ill,
In nights of pain and helplessness,
To heal, to comfort, and to bless!

O love of God, our shield and stay
Through all the perils of our way –
Eternal love, in you we rest,
For ever safe, for ever blest.

PSALM 125

The Lord of hosts shall shield his people, to protect and deliver, to spare and rescue. (cf. Is 31: 5)

Strong is God's love for us, faithful his care. Let us fear no evil but put our trust in him.

Those who put their trust in the Lord
are like Mount Zion, that cannot be shaken,
that stands for ever.

Jerusalem! The mountains surround her,
so the Lord surrounds his people
both now and for ever.

For the scepter of the wicked shall not rest
over the land of the just
for fear that the hands of the just
should turn to evil.

Do good, Lord, to those who are good,
to the upright of heart;
but the crooked and those who do evil,
drive them away!

On Israel, peace!

Glory to the Father...

Word of God   Isaiah 65: 24-25

Before [MY PEOPLE] call, I will answer; while they are yet speaking, I will hearken to them. The wolf and the lamb shall graze alike, and the lion shall eat hay like the ox [but the serpent's food shall be dust]. None shall hurt or destroy on all my holy mountain, says the Lord.

God is a shield to those who take refuge in him. (Prv 30: 5)

CANTICLE OF MARY   (Text, back cover A)
I will be for them an encircling wall of fire, says the Lord, and I will be the glory in their midst. (cf. Zec 2: 9)

INTERCESSIONS

God is our shield and defender. Let us put our trust in him, as we pray:

℟   O God our strength, to you we turn.

O God, those who put their trust in you cannot be shaken:
– strengthen in faith those who are afraid. ℟

O God, you surround your people with your all-power-ful love:
– open the eyes of faith to see your presence. ℟

O God, the rule of wickedness shall not rest on your people:
– guard the hearts of the young and uncertain. ℟

O God, you drive away crookedness and evil:
– drive the moneychangers from the temples of our heart. ℟

O God, your peace dwells all around your people:
– let those who have died live on in your peace. ℟

Personal intentions

Our Father…

May the Lord guard our going and coming both now and for ever. Amen. (cf. Ps 121: 8)

MARIAN ANTIPHON   (Text, page 25)

SAINTS
OF TODAY AND YESTERDAY

Hail, holy wounds of Jesus.

SAINT PAMBO
Monk († c. 390)

The monk Pambo, one of the founders of Egypt's Nitrian desert monasteries, spent his life in long periods of uninterrupted prayer combined with strict mortification and manual labor. He was particularly distinguished by his vigilance in governing his tongue, both to avoid sinning in speech and to preserve the silence necessary for turning his mind to God. He once devoted six months to meditation on the first verse from Psalm 39, "I will guard my ways, that I may not sin with my tongue."

SAINT PHILASTRIUS
Bishop († before 397)

Even before becoming bishop of the northern Italian diocese of Brescia, Philastrius had devoted himself to fighting heresies, preaching against doctrinal errors, and engaging heretics in debate. Because of his defense of the divinity of Christ in opposition to the Arian heresy's denial of this dogma, he suffered a severe scourging. As bishop of Brescia, Philastrius gave himself with renewed zeal to the cause of upholding Church teaching, even composing a Catalogue of Heresies for this purpose. Generous to the poor, the bishop was also remembered for his modesty and quietness.

May your soul be another Bethany
where Jesus may come to rest…
Blessed Elizabeth of the Trinity

THURSDAY, JULY 19

Prayer for the Morning

Here God dwells in our midst:
come, let us adore!

Glory to the Father, and to the Son,
and to the Holy Spirit, as it was in the beginning,
is now, and will be for ever. Amen. Alleluia!

HYMN
Meter: CM
This hymn can be sung to the tune used for
Lord, Who Throughout These Forty Days

We walk by faith, and not by sight;
No gracious words we hear
From him who spoke as none e'er spoke;
But we believe him near.

Help then, O Lord, our unbelief;
And may our faith abound,
To call on you when you are near
And seek where you are found:

That, when our life of faith is done,
In realms of clearer light
We may behold you as you are,
With full and endless sight.

PSALM 25
1-11

Jesus said, "I am the way and the truth and the life. No one comes to
the Father except through me." (cf. Jn 14: 6)

Let us turn from the paths of selfishness into the way of Christ,
follow him in faith and in hope toward the promised kingdom of
God.

To you, O Lord, I lift up my soul.
I trust you, let me not be disappointed;
do not let my enemies triumph.
Those who hope in you shall not be disappointed,
but only those who wantonly break faith.

Lord, make me know your ways.
Lord, teach me your paths.
Make me walk in your truth, and teach me:
for you are God my savior.

In you I hope all day long
because of your goodness, O Lord.
Remember your mercy, Lord,
and the love you have shown from of old.
Do not remember the sins of my youth.
In your love remember me.

The Lord is good and upright.
He shows the path to those who stray,
he guides the humble in the right path;
he teaches his way to the poor.

His ways are faithfulness and love
for those who keep his covenant and law.
Lord, for the sake of your name
forgive my guilt, for it is great.

Glory to the Father…

Word of God   Hebrews 11: 1-2; 12: 1

FAITH IS THE REALIZATION of what is hoped for and evidence of things not seen. Because of it the ancients were well attested. Since we are surrounded by so great a cloud of witnesses, let us rid ourselves of every burden and sin that clings to us and persevere in running the race that lies before us.

> *Hold firm and take heart. Hope in the Lord!*
> *(Ps 27: 14)*

CANTICLE OF ZECHARIAH   (Text, back cover B)
We look not to what is seen but to what is unseen; for what is seen is transitory, but what is unseen is eternal. (2 Cor 4: 18)

INTERCESSIONS

Let us pray to the Lord who is the origin, companion, and goal of our life's journey.

℟   Stay with us, Lord.

Lord Jesus, you accompanied your doubting disciples on the road to Emmaus:
– sustain your Church in our daily journey of faith. ℟

You do not disappoint those who hope in your mercy:
– remember that we are slow to believe, and strengthen our faith. ℟

You guide those who walk in darkness:
– teach your paths to all those who seek the road to life. ℟

                                        Personal intentions

Our Father...

O God, you are our guide and guard along life's paths. Lead us in the ways of justice and love, righteousness and peace, through your Son, our Lord Jesus Christ, who lives and reigns with you and the Holy Spirit, one God for ever and ever. Amen.

MASS

Thursday of the Fifteenth Week of the Year

(The prayers suggested today are those of the Fifth Week in Ordinary Time.)

ENTRANCE ANTIPHON

Come, let us worship the Lord. Let us bow down in the presence of our maker, for he is the Lord our God. (Ps 94: 6-7)

OPENING PRAYER
> Father,
> watch over your family
> and keep us safe in your care,
> for all our hope is in you.
> Grant this through our Lord Jesus Christ, your Son,
> who lives and reigns with you and the Holy Spirit,
> one God, for ever and ever.

● *I am who am. I am has sent me to you.* ●

A reading from
the Book of Exodus

3: 13-20

MOSES, hearing the voice from the burning bush, said to God, "Who am I that I should go to Pharaoh and lead the Israelites out of Egypt?" He answered, "I will be with you; and this shall be your proof that it is I who have sent you: when you bring my people out of Egypt, you will worship God on this very mountain."

"But," said Moses to God, "when I go to the Israelites and say to them, 'The God of your fathers has sent me to you,' if they ask me, 'What is his name?' what am I to tell them?" God replied, "I am who am." Then he added, "This is what you shall tell the Israelites: I AM sent me to you."

God spoke further to Moses, "Thus shall you say to the Israelites: The Lord, the God of your fathers, the God of Abraham, the God of Isaac, the God of Jacob, has sent me to you.

"This is my name forever;/ this is my title for all generations.

"Go and assemble the elders of the Israelites, and tell them: The Lord, the God of your fathers, the God of Abraham, Isaac and Jacob, has appeared to me and said: I am concerned about you and about the way you are being treated in Egypt; so I have decided to lead you up out of the misery of Egypt into the land of the Canaanites, Hittites, Amorites, Perizzites, Hivites and Jebusites, a land flowing with milk and honey.

"Thus they will heed your message. Then you and the elders of Israel shall go to the king of Egypt and say to him: The Lord, the God of the Hebrews, has sent us word. Permit us, then, to go a three days' journey in the desert, that we may offer sacrifice to the Lord, our God.

"Yet I know that the king of Egypt will not allow you to go unless he is forced. I will stretch out my hand, therefore, and smite Egypt by doing all kinds of wondrous deeds there. After that he will send you away."
The word of the Lord.

———— • PSALM 105 • ————

℟ (8) **The Lord remembers his covenant for ever.**

Or: Alleluia.

Give thanks to the Lord, invoke his name;
  make known among the nations his deeds.
Recall the wondrous deeds that he has wrought,
  his portents, and the judgments he has uttered. ℟

He remembers forever his covenant
  which he made binding for a thousand generations –
Which he entered into with Abraham
  and by his oath to Isaac. ℟

He greatly increased his people
  and made them stronger than their foes,
Whose hearts he changed, so that they hated his people,
  and dealt deceitfully with his servants. ℟

He sent Moses his servant;
  Aaron, whom he had chosen.
They wrought his signs among them,
  and wonders in the land of Ham. ℟

Alleluia. Your words, Lord, are spirit and life, you have
the words of everlasting life. Alleluia.

● *I am gentle and humble in heart.* ●

A reading from
the holy Gospel according to Matthew   11: 28-30

JESUS SPOKE THUS: "Come to
me, all you who are weary
and find life burdensome, and I will refresh you. Take
my yoke upon your shoulders and learn from me, for I
am gentle and humble of heart. Your souls will find rest,
for my yoke is easy and my burden light."
The Gospel of the Lord.

PRAYER OVER THE GIFTS
  Lord our God,
  may the bread and wine
  you give us for our nourishment on earth
  become the sacrament of our eternal life.
  We ask this through Christ our Lord.

COMMUNION ANTIPHON

Give praise to the Lord for his kindness, for his wonderful deeds toward men. He has filled the hungry with good things, he has satisfied the thirsty. (Ps 106: 8-9)

PRAYER AFTER COMMUNION

God our Father,
you give us a share in the one bread and the one cup
and make us one in Christ.
Help us to bring your salvation and joy
to all the world.
We ask this through Christ our Lord.

MEDITATION OF THE DAY

The Humanity of Jesus

Why is it that God, in the Scriptures, seems to detest pride so much? Because God gives all, receiving nothing; and therefore the pride which asserts itself before him contains a radical misunderstanding of their mutual relations, like an infinite usurpation. André Suarès compares pride, applied as a cure for the vices, to "those acids which disinfect the sore while eating into the tissue." God loves that which is not in order that it may be. God loves him who knows he is not that he may learn to be. The power of God in us consists precisely in our weakness, and the being of God in us of our own non-existence. It is pride which conceives the basest ideas about man, and humility which tastes of his greatness. Pride aspires to the least height, disdaining to surpass itself; humility is quite ready for the sublimest prospects. Some men would be capable of great things if they did not think themselves great. Humility is truth accepted and revered, and the truth about man is at once misery and greatness. Pride, on the other hand, in conflict with truth, reverses it, becomes puffed up at the misery and rejects the greatness. Identifying humility with modesty is an error. The difference between them is great. Modesty is a kind of deliberate timidity and therefore a pretense. It does not exclude pride. Humility is the opposite of pride, a genuine state of soul rather than a disguise. Humility is but the reverse side of adoration and possessed of its grandeur.

FATHER ANTONIN GILBERT SERTILLANGES, O.P.

Father Sertillanges († 1948) was a renowned Dominican preacher, apologist, and philosopher.

Prayer for the Evening

In peace, let us pray to the Lord.

**Glory to the Father, and to the Son,
and to the Holy Spirit, as it was in the beginning,
is now, and will be for ever. Amen. Alleluia!**

HYMN   Meter: CM
This hymn can be sung to the tune used for
Let Saints on Earth in Concert Sing

Our God is love, and all his saints
His image bear below;
The heart inspired with love for God
With love for all will glow.

Teach us to love each other, Lord,
As we are loved by you;
May hatred for each other cease,
Our spirits, Lord, renew.

Heirs of the same immortal bliss,
Our hopes and fears the same,
With bonds of love our hearts unite,
With mutual love inflame.

PSALM 25   14-22

Think of the commandments, hate not your neighbor; of the Most High's covenant, and overlook faults. (Sir 28: 7)

If the Lord rescues me from the snare of my faults, should I not extend the same hand of rescue to my neighbor? Resentment, grudges, retaliation do not help the one who offends me. They merely confirm the breach between us. Bridge-building is costly, as the cross demonstrates, but the people stranded on both banks are all freed by the bridge.

The Lord's friendship is for those who revere him;
to them he reveals his covenant.

My eyes are always on the Lord;
for he rescues my feet from the snare.
Turn to me and have mercy
for I am lonely and poor.

Relieve the anguish of my heart
and set me free from my distress.
See my affliction and my toil
and take all my sins away.

See how many are my foes;
how violent their hatred for me.
Preserve my life and rescue me.
Do not disappoint me, you are my refuge.
May innocence and uprightness protect me:
for my hope is in you, O Lord.
Redeem Israel, O God, from all its distress.

Glory to the Father…

Word of God   Colossians 3: 13-14

Bear with one another; forgive whatever grievances you have against one another. Forgive as the Lord has forgiven you. Over all these virtues, put on love, which binds the rest together and makes them perfect.

Forgive from the heart!

CANTICLE OF MARY   (Text, back cover A)
This is my commandment: love one another as I have loved you.
(cf. Jn 13: 34)

INTERCESSIONS

The world is rent asunder by our refusal to forgive.
In repentance we pray:

℟   Lord, hear our prayer.

For peace among warring nations and peoples:
– let us pray to the Lord. ℟

For reconciliation among friends and relatives divided
by old resentments:
– let us pray to the Lord. ℟

For freedom from the desire for revenge:
– let us pray to the Lord. ℟

Personal intentions

Our Father...

*May the Lord rescue us from every evil threat and bring
us safe to his heavenly kingdom. To him be glory for ever
and ever. Amen. (cf. 2 Tm 4: 18)*

MARIAN ANTIPHON   (Text, page 25)

SAINTS
OF TODAY AND YESTERDAY

Blood of Christ, bringing forth virgins, save us.

SAINTS JUSTA AND RUFINA
Virgins and Martyrs († late 3rd century)

Justa and Rufina were two third-century Christian virgins of Seville, Spain, who earned their living by selling earthenware. A confrontation with a passing parade of the pagan idol Venus led to the two women being arrested and tortured for their faith. In the end Justa died while being tortured on a rack, Rufina was either strangled to death or beheaded, and the bodies of the two were burned. For centuries they have been honored as the patronesses of Seville, portrayed repeatedly in the artwork of the city's cathedral.

BLESSED JOHN PLESSINGTON
Priest and Martyr (c. 1637-1679)

A native of Lancashire, England, John Plessington was ordained to the priesthood in Segovia, Spain. Having returned to England he was captured after seven years of priestly ministry. Indicted on the charge of being a Catholic priest, he was sentenced to death but spent over two months in prison before his execution was carried out. Before dying he told the onlookers: "I profess that I undoubtedly believe and firmly hold all the articles of the Roman Catholic Faith, and for the truth of any of them, by the assistance of God, I am willing to die."

Precious is the death of a good priest.
Saint Vincent Pallotti

FRIDAY, JULY 20

Prayer for the Morning

O Lord, open my lips
and my mouth shall declare your praise.

Glory to the Father, and to the Son,
and to the Holy Spirit, as it was in the beginning,
is now, and will be for ever. Amen. Alleluia!

HYMN   Meter: SM

> Have mercy, Lord, on me,
> For you are ever kind;
> Let me, oppressed with loads of guilt,
> Your faithful mercy find.
>
> Blot out my crying sins,
> Nor me in anger view;
> Create in me a heart that's clean,
> An upright mind renew.
>
> The joy your favors give
> Let me again obtain,
> And your free Spirit's firm support
> My fainting soul sustain.

PSALM 51   3-6, 8-9, 12-15

I have not come to call the righteous to repentance but sinners.
(Lk 5: 32)

The most difficult part of ongoing conversion is admitting that we really are sinners and allowing God to see and forgive us as we are, with all our faults unmended and all our flaws showing, especially the ones over which we seem to have no control.

Have mercy on me, God, in your kindness.
In your compassion blot out my offense.

O wash me more and more from my guilt
and cleanse me from my sin.

My offenses truly I know them;
my sin is always before me.
Against you, you alone, have I sinned;
what is evil in your sight I have done.

Indeed you love truth in the heart;
then in the secret of my heart teach me wisdom.
O purify me, then I shall be clean;
O wash me, I shall be whiter than snow.

A pure heart create for me, O God,
put a steadfast spirit within me.
Do not cast me away from your presence,
nor deprive me of your holy spirit.

Give me again the joy of your help;
with a spirit of fervor sustain me,
that I may teach transgressors your ways
and sinners may return to you.

Glory to the Father...

Word of God   1 John 1: 8-10

IF WE SAY, "We are without sin," we deceive ourselves, and the truth is not in us. If we acknowledge our sins, he is faithful and just and will forgive our sins and cleanse us from every wrongdoing. If we say, "We have not sinned," we make him a liar, and his word is not in us.

Lord, have mercy!

CANTICLE OF ZECHARIAH   (Text, back cover B)
Jesus said to them, "Those who are healthy do not need a physician, but the sick do." (Lk 5: 31)

INTERCESSIONS

God knows our failings through and through, yet never turns away from us. With humble, contrite hearts, let us pray:

℟   Have mercy, God, in your kindness.

When we are reluctant to own our sins as sins: ℟

When we are afraid, in our sinfulness, to pray: ℟

When we feel hopeless about the sinful patterns in which we are trapped: ℟

When we refuse to forgive others because we cannot forgive ourselves: ℟

Personal intentions

Our Father…

O God of forgiveness, you sent your only Son to live and die among us in order to set us free from the merciless snares of sin and death. Forgive what we cannot forgive; heal what we dare not face; grant humility where we take refuge in false pride. Grant us singleness of heart and a steadfast spirit, through Christ our Lord. Amen.

MASS

Friday of the Fifteenth Week of the Year

(Today, the prayers of the Votive Mass of the Sacred Heart, given below, could be used.)

ENTRANCE ANTIPHON

The thoughts of his heart last through every generation, that he will rescue them from death and feed them in time of famine. (Ps 32: 11, 19)

OPENING PRAYER

Lord God,
give us the strength and love of the heart of your Son
that, by becoming one with him,
we may have eternal salvation.
We ask this through our Lord Jesus Christ, your Son,
who lives and reigns with you and the Holy Spirit,
one God, for ever and ever.

● *The lamb must be slain in the evening; when I see
the blood I will pass over it.* ●

A reading from
the Book of Exodus
                                                    11: 10–12: 14

MOSES AND AARON per-
formed various wonders
in Pharaoh's presence, but the Lord made Pharaoh obstinate, and he would not let the Israelites leave his land.

The Lord said to Moses and Aaron in the land of
Egypt, "This month shall stand at the head of your cal-
endar; you shall reckon it the first month of the year.
Tell the whole community of Israel: On the tenth of this
month every one of your families must procure for itself
a lamb, one apiece for each household. If a family is too
small for a whole lamb, it shall join the nearest household in procuring one and shall share in the lamb in
proportion to the number of persons who partake of it.
The lamb must be a year-old male and without blemish.
You may take it from either the sheep or the goats. You
shall keep it until the fourteenth day of this month, and
then, with the whole assembly of Israel present, it shall
be slaughtered during the evening twilight. They shall
take some of its blood and apply it to the two doorposts
and the lintel of every house in which they partake of
the lamb. That same night they shall eat its roasted flesh

with unleavened bread and bitter herbs. It shall not be eaten raw or boiled, but roasted whole, with its head and shanks and inner organs. None of it must be kept beyond the next morning; whatever is left over in the morning shall be burned up.

"This is how you are to eat it: with your loins girt, sandals on your feet and your staff in hand, you shall eat like those who are in flight. It is the Passover of the Lord. For on this same night I will go through Egypt, striking down every first-born of the land, both man and beast, and executing judgment on all the gods of Egypt – I, the Lord! But the blood will mark the houses where you are. Seeing the blood, I will pass over you; thus, when I strike the land of Egypt, no destructive blow will come upon you.

"This day shall be a memorial feast for you, which all your generations shall celebrate with pilgrimage to the Lord, as a perpetual institution."

The word of the Lord.

• PSALM 116 •

℟ (13) I will take the cup of salvation,
and call on the name of the Lord.

Or: **Alleluia.**

How shall I make a return to the Lord
for all the good he has done for me?
The cup of salvation I will take up,
and I will call upon the name of the Lord. ℟

Precious in the eyes of the Lord
is the death of his faithful ones.
I am your servant, the son of your handmaid;
you have loosed my bonds. ℟

To you will I offer sacrifice of thanksgiving,
and I will call upon the name of the Lord.
My vows to the Lord I will pay
in the presence of all his people. ℟

Alleluia. Teach me the meaning of your law, O Lord, and
I will guard it with all my heart. Alleluia.

● *The Son of Man is master of the Sabbath.* ●

A reading from
the holy Gospel according to Matthew   12: 1-8

ONCE ON A SABBATH Jesus
walked through the stand-
ing grain. His disciples felt hungry, so they began to pull
off the heads of grain and eat them. When the Pharisees
spied this, they protested: "See here! Your disciples are
doing what is not permitted on the sabbath." He replied:
"Have you not read what David did when he and his
men were hungry, how he entered God's house and ate
the holy bread, a thing forbidden to him and his men or
anyone other than priests? Have you not read in the law
how the priests on temple duty can break the sabbath
rest without incurring guilt? I assure you, there is something greater than the temple here. If you understood
the meaning of the text, 'It is mercy I desire and not sacrifice,' you would not have condemned these innocent
men. The Son of Man is indeed the Lord of the sabbath."
The Gospel of the Lord.

PRAYER OVER THE GIFTS
Father of mercy,
in your great love for us
you have given us your only Son.
May he take us up into his own perfect sacrifice,

that we may offer you fitting worship.
We ask this through Christ our Lord.

COMMUNION ANTIPHON

The Lord says: If anyone is thirsty, let him come to me; whoever believes in me, let him drink. Streams of living water
shall flow out from within him. (Jn 7: 37-38)

PRAYER AFTER COMMUNION

Lord,
we have received your sacrament of love.
By becoming more like Christ on earth
may we share his glory in heaven,
where he lives and reigns for ever and ever.

MEDITATION OF THE DAY

"It is mercy I desire"

[Jesus says:] "You cannot live without being loved and
without loving. When it is not God or some of your fellow
creatures that you love, you love yourself. Love is as the
breath of your soul. Love must be spoken of with respect
because it comes from God. It must be received as a
messenger from God, as his Spirit. It is an impulse which
you receive, but which does not come from you, and
which is divine in its source. Keep it in its purity and
strength by using it for others, not for yourselves, and by
directing it back to him who gives it to you, to the Savior
who waits, unwearyingly, for your gratitude.

The souls who surrender themselves to love never
regret it. It is true that I break down the boundaries of their
hearts, for the narrow horizon of their knowledge must be
rent that they may catch a glimpse of the splendors of my
kingdom, the boundless world of the Spirit...

I do not hide myself, I am very near you, within you...
I am very simple. You seek me too far away, as an inac-
cessible God... I am a God who has made himself your
brother... Because you seek me too far off, you pass

beside me without seeing me, and you no longer feel the infinite sweetness that my presence brings in your soul.

The interests of this world fascinate you, but they wither in a flash of the eye... Whereas I live on, and one can never finish discovering me – and one can never exhaust the source of my treasures... As soon as hands are outstretched to me, empty, and pleading, I fill them."

SISTER MARY OF THE HOLY TRINITY

Sister Mary of the Holy Trinity († 1942) was a Poor Clare of Jerusalem.

Prayer for the Evening

Christ suffered that we might rejoice:
come, let us give thanks and praise!

Glory to the Father, and to the Son,
and to the Holy Spirit, as it was in the beginning,
is now, and will be for ever. Amen. Alleluia!

HYMN

Meter: 87 87 D
This hymn can be sung to the tune used for
Praise the Lord, Ye Heavens Adore Him

See, the streams of living waters,
Springing from eternal love,
Well supply thy sons and daughters,
And all fear of want remove.
Who can faint while such a river
Ever flows their thirst to assuage?
Grace which like the Lord, the giver,
Never fails from age to age.

PSALM 69

2-4, 14-16

My friends it is who wrong me; before God my eyes drop tears. (Jb 16: 20)

Jesus wept the tears of suffering humanity and, weeping, transformed them into the waters of life. These waters, flowing from his wounded side, wash away all the tears that stain the face of a sorrowing world.

Save me, O God,
for the waters have risen to my neck.

I have sunk into the mud of the deep
and there is no foothold.
I have entered the waters of the deep
and the waves overwhelm me.

I am wearied with all my crying,
my throat is parched.
My eyes are wasted away
from looking for my God.

This is my prayer to you,
my prayer for your favor.
In your great love, answer me, O God,
with your help that never fails:
rescue me from sinking in the mud;
save me from my foes.

Save me from the waters of the deep
lest the waves overwhelm me.
Do not let the deep engulf me
nor death close its mouth on me.

Glory to the Father...

Word of God   Ezekiel 47: 1, 8-9

I SAW WATER FLOWING OUT from beneath the threshold of the temple toward the east, for the facade of the temple was toward the east. He said to me, "This water flows into the eastern district down upon the Arabah, and empties into the sea, the salt waters, which it makes fresh.

Wherever the river flows, every sort of living creature that can multiply shall live."

One soldier thrust his lance into his side,
and immediately blood and water flowed out.
(Jn 19: 34)

CANTICLE OF MARY   (Text, back cover A)
Jesus said, "Destroy this temple and in three days I will raise it up."
He was speaking about the temple of his body. (cf. Jn 2: 19, 21)

INTERCESSIONS

Let us pray to Jesus Christ, our compassionate high priest, who was tempted in every way that we are but did not sin. (cf. Heb 4: 14-15)

℟   Listen to your people's plea!

Lord Jesus, you wept over Jerusalem:
– grant conversion of heart to all those who have rejected you. ℟

Lord Jesus, you wept over the death of Lazarus:
– comfort those who mourn. ℟

Lord Jesus, you suffered sorrow and distress in the garden of Gethsemane:
– abide with those who watch alone tonight in pain and fear. ℟

Personal intentions

Our Father...

May the God of all grace who called us to his eternal glory through Christ Jesus restore, confirm, strengthen, and establish us after we have suffered a little. Amen. (cf. 1 Pt 5: 10)

MARIAN ANTIPHON   (Text, page 25)

SAINTS
OF TODAY AND YESTERDAY

The Lord will save me.

SAINT VULMAR (WULMAR)
Abbot († c. 700)

Vulmar, upon learning that he had unknowingly married a girl betrothed to another man, separated from her and entered the French monastery of Hautmont where he served by tending the cattle and cutting wood. Every night as the monks slept he quietly entered their cells to clean their shoes as a secret act of charity. It was the abbot who finally discovered Vulmar taking his muddy shoes for this purpose – out of respect for Vulmar's humility the abbot did not disclose this to the other monks. After being ordained a priest Vulmar retired into the forest to live as a hermit, bringing with him vestments and sacred vessels for saying Mass in his solitude. Later he founded a new abbey, Samer, near Calais.

SAINT ANSEGISUS
Abbot (c. 770-833)

After entering the French monastery of Fontanelle at the age of eighteen, Ansegisus came to the attention of the Holy Roman Emperor Charlemagne, who asked the young monk to oversee two abbeys. Subsequently he was made abbot of three more abbeys, including the renowned monastery of Luxeuil and his own abbey of Fontanelle. In each he restored the original discipline and observance of the rule.

We should be so happy if we loved God with all the might of our being.
Saint Peter Julian Eymard

SATURDAY, JULY 21
Saint Lawrence of Brindisi
Prayer for the Morning

God has come among his people:
let us give thanks and praise!

Glory to the Father, and to the Son,
and to the Holy Spirit, as it was in the beginning,
is now, and will be for ever. Amen. Alleluia!

HYMN

Meter: 87 87 D
This hymn can be sung to the tune used for
Praise the Lord, Ye Heavens Adore Him

Sing we of the blessed Mother
Who received the angel's word,
And obedient to the summons
Bore in love the infant Lord;
Sing we of the joys of Mary
At whose breast that child was fed
Who is Son of God eternal
And the everlasting bread.

Sing we, too, of Mary's sorrows,
Of the sword that pierced her through,
When beneath the cross of Jesus
She his weight of suff'ring knew,
Looked upon her Son and Savior
Reigning from the awful tree,
Saw the price of our redemption
Paid to set the sinner free.

Sing again the joys of Mary
When she saw the risen Lord,
And in prayer with Christ's apostles,
Waited on his promised word:

From on high the blazing glory
Of the Spirit's presence came,
Heav'nly breath of God's own being,
Tokened in the wind and flame.

PSALM 106   1-5

In him we were also chosen, destined in accord with the purpose of
the One who accomplishes all things according to the intention of
his will, so that we might exist for the praise of his glory, we who first
hoped in Christ. (Eph 1: 11-12)

Mary told the Lord's mighty deeds and sang his praise. She who is
called blessed from age to age seeks only that all people know the joy
of blessing God through her Son Jesus Christ, in whom God's enduring love became visible among us.

O give thanks to the Lord for he is good;
for his love endures for ever.
Who can tell the Lord's mighty deeds?
Who can recount all his praise?

They are happy who do what is right,
who at all times do what is just.
O Lord, remember me
out of the love you have for your people.

Come to me, Lord, with your help
that I may see the joy of your chosen ones
and may rejoice in the gladness of your nation
and share the glory of your people.

Glory to the Father...

Word of God   Romans 8: 38-39

I AM CONVINCED that neither
death, nor life, nor angels,
nor principalities, nor present things, nor future things,

nor powers, nor height, nor depth, nor any other creature will be able to separate us from the love of God in
Christ Jesus our Lord.

Praised be Jesus Christ, now and for ever!

CANTICLE OF ZECHARIAH   (Text, back cover B)
He who did not spare his own Son but handed him over for us all, how
will he not also give us everything else along with him? (Rom 8: 32)

INTERCESSIONS

God so loved the world that he gave his only begotten
Son for our salvation. With joyful trust, we pray:

℟   Give thanks to the Lord, for he is good!

God all-powerful, you created all things by your
almighty word:
– for the gift of the created world, we pray: ℟

God all-merciful, you delivered your people from
slavery in Egypt:
– for the gift of freedom in Christ, we pray: ℟

God all-loving, you entrusted to Mary's faithful obedience the care of your Church:
– for the gift of redemption made manifest in her, we
pray: ℟

God all-giving, you raise up preachers to inspire us with
your word:
– through the intercession of Saint Lawrence of
Brindisi, we pray: ℟

Personal intentions

Our Father...

O God, no power on earth can silence your enduring
Word of love, born of the Virgin, put to death on the

cross, buried in the earth, raised to eternal glory. Pour forth upon your people the Spirit who set the first disciples afire with your praise and with zeal to proclaim the Gospel. We ask this through our Lord Jesus Christ your Son, who lives and reigns with you and the Holy Spirit, one God for ever and ever. Amen.

MASS

Saturday of the Fifteenth Week of the Year

LAWRENCE OF BRINDISI   *Optional memorial*

● *Saint Lawrence was born in 1559. He entered the Capuchin Friars, taught theology to his fellow religious, and was chosen to fill positions of leadership in his order. He became famous throughout Europe as an effective and forceful preacher. He wrote many works explaining the faith and died in Lisbon in 1619.* ●

ENTRANCE ANTIPHON
The Lord opened his mouth in the assembly, and filled him with the spirit of wisdom and understanding, and clothed him in a robe of glory. (Sir 15: 5)

OPENING PRAYER
Lord,
for the glory of your name and the salvation of souls
you gave Lawrence of Brindisi
courage and right judgment.
By his prayers,
help us to know what we should do
and give us the courage to do it.
We ask this through our Lord Jesus Christ, your Son,
who lives and reigns with you and the Holy Spirit,
one God, for ever and ever.

● *The night is here when the Lord will lead Israel out of the land of Egypt.* ●

A reading from
the Book of Exodus

12: 37-42

T HE ISRAELITES SET OUT from Rameses for Succoth, about six hundred thousand men on foot, not counting the children. A crowd of mixed ancestry also went up with them, besides their livestock, very numerous flocks and herds. Since the dough they had brought out of Egypt was not leavened, they baked it into unleavened loaves. They had been rushed out of Egypt and had no opportunity even to prepare food for the journey.

The time the Israelites had stayed in Egypt was four hundred and thirty years. At the end of four hundred and thirty years, all the hosts of the Lord left the land of Egypt on this very date. This was a night of vigil for the Lord, as he led them out of the land of Egypt; so on this same night all the Israelites must keep a vigil for the Lord throughout their generations.

The word of the Lord.

──── ● PSALM 136 ● ────

℟ **His love is everlasting.**

Or: **Alleluia.**

Give thanks to the Lord, for he is good,
    for his mercy endures forever;
Who remembered us in our abjection,
    for his mercy endures forever;
And freed us from our foes,
    for his mercy endures forever. ℟

Who smote the Egyptians in their first-born,
  for his mercy endures forever;
And brought out Israel from their midst,
  for his mercy endures forever;
With a mighty hand and an outstretched arm,
  for his mercy endures forever. ℟

Who split the Red Sea in twain,
  for his mercy endures forever;
And led Israel through its midst,
  for his mercy endures forever;
But swept Pharaoh and his army into the Red Sea,
  for his mercy endures forever. ℟

Alleluia. The word of the Lord stands for ever; it is the word given to you, the Good News. Alleluia.

● *He did not show himself to them that what had been said would be fulfilled.* ●

A reading from
the holy Gospel according to Matthew   12: 14-21

WHEN THE PHARISEES were outside they began to plot against Jesus to find a way to destroy him. Jesus was aware of this, and so he withdrew from that place.

Many people followed him and he cured them all, though he sternly ordered them not to make public what he had done. This was to fulfill what had been said through Isaiah the prophet:

"Here is my servant whom I have chosen,/ my loved one in whom I delight./ I will endow him with my spirit/ and he will proclaim justice to the Gentiles./ He will not contend or cry out,/ nor will his voice be heard in the streets./ The bruised reed he will not crush;/ The

smoldering wick he will not quench/ until judgment is made victorious./ In his name, the Gentiles will find hope."
The Gospel of the Lord.

PRAYER OVER THE GIFTS

Lord,
accept our sacrifice on this feast of Saint Lawrence
of Brindisi,
and following his example
may we give you our praise
and offer you all we have.
Grant this in the name of Jesus the Lord.

COMMUNION ANTIPHON

The Lord has put his faithful servant in charge of his household, to give them their share of bread at the proper time. (Lk 12: 42)

PRAYER AFTER COMMUNION

God our Father,
Christ the living bread renews us.
Let Christ our teacher instruct us
that on this feast of Saint Lawrence of Brindisi
we may learn your truth
and practice it in love.
We ask this through Christ our Lord.

MEDITATION OF THE DAY

Suffering Servant

By faith, I believe that God chastises those whom he loves. I believe that for those whom God loves he makes all things work for their good. I believe that God loves me with an everlasting love. He loves me more than I love myself. He loves me to such an extent that he sends his only son, Jesus Christ, as a living sacrifice to redeem me.

He loves me so much that he sends anew each day his son, Jesus Christ, as my food and drink in the Eucharist. So, I believe, that ALS [amyotrophic lateral sclerosis] is sent to me as a sign of God's love and it is given to me for my own good and happiness. The object of faith is not what is seen but what is not seen. Who can grasp the designs of God? Who can understand his wisdom? "My ways are above your ways, as the heavens are above the earth and my thoughts are different from your thoughts," says the Lord. No, I do not understand with my reason and my intellect why this should be so, but I believe he has sent me ALS as a sign of his love and special favor. I believe this and I try to renew this belief at each instant. So it is, I do not look at ALS as an enemy which I fight. I accept it, embrace it, and welcome it as a friend.

I believe in the words of Saint Paul that God is faithful and he does not permit us to be tried beyond our strength. With every trial he gives us the strength to endure it and he shows us the way to overcome it. I believe God gives me this pain and suffering. I believe at the same time he gives me the strength and grace to accept it, endure it, and cope with it… I believe the grace of Jesus will always be adequate. The problem is, I would like it to be more than adequate. But it is enough, just enough, for that moment, and that instant. As Jesus on the cross, I do not look back. I do not consider the future but I trust God. I believe in his grace from instant to instant.

MONSIGNOR ALOYSIUS SCHWARTZ

Monsignor Schwartz († 1992) was an American missionary priest who was nominated for the Nobel Peace Prize twice, and who died of Lou Gehrig's disease.

Prayer for the Evening

Vigil of the Sixteenth Sunday in Ordinary Time

Great in our midst is the Holy One of Israel!
Let us sing and give praise, alleluia!

Glory to the Father, and to the Son,
and to the Holy Spirit, as it was in the beginning,
is now, and will be for ever. Amen. Alleluia!

HYMN
Meter: 77 77 77
This hymn can be sung to the tune used for
As With Gladness Men of Old

God of mercy, God of grace,
Show the brightness of thy face;
Shine upon us, Savior, shine,
Fill thy Church with light divine.
And thy saving health extend
Unto earth's remotest end.

Let the people praise thee, Lord;
Be by all that live adored;
Let the nations shout and sing,
Glory to their Savior King;
At thy feet their tribute pay,
And thy holy will obey.

CANTICLE
Colossians 1: 12-20

The Word became flesh and made his dwelling among us, and we saw
his glory. (Jn 1:14)

In the earthly Jesus, the Word made flesh, the light of God's glory
shone in a hidden way; in Jesus Christ risen from the dead, the light
of God's glory shines in its fullness.

Let us give thanks to the Father
for having made you worthy

to share the lot of the saints
in light.

He rescued us
from the power of darkness
and brought us
into the kingdom of his beloved Son.
Through him we have redemption,
the forgiveness of our sins.

He is the image of the invisible God,
the first-born of all creatures.
In him everything in heaven and on earth was created,
things visible and invisible.

All were created through him;
all were created for him.
He is before all else that is.
In him everything continues in being.

It is he who is head of the body, the church!
he who is the beginning,
the first-born of the dead,
so that primacy may be his in everything.

It pleased God to make absolute fullness reside in him
and, by means of him, to reconcile everything in his
   person,
both on earth and in the heavens,
making peace through the blood of his cross.

Word of God   John 1: 1-5

I N THE BEGINNING was the
   Word, and the Word was with
God, and the Word was God. He was in the beginning
with God. All things came to be through him, and without him nothing came to be. What came to be through

him was life, and this life was the light of the human race; the light shines in the darkness, and the darkness has not overcome it.

Your Word, O Lord, is Spirit and life!

CANTICLE OF MARY   (Text, back cover A)
I came so that they might have life and have it more abundantly. (Jn 10: 10)

INTERCESSIONS

Through the intercession of Mary, the mother of Jesus, let us pray to Christ who is our life and our light, our resurrection and our hope:

℟   Son of the living God, save your people!

We pray you for your holy Catholic Church:
– make her holy that she may be a light for all nations. ℟

We pray you for those who suffer sickness, grief, and servitude:
– set them free that their joy may be a light of hope for all sufferers. ℟

We pray you for those who have left your way:
– restore them, that their homecoming may be a beacon of light for all wanderers. ℟

We pray you for those who have died:
– raise them up, that their glory may be a light for all who still struggle. ℟

Personal intentions

Our Father…

May the light of Jesus Christ our risen Savior lead us to life everlasting! Amen.

MARIAN ANTIPHON   (Text, page 25)

SAINTS
OF TODAY AND YESTERDAY

Your will be done.

BLESSED PETER TO ROT
Martyr (1912-1945)

The son of first generation Catholics on the South Pacific island of New Britain, Peter To Rot at the age of twenty-one was appointed catechist to his own village of Rakunai after three years of training. At twenty-four he married one of his own catechetical students and the couple had three children. When during the World War II occupation of the island by the Japanese all missionaries and missionary workers were arrested, Peter was left alone to maintain the Catholic life in his village. He led prayer services, administered baptism, and safeguarded the reserved Blessed Sacrament for the sick and dying. When Peter openly opposed the Japanese forces' attempts to re-introduce the pagan practice of polygamy among his people, he was arrested. Of his imprisonment he observed, "I am here because of those who broke their marriage vows and because of those who do not want the growth of God's kingdom." Aware of the fate that awaited him, he asked his wife to send him his best clothes in preparation for martyrdom. On July 17, 1945 he was given a lethal injection and died after several hours of torment.

> *Would not all the labors of a thousand men be well rewarded in the conversion of one single soul to Jesus Christ?*
> Saint Isaac Jogues

Word of God

for a Sunday

© Dover Publications.

Luke 10: 38-42

"Mary sat beside the Lord at his feet listening to him speak." For a Near East readership this must have a jarring impact: Jesus praises a woman not for doing household chores (typical and expected of women in that culture) but rather Mary is commended for sitting down to listen and learn from him. In the first century it was not customary for women to sit at the feet of the teacher, that is, to be disciples.

J. T.

■ **Suggested Prayer of the Faithful** ■

(Each local community should compose its own Universal Prayer, but may find inspiration in the texts proposed here.)

Let us open our hearts to God our Father in petition for the needs of all for whom we wish to pray.

That the Church may preach the mystery of Christ in all its fullness, making known to the world the hope of glory beyond price that lies in store for all, redeemed by his Blood.

That our Holy Father the Pope may find in his fellow bishops, priests, and deacons a source of encouragement in his concern for all the churches.

That we may gladly offer hospitality to our friends and neighbors during these days of vacation and relaxation, and so discover the blessings God holds in store for us through them.

For married couples who long for children, that they may be given the desire of their hearts and be enabled through God's gift to bring new life and joy into the world.

For those who struggle with the stress and burden of overwork, that they may be comforted by Saint Martha, who found relief in the gentle teaching of Christ on priorities.

That those called to the contemplative life may not be deterred, but rather encouraged by family and friends to follow this arduous vocation at the heart of the Church.

For our beloved dead, that they may be welcomed to the banquet of life in God's kingdom, prepared for them from all eternity.

Heavenly Father, you open your heart and your kingdom to the least of your children, asking only that we believe in your love. Grant us to follow in the footsteps of your Son, and so come to you, through the same Christ our Lord.

SUNDAY, JULY 22
Sixteenth Sunday in Ordinary Time
Prayer for the Morning

Arise, bless the Lord, your God,
from eternity to eternity! (cf. Neh 9: 5)

Glory to the Father... Alleluia!

HYMN   Meter: LM

Lift up your heads, ye mighty gates;
Behold, the King of glory waits;
The King of kings is drawing near;
The Savior of the world is here!

The Lord is just, a Helper tried,
Mercy is ever at his side,
His kingly crown is holiness,
His scepter, pity in distress.

O blest the land, the city blest
Where Christ the Ruler is confessed!
O happy hearts and happy homes
To whom this King in triumph comes!

PSALM 24   1-2, 7-10

Behold, I stand at the door and knock. If anyone hears my voice and
opens the door, [then] I will enter his house and dine with him, and
he with me. (Rv 3: 20)

Doors are a poignant paradox. Christ has promised to open God's
door to anyone who knocks, but the Lord of heaven and earth has no
guarantee the courtesy will be returned when he knocks at the door
of our hearts, awaiting in patient hope an invitation to come in.

The Lord's is the earth and its fullness,
the world and all its peoples.
It is he who set it on the seas;
on the waters he made it firm.

O gates, lift high your heads;
grow higher, ancient doors.
Let him enter, the king of glory!

Who is the king of glory?
The Lord, the mighty, the valiant,
the Lord, the valiant in war.

O gates, lift high your heads;
grow higher, ancient doors.
Let him enter, the king of glory!

Who is he, the king of glory?
He, the Lord of armies,
he is the king of glory.

Glory to the Father...

Word of God   Genesis 28: 16-17

WHEN JACOB AWOKE from his sleep, he exclaimed, "Truly, the Lord is in this spot, although I did not know it!" In solemn wonder he cried out: "How awesome is this shrine! This is nothing else but an abode of God, and that is the gateway to heaven!"

How lovely is your dwelling place, O Lord of hosts!
(Ps 84: 1)

CANTICLE OF ZECHARIAH   (Text, back cover B)
I have left an open door before you, which no one can close. (Rv 3: 8)

INTERCESSIONS

Let us pray in faith to the One who has promised that the one who asks will receive, the one who seeks will find, and to the one who knocks, the door will be opened:

℟   Lord, hear our prayer.

Lord, you have chosen to make our hearts your dwelling place:
– grant us the wisdom, courage, and love to open our doors to your knock. ℟

Lord, you have called us to worship in your house, your dwelling place among us, on this holy day:
– gather us in joyful gratitude to praise your holy name. ℟

Lord, you have opened to us the doors to your heavenly dwelling place:
– bring into your presence all our beloved dead. ℟

Personal intentions

Our Father...

Lord God of heaven and earth, your door stands ever open to all who turn to you in faith. Pour forth your love into our hearts, that we may fling open whatever gates and doors we have closed before your presence; come to dwell with us today, and bring us one day to dwell with you in the place prepared for us by our Lord Jesus Christ, your Son, who lives and reigns with you and the Holy Spirit, one God, for ever and ever. Amen.

MASS

Sixteenth Sunday in Ordinary Time

ENTRANCE ANTIPHON
God himself is my help. The Lord upholds my life. I will offer you a willing sacrifice; I will praise your name, O Lord, for its goodness. (Ps 53: 6, 8)

GLORIA ———————————————— page 226

OPENING PRAYER

> Lord,
> be merciful to your people.
> Fill us with your gifts
> and make us always eager to serve you
> in faith, hope, and love.
> Grant this through our Lord Jesus Christ, your Son,
> who lives and reigns with you and the Holy Spirit,
> one God, for ever and ever.

ALTERNATIVE OPENING PRAYER

> Father,
> let the gift of your life
> continue to grow in us,
> drawing us from death to faith, hope, and love.
> Keep us alive in Christ Jesus.
> Keep us watchful in prayer
> and true to his teaching
> till your glory is revealed in us.
> Grant this through Christ our Lord.

● *Lord, do not go on past your servant.* ●

A reading from
the Book of Genesis   18: 1-10a

THE LORD APPEARED TO Abraham by the terebinth of Mamre, as he sat in the entrance of his tent, while the day was growing hot. Looking up, Abraham saw three men standing nearby. When he saw them, he ran from the entrance of the tent to greet them; and bowing to the ground, he said: "Sir, if I may ask you this favor, please do not go on past your servant. Let some water be brought, that you may bathe your feet, and then rest yourselves under the tree. Now that you have come this close to your servant, let me bring you a little food, that you may refresh yourselves; and afterward you may go on your way." The men replied, "Very well, do as you have said."

Abraham hastened into the tent and told Sarah, "Quick, three measures of fine flour! Knead it and make rolls." He ran to the herd, picked out a tender, choice steer, and gave it to a servant, who quickly prepared it. Then Abraham got some curds and milk, as well as the steer that had been prepared, and set these before the three men; and he waited on them under the tree while they ate.

They asked Abraham, "Where is your wife Sarah?" He replied, "There in the tent." One of them said, "I will surely return to you about this time next year, and Sarah will then have a son."
The word of the Lord.

———• Psalm 15 •———

℟ (1a) He who does justice will live in the presence of the Lord.

One who walks blamelessly and does justice;
　who thinks the truth in his heart
　and slanders not with his tongue. ℟

Who harms not his fellow man,
　nor takes up a reproach against his neighbor;
by whom the reprobate is despised,
　while he honors those who fear the Lord. ℟

Who lends not his money at usury
　and accepts no bribe against the innocent.
One who does these things
　shall never be disturbed. ℟

● *The mystery hidden from ages has now been mani-*
fested to his holy ones. ●

A reading from
the Letter of Saint Paul to the Colossians   1: 24-28

B ROTHERS AND SISTERS: Now I
rejoice in my sufferings for
your sake, and in my flesh I am filling up what is lacking
in the afflictions of Christ on behalf of his body, which
is the church, of which I am a minister in accordance
with God's stewardship given to me to bring to completion for you the word of God, the mystery hidden from
ages and from generations past. But now it has been
manifested to his holy ones, to whom God chose to
make known the riches of the glory of this mystery
among the Gentiles; it is Christ in you, the hope for
glory. It is he whom we proclaim, admonishing everyone and teaching everyone with all wisdom, that we may
present everyone perfect in Christ.
The word of the Lord.

Alleluia, alleluia. Blessed are they who have kept the
word with a generous heart and yield a harvest through
perseverance. Alleluia, alleluia.

● *Martha welcomed him. Mary has chosen the better*
part. ●

A reading from
the holy Gospel according to Luke   10: 38-42

J ESUS ENTERED A VILLAGE where
a woman whose name was
Martha welcomed him. She had a sister named Mary
who sat beside the Lord at his feet listening to him

speak. Martha, burdened with much serving, came to him and said, "Lord, do you not care that my sister has left me by myself to do the serving? Tell her to help me." The Lord said to her in reply, "Martha, Martha, you are anxious and worried about many things. There is need of only one thing. Mary has chosen the better part and it will not be taken from her."
The Gospel of the Lord.

CREDO ———————————————————— page 227

PRAYER OVER THE GIFTS
Lord,
bring us closer to salvation
through these gifts which we bring in your honor.
Accept the perfect sacrifice you have given us,
bless it as you blessed the gifts of Abel.
We ask this through Christ our Lord.

PREFACE OF SUNDAYS IN ORDINARY TIME ———— page 231

COMMUNION ANTIPHON
The Lord keeps in our minds the wonderful things he has done. He is compassion and love; he always provides for his faithful. (Ps 110: 4-5)

Or:

I stand at the door and knock, says the Lord. If anyone hears my voice and opens the door, I will come in and sit down to supper with him, and he with me. (Rv 3: 20)

PRAYER AFTER COMMUNION
Merciful Father,
may these mysteries
give us new purpose
and bring us to a new life in you.
We ask this in the name of Jesus the Lord.

D A Y   B Y   D A Y

Martha, Mary, and Us

To live by faith is to live joyfully, to live with assurance, untroubled by doubts and with complete confidence in all we have to do and suffer at each moment by the will of God. We must realize that it is in order to stimulate and sustain this faith that God allows the soul to be buffeted and swept away by the raging torrent of so much distress, so many troubles, so much embarrassment, and weakness, and so many setbacks. For it is essential to have faith to find God behind all this. The divine life is neither seen nor felt, but there is never a moment when it is not acting in an unknown but very sure manner. It is hidden under such things as death of the body, damnation of the soul, and the general disorder of all earthly affairs. Faith is nourished and strengthened by these happenings. It cuts through them all and takes the hand of God, who keeps it alive through everything except sin. A faithful soul should always advance with confidence, regarding all these things as the disguise God assumes, for his immediate presence would terrify us. But God, who comforts the humble, always gives us, however great our feeling of desolation, an inner assurance that we need be afraid of nothing as long as we allow him to act and abandon ourselves to him. Although we are distressed at the loss of our beloved, we somehow feel that we still possess him, and in spite of all our troubles and disturbance, there is something deep-seated within us which keeps us steadfastly attached to God. "Truly," said Jacob, "God is in this place and I never knew it" (Gn 28: 16). You seek for God, beloved soul, and he is everywhere, everything speaks of him, everything offers him to you, he walks beside you, he surrounds you and is within you. He lives with you and yet you try to find him. You seek your own idea of God, although you have him in his reality. You seek perfection and you meet it in all that happens to you. All you suffer, all you do, all your inclinations are mysteries under which

God gives himself to you while you are vainly straining after high-flown fancies. God will never come to dwell with you clothed in these imaginings. Martha tried to please Jesus by cooking him good food, but Mary was content to receive him and listen to him. Yet he deceived even her, and when, after the resurrection, she looked for him as she imagined he would be, he appeared to her as a gardener. When the apostles saw Jesus they thought he was a ghost. God disguises himself so that we may reach that pure faith which enables us to recognize him under any appearance.

FATHER JEAN-PIERRE DE CAUSSADE, S.J.
Father de Caussade († 1751) was a French Jesuit, a writer, and a revered spiritual director.

Prayer for the Evening

The Lord feeds us with finest wheat:
come, let us give thanks and praise!

Glory to the Father, and to the Son,
and to the Holy Spirit, as it was in the beginning,
is now, and will be for ever. Amen. Alleluia!

HYMN   Meter: 7 8 7 8 88

Word of God, come down on earth,
Living rain from heav'n descending,
Touch our hearts and bring to birth
Faith and hope and love unending.
Word almighty, we revere you;
Word made flesh, we long to hear you.

Word eternal, throned on high,
Word that brought to life creation,
Word that comes from heav'n to die,
Crucified for our salvation,
Saving Word, the world restoring,
Speak to us, your love outpouring.

PSALM 147 12-20

Taste and see that the Lord is good. (Ps 34: 9)

The Church is the new Jerusalem, sustained by God's life-giving word, nourished with the finest wheat, kept in peace by his blessing. On Sunday we give thanks for all these gifts, given in the Eucharist through the death and resurrection of Jesus Christ.

O praise the Lord, Jerusalem!
Zion, praise your God!

He has strengthened the bars of your gates,
he has blessed the children within you.
He established peace on your borders,
he feeds you with finest wheat.

He sends out his word to the earth
and swiftly runs his command.
He showers down snow white as wool,
he scatters hoar-frost like ashes.

He hurls down hailstones like crumbs.
The waters are frozen at his touch;
he sends forth his word and it melts them:
at the breath of his mouth the waters flow.

He makes his word known to Jacob,
to Israel his laws and decrees.
He has not dealt thus with other nations;
he has not taught them his decrees.

Glory to the Father...

Word of God
1 Corinthians 11: 23-25

I RECEIVED FROM THE LORD what I also handed on to you, that the Lord Jesus, on the night he was handed over, took bread, and, after he had given thanks, broke it and said, "This is my body that is for you. Do this in remembrance of me." In the same way also the cup, after supper, saying, "This cup is the new covenant in my blood. Do this, as often as you drink it, in remembrance of me."

This is "the blood of the covenant which
God has enjoined upon you." (Heb 9: 20)

CANTICLE OF MARY   (Text, back cover A)
Jesus is the mediator of a new covenant. (cf. Heb 12: 24)

INTERCESSIONS

In peace let us pray to the Lord:

℞   Hear, O Lord, the cry of your people!

Bread of life,
– feed those who hunger and thirst: ℞

Priest of the new and eternal covenant,
– make holy all those whom you have called to the priesthood: ℞

Pledge of eternal life,
– bring to the fullness of life all those who have died: ℞

Personal intentions

Our Father…

May the God of peace, who brought up from the dead the great shepherd of the sheep by the blood of the eternal covenant, Jesus our Lord, furnish us with all that is good, that we may do his will. Amen. (cf. Heb 13: 20-21)

MARIAN ANTIPHON   (Text, page 25)

MONDAY, JULY 23
Saint Bridget of Sweden
Prayer for the Morning

Let us bless God all our lives!
Let us praise him with joy!

Glory to the Father, and to the Son,
and to the Holy Spirit, as it was in the beginning,
is now, and will be for ever. Amen. Alleluia!

HYMN
                                                                Meter: LM
This hymn can be sung to the tune used for
Around the Throne a Glorious Band

For God, the living God, I thirst.
Like dew upon the fleece come down,
Like rain upon the desert sand,
Like light into a darkened room.

As parched earth breaks for need of rain
So my heart breaks but not in vain.
When wilt thou on my vision burst?
For thee my living God I thirst.

PSALM 63   2-9

Food from heaven you gave your people in their hunger, water from
a rock you sent them in their thirst. (Neh 9: 15)

Without food or water, we perish in time. Without the love of God, we
would perish even faster. God is present before we yearn, found before
we seek, offering life-giving love before we know our need for it.

O God, you are my God, for you I long;
for you my soul is thirsting.
My body pines for you
like a dry, weary land without water.
So I gaze on you in the sanctuary
to see your strength and your glory.

For your love is better than life,
my lips will speak your praise.
So I will bless you all my life,
in your name I will lift up my hands.
My soul shall be filled as with a banquet,
my mouth shall praise you with joy.

On my bed I remember you.
On you I muse through the night
for you have been my help;
in the shadow of your wings I rejoice.
My soul clings to you;
your right hand holds me fast.

Glory to the Father...

Word of God   1 John 4: 10-11

I N THIS IS LOVE: not that we
have loved God, but that he
loved us and sent his Son as expiation for our sins.
Beloved, if God so loved us, we also must love one
another.

We love because he first loved us. (1 Jn 4: 19)

CANTICLE OF ZECHARIAH   (Text, back cover B)
I [am] the Alpha and the Omega, the beginning and the end. To the
thirsty I will give a gift from the spring of life-giving water. (Rv 21: 6)

INTERCESSIONS

Jesus Christ invites us to the banquet of life, where he
offers himself as real food and real drink. To him we
pray:

℟   For you we long!

You are the spring of life-giving water:
– refresh those who grow weary in their search for you. ℟

You are the bread from heaven:
– feed those who hunger for your love. ℟

You are the source of the Spirit of God's love:
– pour your love into our hearts that we may love one another. ℟

You are the life of all the living:
– bring to the joy of everlasting life all those who have died. ℟

You have spoken to us through the great mystics and reformers:
– by the intercession and example of Saint Bridget of Sweden, teach us to listen for your voice in prayer. ℟

Personal intentions

Our Father…

God our Father, you feed your people with the finest wheat and give us water to drink from the rock, who is Christ. Sustain all those who hunger and thirst for you without knowing it, through the same Christ our Lord. Amen.

MASS

Monday of the Sixteenth Week of the Year

BRIDGET   *Optional memorial*

● *Saint Bridget was born in Sweden in 1303. She married and gave birth to eight children for whom she was a devoted mother. After her husband's death she continued to live in the world but devoted herself to the ascetic life as a member of the Third Order of Saint Francis. She then founded a religious order and, journeying to Rome for the sake of penance, became a model of great virtue to all. She also wrote many works in which she related her mystical experiences. Saint Bridget died in Rome in 1373.* ●

ENTRANCE ANTIPHON

Honor the woman who fears the Lord. Her sons will bless her, and her husband praise her. (See Prv 31: 30, 28)

OPENING PRAYER

Lord our God,
you revealed the secrets of heaven to Saint Bridget
as she meditated on the suffering and death of your Son.
May your people rejoice in the revelation of your glory.
Grant this through our Lord Jesus Christ, your Son,
who lives and reigns with you and the Holy Spirit,
one God, for ever and ever.

● *They will know that I am the Lord God when I glorify myself at the expense of Pharaoh.* ●

A reading from
the Book of Exodus   14: 5-18

WHEN IT WAS REPORTED to the king of Egypt that the people had fled, Pharaoh and his servants changed their minds about them. "What have we done!" they exclaimed. "Why, we released Israel from our service!" So Pharaoh made his chariots ready and mustered his soldiers – six hundred first-class chariots and all the other chariots of Egypt, with warriors on them all. So obstinate had the Lord made Pharaoh that he pursued the Israelites even while they were marching away in triumph. The Egyptians, then, pursued them; Pharaoh's whole army, his horses, chariots and charioteers, caught up with them as they lay encamped by the sea, at Pi-hahiroth, in front of Baal-zephon.

Pharaoh was already near when the Israelites looked up and saw that the Egyptians were on the march in pursuit of them. In great fright they cried out to the Lord. And they complained to Moses, "Were there no burial places in Egypt that you had to bring us out here to die in the desert? Why did you do this to us? Why did you bring us out of Egypt? Did we not tell you this in Egypt, when we said, 'Leave us alone. Let us serve the Egyptians'? Far better for us to be the slaves of the Egyptians than to die in the desert." But Moses answered the people, "Fear not! Stand your ground, and you will see the victory the Lord will win for you today. These Egyptians whom you see today you will never see again. The Lord himself will fight for you; you have only to keep still."

Then the Lord said to Moses, "Why are you crying out to me? Tell the Israelites to go forward. And you, lift up your staff and, with hand outstretched over the sea, split the sea in two, that the Israelites may pass through it on dry land. But I will make the Egyptians so obstinate that they will go in after them. Then I will receive glory through Pharaoh and all his army, his chariots and charioteers. The Egyptians shall know that I am the Lord, when I receive glory through Pharaoh and his chariots and charioteers."

The word of the Lord.

———— • CANTICLE (Exodus 15) • ————

℟ (1) **Let us sing to the Lord;**
he has covered himself in glory.

I will sing to the Lord, for he is gloriously triumphant;
  horse and chariot he has cast into the sea.

My strength and my courage is the Lord,
  and he has been my savior.
He is my God, I praise him;
  the God of my father, I extol him. ℟

The Lord is a warrior,
  Lord is his name!
Pharaoh's chariots and army he hurled into the sea;
  the elite of his officers were submerged in the Red
    Sea. ℟

The flood waters covered them,
  they sank into the depths like a stone.
Your right hand, O Lord, magnificent in power,
  your right hand, O Lord, has shattered the enemy. ℟

Alleluia. Open our hearts, O Lord, to listen to the words
of your Son. Alleluia.

  ● On Judgment Day the Queen of the South will rise
  up with this generation and condemn it. ●

A reading from
the holy Gospel according to Matthew   12: 38-42

SOME OF THE SCRIBES and
Pharisees then spoke up,
saying, "Teacher, we want to see you work some signs."
Jesus answered: "An evil and unfaithful age is eager for a
sign! No sign will be given it but that of the prophet
Jonah. Just as Jonah spent three days and three nights in
the belly of the whale, so will the Son of Man spend
three days and three nights in the bowels of the earth. At
the judgment, the citizens of Nineveh will rise with the
present generation and be the ones to condemn it. At
the preaching of Jonah they reformed their lives; but
you have a greater than Jonah here. At the judgment, the

queen of the South will rise with the present generation and be the one to condemn it. She came from the farthest corner of the earth to listen to the wisdom of Solomon; but you have a greater than Solomon here." The Gospel of the Lord.

PRAYER OVER THE GIFTS
Lord,
may the gifts we present in memory of Saint Bridget
bring us your forgiveness and salvation.
We ask this in the name of Jesus the Lord.

COMMUNION ANTIPHON
The kingdom of heaven is like a merchant in search of fine pearls; on finding one rare pearl he sells everything he has and buys it. (Mt 13: 45-46)

PRAYER AFTER COMMUNION
All-powerful God,
fill us with your light and love
by the sacrament we receive on the feast of Saint Bridget.
May we burn with love for your kingdom
and let our light shine before men.
We ask this through Christ our Lord.

MEDITATION OF THE DAY

The True Sign

The values through which to judge are those that pay attention to the word of the Word as presence of Jesus: as Presence. But this is the community of the Church to which we belong, the face of this Presence, or that in which the face of this presence becomes perceivable, becomes sign, a sign, though, that contains that which it signifies. The community of the Church is the locus where the event of Christ's presence is renewed, is new, is born.

The method the mystery has used to give himself, to reveal himself to his creature is the sacramental method: a sign that contains, in this sense, the mystery of which it is the sign. The community of the Church is the aspect of this sign, of that face, is the visible aspect of that face. It is the clothing of that presence, as the clothes of Jesus for the little children who stayed close to him. The very small children, [four to five] years old, who surrounded Jesus and grabbed hold of his legs, sticking their noses into his clothes, and didn't see his face, they didn't remember his face, perhaps didn't even look at it. But they were there with him. So that the clothes, the seamless tunic in which Jesus was clad, were fixed in their eyes more than his face. Thus Jesus makes himself perceivable to us in the ecclesial community, as if it were clothing with which our smallness enters into relationship with his real presence.

MONSIGNOR LUIGI GIUSSANI

Monsignor Giussani is the founder of the ecclesial movement Communion and Liberation.

Prayer for the Evening

Christ is our light and guide:
come, let us give thanks and praise!

Glory to the Father, and to the Son,
and to the Holy Spirit, as it was in the beginning,
is now, and will be for ever. Amen. Alleluia!

HYMN   Meter: CM
This hymn can be sung to the tune used for
Let Saints on Earth in Concert Sing

Rejoice, you righteous, in the Lord,
This work belongs to you;
Sing of his name, his ways, his word,
How holy, just and true!

His mercy and his righteousness
Let heav'n and earth proclaim;

His works of nature and of grace
Reveal his wondrous name.

PSALM 119   1-8

If they obey and serve him, they spend their days in prosperity, their
years in happiness. (Jb 36: 11)

Obedience to God's law seems an unlikely road to happiness. Indeed,
at times it seems to bring us conflict, trial, and great loss. What we
lose, though, is far less than what we gain if we do the will of the God
who wills nothing less for us than the joy of life everlasting in his
presence.

They are happy whose life is blameless,
who follow God's law!
They are happy who do his will,
seeking him with all their hearts,
who never do anything evil
but walk in his ways.

You have laid down your precepts
to be obeyed with care.
May my footsteps be firm
to obey your statutes.
Then I shall not be put to shame
as I heed your commands.

I will thank you with an upright heart
as I learn your decrees.
I will obey your statutes:
do not forsake me.

Glory to the Father...

Word of God   1 Peter 1: 22-23

SINCE YOU HAVE PURIFIED yourselves by obedience to the
truth for sincere mutual love, love one another intense-

ly from a [pure] heart. You have been born anew, not from perishable but from imperishable seed, through the living and abiding word of God.

All who inhabit the world shall understand, that nothing is better than the fear of the Lord, nothing more salutary than to obey his commandments.
(Sir 23: 27)

CANTICLE OF MARY (Text, back cover A)
Whoever loves me will keep my word, and my Father will love him, and we will come to him and make our dwelling with him. (Jn 14: 23)

INTERCESSIONS

In hope of God's promise, we pray:

℟   Abide with us always!

In our evening activities:
– grant that we may follow your law. ℟

In the day that lies before us tomorrow:
– grant that we may do your will. ℟

In the times ahead of us:
– grant that we may never do anything evil. ℟

In all the moments of our life:
– grant that we may walk in your ways. ℟

Personal intentions

Our Father...

May the Lord our God bless us in all our works and undertakings. Amen. (cf. Dt 15: 10)

MARIAN ANTIPHON (Text, page 25)

SAINTS
OF TODAY AND YESTERDAY

Love your enemies.

BLESSED JANE OF ORVIETO
Virgin († 1306)

As a peasant girl of Carnaiola, Italy, orphaned from the age of five, Jane was taunted by her companions who reminded her of how she had no one to care for her. To this she would respond, "I've got a better father than you have!", which she explained by pointing to a statue of a guardian angel in her parish church, adding, "He will look after me!" Jane was to have a lifelong devotion to the angels. A family of Orvieto took her in and provided for her. When they attempted to arrange a marriage for her, Jane instead resolved to live as a consecrated virgin and became a Third Order Dominican. She particularly directed her charity, prayers, and penances toward those who treated her unkindly, such that it became a running joke in Orvieto that anyone who wished for Jane to pray for them should simply act against her. Jane's personal devotion to the Passion was especially manifest each year on Good Friday (during the last ten years of her life) when she experienced an ecstasy from midday until evening, stretched out upon the floor as if she were participating in the crucifixion.

Do not cease to pray for all other men, for there is hope of their conversion and of their finding God.
Saint Ignatius of Antioch

TUESDAY, JULY 24

Prayer for the Morning

With God is wisdom: come, let us adore!

Glory to the Father, and to the Son,
and to the Holy Spirit, as it was in the beginning,
is now, and will be for ever. Amen. Alleluia!

HYMN
Meter: 12 11 12 11
This hymn can be sung to the tune used for
We Gather Together

The works of the Lord are created in wisdom!
We view the earth's wonders and call him to mind;
We hear what he says in the world we discover,
And God shows his glory in all that we find.

The sun ev'ry morning lights up all creation,
The moon marks the rhythm of months in their
turn;
The glittering stars are arrayed in God's honor,
Adorning the years as they ceaselessly burn.

The song is unfinished; how shall we complete it,
And where find the skill to perfect all his praise?
At work in all places, he cares for all peoples –
How great is the Lord to the end of all days!

PSALM 104
1, 19-24, 33-34, 35b

With him are wisdom and might; his are counsel and understanding.
(Jb 12: 13)

In the Scriptures, wisdom puts all of life in right order. Here the
psalmist celebrates the wisdom with which God has ordered time so
that day and night, months and seasons all serve the purpose of life.
Time reaches its intended culmination in the gift of everlasting life
bestowed through Jesus Christ.

Bless the Lord, my soul!
Lord God, how great you are!

You made the moon to mark the months;
the sun knows the time for its setting.
When you spread the darkness it is night
and all the beasts of the forest creep forth.
The young lions roar for their prey
and ask their food from God.

At the rising of the sun they steal away
and go to rest in their dens.
Man goes forth to his work,
to labor till evening falls.

How many are your works, O Lord!
In wisdom you have made them all.
The earth is full of your riches.

I will sing to the Lord all my life,
make music to my God while I live.
May my thoughts be pleasing to him.
I find my joy in the Lord.
Bless the Lord, my soul.

Glory to the Father...

Word of God   Job 12: 7-10

NOW ASK THE BEASTS to teach you, and the birds of the air to tell you; or the reptiles on earth to instruct you, and the fish of the sea to inform you. Which of all these does not know that the hand of God has done this? In his hand is the soul of every living thing, and the life breath of all mankind.

The Lord by wisdom founded the earth,
established the heavens by understanding. (Prv 3: 19)

CANTICLE OF ZECHARIAH   (Text, back cover B)
When the fullness of time had come, God sent his Son, born of a
woman, born under the law, to ransom those under the law, so that
we might receive adoption. (Gal 4: 4-5)

INTERCESSIONS

All times and all seasons are in God's hand; all times and
all seasons are fulfilled in Christ. Let us pray:

℟   You are our life and our salvation!

Yours is the night and yours the day:
– enlighten us with your wisdom at every hour of our
lives. ℟

Yours are the years and yours the seasons:
– teach us to trust in your provident designs. ℟

Yours is the fullness of life:
– bring us to dwell in your presence for ever. ℟

                                            Personal intentions

Our Father…

Lord God of time and timelessness, you order all things
according to your wise designs. Grant us discerning
hearts, that we may know and love and serve your plan,
through Christ our Lord. Amen.

MASS

Tuesday of the Sixteenth Week of the Year

(The prayers suggested today are those of the Sixteenth
Week in Ordinary Time.)

ENTRANCE ANTIPHON
God himself is my help. The Lord upholds my life. I will offer
you a willing sacrifice; I will praise your name, O Lord, for its
goodness. (Ps 53: 6, 8)

OPENING PRAYER
> Father,
> let the gift of your life
> continue to grow in us,
> drawing us from death to faith, hope, and love.
> Keep us alive in Christ Jesus.
> Keep us watchful in prayer
> and true to his teaching
> till your glory is revealed in us.
> Grant this through Christ our Lord.

● *The sons of Israel went on dry ground right into the sea.* ●

A reading from the Book of Exodus

14: 21–15: 1

MOSES STRETCHED OUT his hand over the sea, and the Lord swept the sea with a strong east wind throughout the night and so turned it into dry land. When the water was thus divided, the Israelites marched into the midst of the sea on dry land, with the water like a wall to their right and to their left.

The Egyptians followed in pursuit; all Pharaoh's horses and chariots and charioteers went after them right into the midst of the sea. In the night watch just before dawn the Lord cast through the column of the fiery cloud upon the Egyptian force a glance that threw it into a panic; and he so clogged their chariot wheels that they could hardly drive. With that the Egyptians sounded the retreat before Israel, because the Lord was fighting for them against the Egyptians.

Then the Lord told Moses, "Stretch out your hand over the sea, that the water may flow back upon the Egyptians, upon their chariots and their charioteers." So

Moses stretched out his hand over the sea, and at dawn the sea flowed back to its normal depth. The Egyptians were fleeing head on toward the sea, when the Lord hurled them into its midst. As the water flowed back, it covered the chariots and the charioteers of Pharaoh's whole army which had followed the Israelites into the sea. Not a single one of them escaped. But the Israelites had marched on dry land through the midst of the sea, with the water like a wall to their right and to their left. Thus the Lord saved Israel on that day from the power of the Egyptians. When Israel saw the Egyptians lying dead on the seashore and beheld the great power that the Lord had shown against the Egyptians, they feared the Lord and believed in him and in his servant Moses.

Then Moses and the Israelites sang this song to the Lord:

I will sing to the Lord, for he is gloriously triumphant;/ horse and chariot he has cast into the sea. The word of the Lord.

———— • CANTICLE (Exodus 15) • ————

℞ (1) **Let us sing to the Lord;**
he has covered himself in glory.

At the breath of your anger the waters piled up,
    the flowing waters stood like a mound,
    the flood waters congealed in the midst of the sea.
The enemy boasted, "I will pursue and overtake them;
    I will divide the spoils and have my fill of them;
    I will draw my sword; my hand shall despoil
        them!" ℞

When your wind blew, the sea covered them;
    like lead they sank in the mighty waters.

When you stretched out your right hand,
  the earth swallowed them! R/

And you brought them in and planted them on
    the mountain of your inheritance –
  the place where you made your seat, O Lord,
  the sanctuary, O Lord, which your hands
    established. R/

Alleluia. He who keeps the word of Christ, grows perfect
in the love of God. Alleluia.

  ● *Extending his hands toward the disciples, he said:*
    Here are my mother and my brothers. ●

A reading from
the holy Gospel according to Matthew   12: 46-50

JESUS WAS ADDRESSING the crowds when his mother and his brothers appeared outside to speak with him. Someone said to him, "Your mother and your brothers are standing out there and they wish to speak to you." He said to the one who had told him, "Who is my mother? Who are my brothers?" Then extending his hands to his disciples, he said, "There are my mother and my brothers. Whoever does the will of my heavenly Father is brother and sister and mother to me."
The Gospel of the Lord.

PRAYER OVER THE GIFTS
  Lord,
  bring us closer to salvation
  through these gifts which we bring in your honor.
  Accept the perfect sacrifice you have given us,
  bless it as you blessed the gifts of Abel.
  We ask this through Christ our Lord.

COMMUNION ANTIPHON

I stand at the door and knock, says the Lord. If anyone hears my voice and opens the door, I will come in and sit down to supper with him, and he with me. (Rv 3: 20)

PRAYER AFTER COMMUNION

Merciful Father,
may these mysteries
give us new purpose
and bring us to a new life in you.
We ask this in the name of Jesus the Lord.

MEDITATION OF THE DAY

"Who is my mother?"

[Mary's] motherhood takes her back totally to [Jesus], in a perfect dispossession of herself, in a sublime poverty making her whole person a living relationship with her Son.

All the beliefs of the Church have been clarified in this sense, and nothing is more moving than to see with what tender rigor the successive definitions or the doctrines in the process of maturation have affirmed and do not cease to affirm in her the primacy of Christ, from the Immaculate Conception which, from the first moment of her existence, placed her soul under the sovereign dependency of the grace of the Savior, down to the Assumption, which places her body itself under the eternal dependency of his glory.

Thus the Mother is always the monstrance of her Son as, under the name of Notre Dame, the great cathedrals are the tabernacles of the Host, so evident is it that devotion could not be directed to any other pole but God alone.

Moreover, the most enthusiastic servants of the Virgin have always been the most ardent apostles of Jesus. They have instinctively understood that she was given to them as the mysterious sacrament of divine Goodness.

They have said to themselves and to each other, and rightly so, that all the tenderness there is in the heart of mothers is derived from the first Love, and that God who has communicated to them such power to love must, more than they, be a mother, be infinitely more mother indeed than the Blessed Virgin herself.

MAURICE ZUNDEL

Maurice Zundel († 1975) was a Swiss mystic, poet, philosopher, liturgist, and author.

Prayer for the Evening

What marvels the Lord has worked for us!
Let us give thanks and praise!

Glory to the Father, and to the Son,
and to the Holy Spirit, as it was in the beginning,
is now, and will be for ever. Amen. Alleluia!

HYMN
Meter: 87 87D
This hymn can be sung to the tune used for
All Who Love and All Who Labor

When from bondage we are summoned
Out of darkness into light,
We must go by hope and patience,
Walk by faith and not by sight.

℟ Let us throw off all that hinders;
Let us run the race to win!
Let us hasten to our homeland
And, rejoicing, enter in.

When our God names us his people,
Then he leads us by the hand
Through a lonely, barren desert,
To a great and glorious land. ℟

PSALM 126

Once more will he fill your mouth with laughter, and your lips with rejoicing. (Jb 8: 21)

Christ sends his disciples out to sow the seed of the Gospel in a world still governed by sin, pain, exile, and death. When the burden seems too great to bear, let us put our hope in his promise that joy awaits those who follow the road faithfully to the end and bring home the harvest of life.

When the Lord delivered Zion from bondage,
it seemed like a dream.
Then was our mouth filled with laughter,
on our lips there were songs.

The heathens themselves said: "What marvels
the Lord worked for them!"
What marvels the Lord worked for us!
Indeed we were glad.

Deliver us, O Lord, from our bondage
as streams in dry land.
Those who are sowing in tears
will sing when they reap.

They go out, they go out, full of tears,
carrying seed for the sowing:
they come back, they come back, full of song,
carrying their sheaves.

Glory to the Father...

Word of God   Baruch 4: 22-23

I HAVE TRUSTED in the Eternal God for your welfare, and joy has come to me from the Holy One because of the mercy that will swiftly reach you from your eternal savior.

With mourning and lament I sent you forth, but God will give you back to me with enduring gladness and joy.

I accomplish my every purpose.
(Is 46: 10)

CANTICLE OF MARY   (Text, back cover A)
I will rejoice in Jerusalem and exult in my people. No longer shall the sound of weeping be heard there, or the sound of crying. (Is 65: 19)

INTERCESSIONS

Let us pray especially for those who have grown discouraged in bearing the heat and burden of the day:

R̸   Deliver your people, O Lord, from bondage.

For all those whose faith has led them into places of exile and sorrow:
– be their deliverance and their joy. R̸

For all those who labor in hopelessness:
– be their hope and their courage. R̸

For all those who have abandoned pastoral ministry in discouragement:
– be their reconciliation and guide. R̸

Personal intentions

Our Father...

May the Lord of peace himself give us peace at all times and in every way. Amen. (cf. 2 Thes 3: 16)

MARIAN ANTIPHON   (Text, page 25)

SAINTS
OF TODAY AND YESTERDAY

A prudent wife is from the Lord.

SAINT KINGA (CUNEGUND) OF POLAND
Virgin, Widow, and Religious (1234-1292)

The Hungarian Princess Kinga, having been given in marriage to the Polish Prince Boleslaus of Sandomierz, convinced her husband that the two should embrace a life of perpetual virginity in the married state and thus the two lived their forty years together, reigning as king and queen of Poland. Imitating the virtues of her famous aunt Saint Elizabeth of Hungary, Kinga devoted herself to the personal care of the poor, and visiting hospitals to tend the sick. As a penance she wore a hair shirt under her royal garments. In answer to the prayers of Kinga valuable salt mines were discovered at a time when Poland was facing a critical shortage of this mineral. Following her husband's death she entered the Polish convent of Poor Clares in Sandek, telling the other nuns, "Forget what I once was; I come only to be your servant." On her deathbed she was to exclaim, "Make room, do you not see our father Francis coming to assist me?"

It is most laudable in a married woman to be devout, but she must never forget that she is a housewife; and sometimes she must leave God at the altar to find him in her housekeeping.
Saint Frances of Rome

WEDNESDAY, JULY 25
Saint James
Prayer for the Morning

God sends workers into the harvest fields of faith:
let us give thanks and praise!

Glory to the Father, and to the Son,
and to the Holy Spirit, as it was in the beginning,
is now, and will be for ever. Amen. Alleluia!

HYMN   Meter: LM
This hymn can be sung to the tune used for
When I Survey the Wondrous Cross

Christ, in whose passion once was sown
All virtue of all saints to be,
For the white field of these thy own
We praise the seed and sower, thee.

Thine was the first and holiest grain
To die and quicken and increase;
And then came these, and died again
That spring and harvest should not cease.

PSALM 65   10-11, 13-14

A sower went out to sow his seed. The seed is the word of God.
(Lk 8: 5, 11)

The mission of the apostles was to prepare the earth and plant the
seed of God's word for the harvest of faith. James, the brother of
John, was the first of the apostles to water the soil with his own
blood. A century later, Tertullian would say that the blood of martyrs was the seed of Christians.

You care for the earth, give it water,
you fill it with riches.
Your river in heaven brims over
to provide its grain.

And thus you provide for the earth;
you drench its furrows,
you level it, soften it with showers,
you bless its growth.

The hills are girded with joy,
the meadows covered with flocks,
the valleys are decked with wheat.
They shout for joy, yes, they sing.

Glory to the Father…

Word of God   Isaiah 55: 10-11

JUST AS FROM THE HEAVENS the rain and snow come down
and do not return there till they have watered the earth,
making it fertile and fruitful, giving seed to him who
sows and bread to him who eats, so shall my word be
that goes forth from my mouth; it shall not return to me
void, but shall do my will, achieving the end for which
I sent it.

*Ground that has absorbed the rain falling upon it
repeatedly and brings forth crops useful to those for
whom it is cultivated receives a blessing from God.*
(Heb 6: 7)

CANTICLE OF ZECHARIAH   (Text, back cover B)
As for the seed that fell on rich soil, they are the ones who, when they
have heard the word, embrace it with a generous and good heart, and
bear fruit through perseverance. (Lk 8: 15)

INTERCESSIONS

Jesus Christ is the grain of wheat that fell into the
ground and died. Let us pray for an abundant harvest:

℟   You came to give life and give it in abundance!

Some seed fell on rocky ground:
– soften all hardened hearts to receive the gift of your word. ℟

Some seed fell in patches of thorn:
– uproot from our hearts all that would choke off the growth of your word. ℟

Some seed fell on good ground and bore much fruit:
– cultivate the love you have poured into our hearts for the good of your kingdom. ℟

Personal intentions

Our Father…

O God and giver of all good gifts, you sent your apostle James to prepare the earth's soil to receive the good seed who is your Word made flesh, our Lord Jesus Christ. Through the works of evangelization, prepare all hearts to welcome with joy the Word of life, who lives and reigns with you and the Holy Spirit, one God for ever and ever. Amen.

MASS

Feast of Saint James

● *Saint James, son of Zebedee and brother of Saint John the apostle, was born in Bethsaida. He was present at most of the miracles performed by Christ and was put to death by Herod around the year 42. He is especially honored in Compostella in Spain where a famous church is dedicated to his name.* ●

ENTRANCE ANTIPHON

Walking by the Sea of Galilee, Jesus saw James and John, the sons of Zebedee, mending their nets, and he called them to follow him. (See Mt 4: 18, 21)

GLORIA ————————————————————————— page 226

OPENING PRAYER

Almighty Father,
by the martyrdom of Saint James
you blessed the work of the early Church.
May his profession of faith give us courage
and his prayers bring us strength.
We ask this through our Lord Jesus Christ, your Son,
who lives and reigns with you and the Holy Spirit,
one God, for ever and ever.

● *We carry always in our bodies the death of Jesus.* ●

A reading from the second Letter
of Paul to the Corinthians   4: 7-15

WE POSSESS a treasure in earthen vessels to make it clear that its surpassing power comes from God and not from us. We are afflicted in every way possible, but we are not crushed; full of doubts, we never despair. We are persecuted but never abandoned; we are struck down but never destroyed. Continually we carry about in our bodies the dying of Jesus, so that in our bodies the life of Jesus may also be revealed. While we live we are constantly being delivered to death for Jesus' sake, so that the life of Jesus may be revealed in our mortal flesh. Death is at work in us, but life in you. We have that spirit of faith of which the Scripture says, "Because I believed, I spoke out." We believe and so we speak, knowing that he who raised up the Lord Jesus will raise us up along with Jesus and place both us and you in his presence. Indeed, everything is ordered to your benefit, so that the grace bestowed in abundance may bring greater glory to God because they who give thanks are many.

The word of the Lord.

• PSALM 126 •

℟ (5)**Those who sow in tears, shall reap with shouts of joy.**

When the Lord brought back the captives of Zion,
  we were like men dreaming.
Then our mouth was filled with laughter,
  and our tongue with rejoicing. ℟

Then they said among the nations,
  "The Lord has done great things for them."
The Lord has done great things for us;
  we are glad indeed. ℟

Restore our fortunes, O Lord,
  like the torrents in the southern desert.
Those that sow in tears
  shall reap rejoicing. ℟

Although they go forth weeping,
  carrying the seed to be sown,
They shall come back rejoicing,
  carrying their sheaves. ℟

Alleluia. I have chosen you from the world, says the Lord, to go and bear fruit that will last. Alleluia.

● *You shall indeed drink my cup.* ●

A reading from
the holy Gospel according to Matthew   20: 20-28

THE MOTHER OF Zebedee's sons came up to Jesus accompanied by her sons, to do him homage and ask of him a favor. "What is it you want?" he said. She answered, "Promise me that these sons of mine will sit, one at your right hand and the other at your left, in your kingdom." In reply Jesus said, "You do not know what you are asking. Can you drink of the cup I am to drink of?" "We can," they said. He told them, "From the cup I drink of you shall drink. Sitting at my right hand or my left is not mine to give. That is for those for whom it has been reserved by my Father." The other ten, on hearing this, became indignant at the two brothers. Jesus then called them together and said: "You know how those who exercise authority among the Gentiles lord it over them; their great ones make their importance felt. It cannot be like that with you. Anyone among you who aspires to greatness must serve the rest, and whoever wants to rank first among you must serve the needs of all. Such is the case with the Son of Man who has come, not to be served by others but to serve, to give his own life as a ransom for the many."
The Gospel of the Lord.

PRAYER OVER THE GIFTS
Lord,
as we honor Saint James,
the first apostle to share the cup of suffering and death,
wash away our sins
by the saving passion of your Son,
and make our sacrifice pleasing to you.
We ask this through Christ our Lord.

PREFACE OF THE APOSTLES I OR II ——————— page 62

COMMUNION ANTIPHON
By sharing the cup of the Lord's suffering, they became the
friends of God. (See Mt 20: 22-23)

PRAYER AFTER COMMUNION
Father,
we have received this holy Eucharist with joy
as we celebrate the feast of the apostle James.
Hear his prayers
and bring us your help.
We ask this in the name of Jesus the Lord.

• ——————————————————— •

M E D I T A T I O N   O F   T H E   D A Y

• ——————————————————— •

Greatness in Serving Others

We learn from Hubert of Besançon that about the year
1070 thirty men from Lorraine went on pilgrimage to
Compostella, to the tomb of Saint James. All of them
except one had sworn to help each other. One of the thirty fell ill, and the rest waited for him for a fortnight, after
which they all left him except the one who had not made
the promise. This man stayed with him at the foot of the
mountain of Saint Michael, where, as evening drew on,
the sick man died. The other was frightened by the loneliness of the place, the presence of the dead man, the
darkness of the night, and the fierceness of the local pop-
ulation; but all of a sudden Saint James appeared to him
in knightly array, comforted him, and said: "Lift the corpse
up to me, and you come behind me on my horse!" They
rode on and before dawn had traveled a fifteen days' journey, arriving at Mount Joy, a short distance from
Compostella and the apostle's tomb. The saint set both
the living and the dead down there, ordering the survivor
to call upon the canons of Saint James to bury the dead
pilgrim, and to tell those who had traveled with him that
their pilgrimage was worthless because they had broken

their oath. The man carried out his orders and told his astonished companions what Saint James had said.

Blessed Jacobus de Voragine

Blessed Jacobus († 1298) was a Dominican friar, archbishop of Genoa, and an esteemed peacemaker and father to the poor.

Prayer for the Evening

Let us thank God for his fidelity and love!

Glory to the Father, and to the Son,
and to the Holy Spirit, as it was in the beginning,
is now, and will be for ever. Amen. Alleluia!

Hymn
Meter: CM
This hymn can be sung to the tune used for
Lord, Who Throughout These Forty Days

R/ The rocks would shout if we kept still
And failed to preach the word.
It is the Lord's insistent will
The truth be told and heard.

We're called to speak disturbing things
Though wealth and power conspire
To hush the messenger who brings
God's purifying fire. R/

We're called to preach by Jesus Christ
Who with the Spirit's breath
Will make our fragile words suffice
To raise new life from death. R/

Psalm 138
1-5, 7b-8

Behold, I am with you always, until the end of the age. (Mt 28: 20b)

The courageous fidelity of the apostles is built upon the rock of the unshakeable fidelity of God.

I thank you, Lord, with all my heart,
you have heard the words of my mouth.
In the presence of the angels I will bless you.
I will adore before your holy temple.

I thank you for your faithfulness and love
which excel all we ever knew of you.
On the day I called, you answered;
you increased the strength of my soul.

All earth's kings shall thank you
when they hear the words of your mouth.
They shall sing of the Lord's ways:
"How great is the glory of the Lord!"

You stretch out your hand and save me,
your hand will do all things for me.
Your love, O Lord, is eternal,
discard not the work of your hands.

Glory to the Father...

Word of God
Matthew 10: 17-20

THEY WILL HAND you over to courts and scourge you in their synagogues, and you will be led before governors and kings for my sake as a witness before them and the pagans. When they hand you over, do not worry about how you are to speak or what you are to say. You will be given at that moment what you are to say. For it will not be you who speak but the Spirit of your Father speaking through you.

You will be hated by all because of my name, but whoever endures to the end will be saved.

(Mt 10: 22)

CANTICLE OF MARY (Text, back cover A)
No disciple is above his teacher, no slave above his master.
(Mt 10: 24)

INTERCESSIONS

Through the intercession of Saint James, we pray:

℟   On the day we call, you answer, Lord!

You sent your apostles into the world to proclaim your
Gospel in the face of hostility:
– make us courageous in our faith and witness. ℟

You sent your apostles to the ends of the earth:
– make us generous in following your will. ℟

You rewarded your apostles with eternal life in your
presence:
– draw to yourself all those who have died in the service
of the Gospel. ℟

Personal intentions

Our Father...

*May God keep us firm to the end, irreproachable on the
day of our Lord Jesus Christ. Amen. (cf. 1 Cor 1: 8)*

MARIAN ANTIPHON (Text, page 25)

You chose Saints Joachim and Ann
to be the parents of the Virgin Mary: keep all parents
faithful to the life to which you have called them.

THURSDAY, JULY 26
Saints Joachim and Ann

Prayer for the Morning

Blessed be God, the Father of us all:
come, let us adore.

Glory to the Father, and to the Son,
and to the Holy Spirit, as it was in the beginning,
is now, and will be for ever. Amen. Alleluia!

HYMN
Meter: 77 77 77
This hymn can be sung to the tune used for
As with Gladness Men of Old

For the beauty of the earth,
For the glory of the skies,
For the love which from our birth
Over and around us lies:

℟ Lord of all, to you we raise
This our hymn of grateful praise.

For the joy of human love,
Brother, sister, parent, child,
Friends on earth and friends above;
For all gentle thoughts and mild: ℟

For yourself, best Gift Divine!
To this world so freely giv'n.
Word Incarnate, God's design,
Peace on earth and joy in heav'n: ℟

PSALM 128

Remember, of these parents you were born; what can you give them
for all they gave you? (Sir 7: 28)

The memorial of the couple identified by tradition as the parents of the Virgin Mary gives reason to rejoice in the gift of family life and to reflect on the mutual responsibility parents and children have to love one another and lead one another to holiness.

O blessed are those who fear the Lord
and walk in his ways!

By the labor of your hands you shall eat.
You will be happy and prosper;
your wife like a fruitful vine
in the heart of your house;
your children like shoots of the olive,
around your table.

Indeed thus shall be blessed
the man who fears the Lord.
May the Lord bless you from Zion
all the days of your life!
May you see your children's children
in a happy Jerusalem!
On Israel, peace!

Glory to the Father...

Word of God   Sirach 3: 1-6

CHILDREN, PAY HEED to a father's right; do so that you may live. For the Lord sets a father in honor over his children; a mother's authority he confirms over her sons. He who honors his father atones for sins; he stores up riches who reveres his mother. He who honors his father is gladdened by children, and when he prays he is heard. He who reveres his father will live a long life; he obeys the Lord who brings comfort to his mother.

Let us love one another!

CANTICLE OF ZECHARIAH (Text, back cover B)
Children, obey your parents in everything, for this is pleasing to the Lord. (Col 3: 20)

INTERCESSIONS

With trust in our Father's love for us, let us pray:

℟ Show mercy to your people, Lord.

You chose Saints Joachim and Ann to be the parents of the Virgin Mary:
– keep all parents faithful to the life to which you have called them. ℟

You entrust all Christian parents with the task of raising their children to live the Gospel:
– grant them the grace to live what they teach. ℟

You have promised that even if father and mother abandon us, you will never abandon us:
– keep in your care all abandoned, orphaned, and abused children. ℟

Personal intentions

Our Father…

God our Father, from whom every family in heaven and on earth is named, grant us in accord with the riches of your glory to be strengthened with power through your Spirit in the inner self, and that Christ may dwell in our hearts through faith; that rooted and grounded in love, we may have strength to comprehend with all the holy ones what is the breadth and length and height and depth, and to know the love of Christ that surpasses knowledge, so that we may be filled with all the fullness of God. Through the same Christ our Lord. Amen. (cf. Eph 3: 14-19)

MASS

Thursday of the Sixteenth Week of the Year

JOACHIM AND ANN   *Memorial*

● *From an ancient tradition, going back even to the second century, the parents of the Virgin Mary are known by the names of Joachim and Ann. Devotion to Saint Ann is found in the sixth century in the East, and by the tenth century it was widespread in the West. Saint Joachim was likewise honored, but at a more recent date.* ●

ENTRANCE ANTIPHON

Praised be Joachim and Ann for the child they bore. The Lord gave them the blessing of all the nations.

OPENING PRAYER

God of our fathers,
you gave Saints Joachim and Ann
the privilege of being the parents of Mary,
the mother of your incarnate Son.
May their prayers help us to attain
the salvation you have promised to your people.
Grant this through our Lord Jesus Christ, your Son,
who lives and reigns with you and the Holy Spirit,
one God, for ever and ever.

● *The Lord descended on Mount Sinai before all the people.* ●

A reading from
the Book of Exodus   19: 1-2, 9-11, 16-20a

IN THE THIRD MONTH after their departure from the land of Egypt, on its first day, the Israelites came to the desert of Sinai. After the journey from Rephidim to the desert of Sinai, they pitched camp. While Israel was encamped here in front of the mountain, the Lord told Moses, "I am coming to you in a dense cloud, so that when the people hear me speaking with you, they may always have faith in you also." When Moses, then, had reported to the Lord the response of the people, the Lord added, "Go to the people and have them sanctify themselves today and tomorrow. Make them wash their garments and be ready for the third day; for on the third day the Lord will come down on Mount Sinai before the eyes of all the people."

On the morning of the third day there were peals of thunder and lightning, and a heavy cloud over the mountain, and a very loud trumpet blast, so that all the people in the camp trembled. But Moses led the people out of the camp to meet God, and they stationed themselves at the foot of the mountain. Mount Sinai was all wrapped in smoke, for the Lord came down upon it in fire. The smoke rose from it as though from a furnace, and the whole mountain trembled violently. The trumpet blast grew louder and louder, while Moses was speaking and God answering him with thunder.

When the Lord came down to the top of Mount Sinai, he summoned Moses to the top of the mountain.
The word of the Lord.

——— • CANTICLE (Daniel 3) • ———

℟ (52) **Glory and praise for ever!**

Blessed are you, O Lord, the God of our fathers,
    praiseworthy and exalted above all forever;
And blessed is your holy and glorious name,
    praiseworthy and exalted above all for all ages. ℟

Blessed are you in the temple of your holy glory,
    praiseworthy and glorious above all forever. ℟

Blessed are you on the throne of your kingdom,
  praiseworthy and exalted above all forever. ℟

Blessed are you who look into the depths
  from your throne upon the cherubim,
  praiseworthy and exalted above all forever. ℟

Blessed are you in the firmament of heaven,
  praiseworthy and glorious forever. ℟

Alleluia. Blessed are you, Father, Lord of heaven and
earth; you have revealed to little ones the mysteries of
the kingdom. Alleluia.

> ● *To you it is given to know the mysteries of the king-*
> *dom of heaven, but to them it has not been given.* ●

A reading from
the holy Gospel according to Matthew   13: 10-17

WHEN THE DISCIPLES appro-
ached Jesus, they asked
him, "Why do you speak to them in parables?" He
answered: "To you has been given a knowledge of the
mysteries of the reign of God, but it has not been given
to the others. To the man who has, more will be given
until he grows rich; the man who has not, will lose what
little he has.

"I use parables when I speak to them because they
look but do not see, they listen but do not hear or
understand. Isaiah's prophecy is fulfilled in them which
says:

'Listen as you will, you shall not understand,/ look
intently as you will, you shall not see./ Sluggish indeed
is this people's heart./ They have scarcely heard with
their ears,/ they have firmly closed their eyes;/ otherwise
they might see with their eyes,/ and hear with their

ears,/ and understand with their hearts,/ and turn back to me,/ and I should heal them.'

"But blest are your eyes because they see and blest are your ears because they hear. I assure you, many a prophet and many a saint longed to see what you see but did not see it, to hear what you hear but did not hear it." The Gospel of the Lord.

PRAYER OVER THE GIFTS

Lord,
receive these gifts as signs of our love
and give us a share in the blessing you promised
to Abraham and his descendants.
We ask this in the name of Jesus the Lord.

COMMUNION ANTIPHON

They received a blessing from the Lord, and kindness from God their Savior. (See Ps 23: 5)

PRAYER AFTER COMMUNION

Father,
your Son was born as a man
so that men could be born again in you.
As you nourish us with the bread of life,
given only to your sons and daughters,
fill us with the Spirit who makes us your children.
We ask this through Christ our Lord.

MEDITATION OF THE DAY

Blessed Are Your Ears Because They Hear

Ultimately, we come to expect God to accept our understanding of what his will ought to be and to help us fulfill that, instead of learning to see and accept his will in the real situations in which he places us daily. The simple soul who each day makes a morning offering of "all the prayers, works, joys, and sufferings of this day" – and who then acts upon it by accepting unquestionably and responding lovingly to all the situations of the day as truly sent by God – has perceived with an almost childlike faith the profound truth about the will of God. To predict what God's will is going to be, to rationalize about what his will must be, is at once a work of human folly and yet the subtlest of all temptations. The plain and simple truth is that his will is what he actually wills to send us each day, in the way of circumstances, places, people, and problems. The trick is to learn to see that – not just in theory, or not just occasionally in a flash of insight granted by God's grace, but every day. Each of us has no need to wonder about what God's will must be for us; his will for us is clearly revealed in every situation of every day, if only we could learn to view all things as he sees them and sends them to us.

The temptation is to overlook these things as God's will. The temptation is to look beyond these things, precisely because they are so constant, so petty, so humdrum, and so routine, and to seek to discover instead some other and nobler "will of God" in the abstract that better fits our notion of what his will should be.

FATHER WALTER J. CISZEK, S.J.

Father Ciszek († 1984) was convicted of being a "Vatican spy" in World War II and spent twenty-three years in Soviet prisons.

Prayer for the Evening

*Blessed are they who honor the Lord:
come, let us adore him!*

*Glory to the Father, and to the Son,
and to the Holy Spirit, as it was in the beginning,
is now, and will be for ever. Amen. Alleluia!*

HYMN   Meter: 10 10 10 with alleluias

For all the saints who from their labors rest,
Who thee by faith before the world confessed,
Thy name, O Jesus, be forever blest.
Alleluia! Alleluia!

O blest communion, fellowship divine!
We feebly struggle, they in glory shine;
Yet all are one in thee for all are thine.
Alleluia! Alleluia!

PSALM 112   1-9

With devoted men was she created from of old, and with their
children her beneficence abides. (Sir 1: 13)

Saint Ann is the patroness of Christian mothers. Both Joachim and
Ann are remembered as worthy, God-fearing parents whose child
was most blessed to give birth to the Savior, the Sun of Justice. He,
their grandson in his humanity, shines as a light in the darkness for
all those who hunger and thirst for righteousness.

Happy the man who fears the Lord,
who takes delight in all his commands.
His sons will be powerful on earth;
the children of the upright are blessed.

Riches and wealth are in his house;
his justice stands firm for ever.
He is a light in the darkness for the upright:
he is generous, merciful and just.

The good man takes pity and lends,
he conducts his affairs with honor.
The just man will never waver:
he will be remembered for ever.

He has no fear of evil news;
with a firm heart he trusts in the Lord.
With a steadfast heart he will not fear;
he will see the downfall of his foes.

Open-handed, he gives to the poor;
his justice stands firm for ever.
His head will be raised in glory.

Glory to the Father...

Word of God   Ephesians 6: 1-4

CHILDREN, OBEY YOUR PARENTS [in the Lord], for this is right. "Honor your father and mother." This is the first commandment with a promise, "that it may go well with you and that you may have a long life on earth." Fathers, do not provoke your children to anger, but bring them up with the training and instruction of the Lord.

Blessed be the one God and Father of all,
who is over all and through all and in all. (cf. Eph 4: 6)

CANTICLE OF MARY   (Text, back cover A)
Through faith you are all children of God in Christ Jesus. (Gal 3: 26)

INTERCESSIONS

God's love endures for ever. Let us pray:

℟   Hear your children, O Lord.

For all grandparents:
– make them strong, loving, and wise. ℟

For all families blessed with living grandparents:
– fill them with respect and love for the aging. ℟

For all the elderly abandoned by their families:
– fill them with peace of heart and grant them the companionship of others in their loneliness. ℟

For all our family members who have died:
– bring them in joy to your eternal home. ℟

Personal intentions

Our Father…
May the Lord be kind and faithful to us. Amen. (cf. 2 Sm 2: 6)

MARIAN ANTIPHON   (Text, page 25)

SAINTS
OF TODAY AND YESTERDAY

I will greatly rejoice in the Lord.

Blessed Andrew of Phu Yen
Martyr (c. 1625-1644)

After being baptized around the age of fifteen along with his mother, Andrew, a native of the Phu Yen province of what is now Vietnam, became a catechist. He worked as an assistant to the Jesuit missionary Father de Rhodes. Andrew joined an association founded by Father de Rhodes known as the Maison Dieu ("House of God") whose members pledged themselves to a lifetime of catechetical service to the Church. The return to Andrew's province of the governing mandarin, instructed by his king to put an end to the spread of Christianity, led to the issuing of threats against Father de Rhodes. When the priest's house was searched, the authorities found Andrew there and beat him, bound him, and took him to the governor's palace. Questioned by the mandarin who considered Andrew's faith nothing but a "foolish opinion," Andrew professed himself ready to suffer anything rather than deny his Catholicism. While in prison the young catechist asked those who visited him to pray that he would "respond with fullness of love to the infinite love of his Lord." On July 26, 1644 Andrew was pierced with a lance and beheaded.

As the power of love is not broken by distance, neither is the efficacy of prayer.
Saint John Chrysostom

FRIDAY, JULY 27

Prayer for the Morning

To God our praise is due!

*Glory to the Father, and to the Son,
and to the Holy Spirit, as it was in the beginning,
is now, and will be for ever. Amen. Alleluia!*

HYMN

Meter: LM
This hymn can be sung to the tune used for
Awake, My Soul, and With the Sun or
O God of Love, O King of Peace

When God restored our captive state,
Joy was our song, and grace our theme,
The grace beyond our hopes so great
That joy appeared a painted dream.

When we review our dismal fears
'Twas hard to think they'd vanish so;
With God we left our flowing tears;
He makes our joys like rivers flow.

PSALM 65   2-4, 6

The Lord God will wipe away the tears from all faces; the reproach of
his people he will remove from the whole earth. (Is 25: 8)

The psalm calls to mind Saint Gregory of Nyssa's word portrait of
Christ, the artist, tenderly wiping away all the grime of sin that disfigures the human face and restoring God's image to its full beauty.

To you our praise is due
in Zion, O God.
To you we pay our vows,
you who hear our prayer.

To you all flesh will come
with its burden of sin.

Too heavy for us, our offenses,
but you wipe them away.

You keep your pledge with wonders,
O God our savior,
the hope of all the earth
and of far distant isles.

Glory to the Father...

Word of God
Isaiah 43: 20-21, 25

I PUT WATER in the desert and
rivers in the wasteland for my
chosen people to drink, the people whom I formed for
myself, that they might announce my praise. It is I,
I, who wipe out, for my own sake, your offenses; your
sins I remember no more.

> *O wash me more and more from my guilt*
> *and cleanse me from my sin. (Ps 51: 4)*

CANTICLE OF ZECHARIAH
(Text, back cover B)
Cease your cries of mourning, wipe the tears from your eyes. The
sorrow you have shown shall have its reward. (Jer 31: 16)

INTERCESSIONS

God rewards with joy those who mourn for their sins
and the sins of all our race. Let us pray with contrite
hearts:

℟   Hear our prayer; forgive our sins.

Where we have failed to be compassionate as you are
compassionate:
– deepen our love for those who have fallen under the
burden of their weakness. ℟

Where we have failed to be faithful as you are faithful:
– renew our commitment to live the vows we made in
baptism. ℟

Where we have failed to be loving as you are loving:
– sharpen our willingness to put you and our neighbor
before our own desires. ℟

Where we have failed to be joyful as you free us to be:
– strengthen our trust in your unfailing love for us. ℟

Personal intentions

Our Father...

Most merciful Lord and Savior, you wash away all our
sins in the blood you shed upon the cross. Grant us the
grace to rejoice in the freedom you have bought for us
and to turn and set others free by the power of the love
you have shown us, who live and reign with God the
Father and the Holy Spirit, one God for ever and ever.
Amen.

MASS

Friday of the Sixteenth Week of the Year

(Today, the prayers of the Votive Mass of the Sacred Heart,
given below, could be used.)

ENTRANCE ANTIPHON
The thoughts of his heart last through every generation, that
he will rescue them from death and feed them in time of
famine. (Ps 32: 11, 19)

OPENING PRAYER
Lord God,
give us the strength and love of the heart of your Son
that, by becoming one with him,
we may have eternal salvation.

We ask this through our Lord Jesus Christ, your Son,
who lives and reigns with you and the Holy Spirit,
one God, for ever and ever.

● *The law was given through Moses.* ●

A reading from
the Book of Exodus

20: 1-17

GOD DELIVERED ALL these commandments:

"I, the Lord, am your God, who brought you out of
the land of Egypt, that place of slavery. You shall not
have other gods besides me. You shall not carve idols for
yourselves in the shape of anything in the sky above or
on the earth below or in the waters beneath the earth;
you shall not bow down before them or worship them.
For I, the Lord, your God, am a jealous God, inflicting
punishment for their fathers' wickedness on the children of those who hate me, down to the third and fourth
generation; but bestowing mercy down to the thou-
sandth generation, on the children of those who love me
and keep my commandments.

"You shall not take the name of the Lord, your God,
in vain. For the Lord will not leave unpunished him who
takes his name in vain.

"Remember to keep holy the sabbath day. Six days
you may labor and do all your work, but the seventh day
is the sabbath of the Lord, your God. No work may be
done then either by you, or your son or daughter, or
your male or female slave, or your beast, or by the alien
who lives with you. In six days the Lord made the heavens and the earth, the sea and all that is in them; but on
the seventh day he rested. That is why the Lord has
blessed the sabbath day and made it holy.

"Honor your father and your mother, that you may have a long life in the land which the Lord, your God, is giving you.

"You shall not kill.

"You shall not commit adultery.

"You shall not steal.

"You shall not bear false witness against your neighbor.

"You shall not covet your neighbor's house. You shall not covet your neighbor's wife, nor his male or female slave, nor his ox or ass, nor anything else that belongs to him."

The word of the Lord.

• PSALM 19 •

R/ (Jn 6: 69) **Lord, you have the words of everlasting life.**

The law of the Lord is perfect,
    refreshing the soul;
The decree of the Lord is trustworthy,
    giving wisdom to the simple. R/

The precepts of the Lord are right,
    rejoicing the heart;
The command of the Lord is clear,
    enlightening the eye; R/

The fear of the Lord is pure,
    enduring forever;
The ordinances of the Lord are true,
    all of them just. R/

They are more precious than gold,
    than a heap of purest gold;

Sweeter also than syrup
or honey from the comb. ℟

Alleluia. Turn my heart to do your will; teach me your
law, O God. Alleluia.

● *He who hears the word of God and understands it,
yields much fruit.* ●

A reading from
the holy Gospel according to Matthew 13: 18-23

JESUS SAID TO HIS DISCIPLES,
"Mark well the parable of the
sower. The seed along the path is the man who hears the
message about God's reign without understanding it.
The evil one approaches him to steal away what was
sown in his mind. The seed that fell on patches of rock
is the man who hears the message and at first receives it
with joy. But he has no roots, so he lasts only for a time.
When some setback or persecution involving the message occurs, he soon falters. What was sown among
briers is the man who hears the message, but then
worldly anxiety and the lure of money choke it off. Such
a one produces no yield. But what was sown on good
soil is the man who hears the message and takes it in.
He it is who bears a yield of a hundred – or sixty – or
thirty-fold."
The Gospel of the Lord.

PRAYER OVER THE GIFTS
Father of mercy,
in your great love for us
you have given us your only Son.
May he take us up into his own perfect sacrifice,
that we may offer you fitting worship.
We ask this through Christ our Lord.

COMMUNION ANTIPHON

The Lord says: If anyone is thirsty, let him come to me; whoever believes in me, let him drink. Streams of living water shall flow out from within him. (Jn 7: 37-38)

PRAYER AFTER COMMUNION

Lord,
we have received your sacrament of love.
By becoming more like Christ on earth
may we share his glory in heaven,
where he lives and reigns for ever and ever.

• ─────────────────────────────── •

M E D I T A T I O N   O F   T H E   D A Y

• ─────────────────────────────── •

Taking in the Word

O Hidden God, Your presence overwhelms my heart,
Now is the time for me to watch with my unknowing
Under the pure and matchless star of Faith;
Now must I vigil keep before the gates of self,
Of my own self, a closely-shuttered tower
Whose secret walls my Lord Himself has shaped,
And had not any light to guide His step.
Our God of Compassion who restores what we have
      ruined –
I know not what He does,
Nor what He gives to me, what He obtains,
How He transforms my sin, to fashion light.
This aspect of myself which God creates in me
Only He knows, because He wills it thus.
With holy darkness He enshrouds my spirit;
Far out of reach is heaven divine
Which burns within my soul to make it god-like.
This is the hour when I touch what Faith conceals;
Let us keep watch by everlasting gates

The long night through
Until the dawn when God shall tell the soul
To enter into self, and into Him.

RAÏSSA MARITAIN

*Raïssa Maritain († 1960) was born in Russia. She was a
convert to Catholicism and the wife of philosopher Jacques
Maritain.*

Prayer for the Evening

*Christ is our peace:
let us give thanks and praise!*

*Glory to the Father, and to the Son,
and to the Holy Spirit, as it was in the beginning,
is now, and will be for ever. Amen. Alleluia!*

HYMN   Meter: 7 7 7 7 D

Hail, Redeemer, King divine!
Priest and Lamb, the throne is thine;
King whose reign shall never cease,
Prince of everlasting peace.
Angels, saints, and nations sing:
"Praised be Jesus Christ, our King;
Lord of earth and sky and sea,
King of love on Calvary."

Christ, thou King of truth and might,
Be to us eternal light,
Till in peace each nation rings
With thy praises, King of kings.
Angels, saints, and nations sing:
"Praised be Jesus Christ, our King;
Lord of earth and sky and sea,
King of love on Calvary."

PSALM 72 1-7, 12-14, 18-19

I will appoint peace your governor, and justice your ruler. (Is 60: 17)

When we pray "Thy kingdom come," we commit ourselves to serve its coming by living in peace and by seeking peace and justice for all who suffer in our homes, our workplaces, our neighborhoods, our world.

O God, give your judgment to the king,
to a king's son your justice,
that he may judge your people in justice
and your poor in right judgment.

May the mountains bring forth peace for the people
and the hills, justice.
May he defend the poor of the people
and save the children of the needy
and crush the oppressor.

In his days justice shall flourish
and peace till the moon fails.

For he shall save the poor when they cry
and the needy who are helpless.
He will have pity on the weak
and save the lives of the poor.
From oppression he will rescue their lives,
to him their blood is dear.

Blessed be the Lord, God of Israel,
who alone works wonders,
ever blessed his glorious name.
Let his glory fill the earth.

Glory to the Father…

Word of God Ephesians 2: 13-16

N OW IN CHRIST JESUS you
who once were far off have

become near by the blood of Christ. For he is our peace, he who made both one and broke down the dividing wall of enmity, through his flesh, that he might create in himself one new person in place of the two, thus establishing peace, and might reconcile both with God, in one body, through the cross, putting that enmity to death by it.

He shall be peace.
(Mi 5: 4)

CANTICLE OF MARY   (Text, back cover A)
Blessed are the peacemakers; they shall be called children of God.
(cf. Mt 5: 9)

INTERCESSIONS

Ours were the sufferings Christ bore; by his death we are healed. Trusting in his love, we pray:

℟   Lamb of God, you take away the sins of the world; grant us peace.

In the name of the poor, we pray: ℟

In the name of the children of the needy, we pray: ℟

In the name of the weak and oppressed, we pray: ℟

Personal intentions

Our Father…

May the peace of God which passes all understanding guard our hearts in Christ Jesus our Lord. Amen.
(cf. Phil 4: 7)

MARIAN ANTIPHON   (Text, page 25)

SAINTS
OF TODAY AND YESTERDAY

> *Cry to God, and he will deliver you*
> *from the power and hand of the enemy.*

BLESSEDS RUDOLPH ACQUAIRVA,
ALPHONSUS PACHECO, PETER BERNO,
ANTHONY FRANCIS, AND FRANCIS ARANHA
Martyrs († 1583)

On July 25, 1583, in Cuncolim, India, five Jesuits –
Fathers Acquairva, Pacheco, Berno and Francis,
and a lay brother, Francis Aranha – were attacked
by an armed band of natives enraged in part by the
missionaries' efforts to erect a church and cross.
Father Acquairva, from Atri, Italy, insisted that no
arms be fired in the missionaries' defense, saying,
"We are not here to fight!" Father Berno, a Swiss,
although successful in winning many converts among
the Hindus, had been convinced that substantial
missionary success in India could only be obtained
through martyrdom. Father Francis, from Portugal,
had prayed daily to die a martyr; once as he elevated
the Host at the consecration he was interiorly assured
that his prayer would be answered. The four priests
were killed by their attackers with lances and swords.
The lay brother Francis Aranha, a Portuguese
architect, was captured and after refusing to worship
an idol was executed bound to a tree and pierced with
arrows.

> *O heavenly city, dwelling-place secure, country in*
> *which is found all that can delight!*
> Saint Peter of Alcantara

SATURDAY, JULY 28

Prayer for the Morning

Come, let us sing a new song to the Lord!

Glory to the Father, and to the Son,
and to the Holy Spirit, as it was in the beginning,
is now, and will be for ever. Amen. Alleluia!

HYMN

Meter: 87 87 D
This hymn can be sung to the tune used for
Sing of Mary

Holy light on earth's horizon,
Star of hope to those who fall,
Light amid a world of shadows,
Dawn of God's design for all,
Chosen from eternal ages,
You alone of all our race,
By your Son's atoning merits
Were conceived in perfect grace.

Mother of the world's Redeemer,
Promised from the dawn of time:
How could one so highly favored
Share the guilt of Adam's crime?
Sun and moon and stars adorn you,
Sinless Eve, triumphant sign;
You it is who crushed the serpent,
Mary, pledge of life divine.

Earth below and highest heaven,
Praise the splendor of your state,
You who now are crowned in glory
Were conceived immaculate.

Hail, beloved of the Father,
Mother of his only Son,
Mystic bride of Love eternal,
Hail, O fair and spotless one!

PSALM 57   8-12

A great sign appeared in the sky, a woman clothed with the sun, with
the moon under her feet, and on her head a crown of twelve stars.
(Rv 12: 1)

Mary the Mother of God, conceived without sin, courageous partic-
ipant in the mystery of redemption wrought by her Son, loving
mother to all the world, is herself the song of salvation sung by all
the human race as the dawn of our own hope.

My heart is ready, O God,
my heart is ready.
I will sing, I will sing your praise.
Awake, my soul,
awake, lyre and harp,
I will awake the dawn.

I will thank you, Lord, among the peoples,
among the nations I will praise you
for your love reaches to the heavens
and your truth to the skies.

O God, arise above the heavens;
may your glory shine on earth!

Glory to the Father...

Word of God   Judith 15: 9-10

YOU ARE THE GLORY of
Jerusalem, the surpassing
joy of Israel; you are the splendid boast of our people.
With your own hand you have done all this; you have

done good to Israel, and God is pleased with what you have wrought. May you be blessed by the Lord Almighty forever and ever!

O sing a new song to the Lord!
(Ps 96: 1)

CANTICLE OF ZECHARIAH   (Text, back cover B)
Who is this that comes forth like the dawn, as beautiful as the moon, as resplendent as the sun? (Song 6: 10)

INTERCESSIONS

Encouraged by the faith of Mary, our Mother, we pray:

℟ Through the intercession of Mary, grant our prayer!

For those who hear only the dissonant clamor of despair:
– fill them with the new song of salvation. ℟

For those who see only the endless night of sin and death:
– awaken them to the day of salvation. ℟

For those who place their hope in you:
– reward their faith with joy. ℟

Personal intentions

Our Father…

God, the Father of lights, let the light of your face shine upon the darkness of our sin. Through the intercession of Mary, our Mother, free us from the shadows to which we cling and draw us into the light of your eternal kingdom, through Jesus Christ our Lord. Amen.

MASS

Saturday of the Sixteenth Week of the Year

Today, the prayers of the Votive Mass of the Blessed Virgin
Mary, given below, could be used.)

ENTRANCE ANTIPHON

Blessed are you, Virgin Mary, who carried the creator of all
things in your womb; you gave birth to your maker, and
remain for ever a virgin.

OPENING PRAYER

> God of mercy,
> give us strength.
> May we who honor the memory of the Mother of God
> rise above our sins and failings with the help of her
>   prayers.
> Grant this through our Lord Jesus Christ, your Son,
> who lives and reigns with you and the Holy Spirit,
> one God, for ever and ever.

● *This is the blood of the covenant which the Lord God
has made with you.* ●

A reading from
the Book of Exodus   24: 3-8

WHEN MOSES CAME to the
people and related all the
words and ordinances of the Lord, they all answered
with one voice, "We will do everything that the Lord has
told us." Moses then wrote down all the words of the
Lord and, rising early the next day, he erected at the foot
of the mountain an altar and twelve pillars for the
twelve tribes of Israel. Then, having sent certain young
men of the Israelites to offer holocausts and sacrifice
young bulls as peace offerings to the Lord, Moses took
half of the blood and put it in large bowls; the other half

he splashed on the altar. Taking the book of the covenant, he read it aloud to the people, who answered, "All that the Lord has said, we will heed and do." Then he took the blood and sprinkled it on the people, saying, "This is the blood of the covenant which the Lord has made with you in accordance with all these words of his." The word of the Lord.

———— • PSALM 50 • ————

℟ (14) **Offer to God a sacrifice of praise.**

God the Lord has spoken and summoned the earth,
    from the rising of the sun to its setting.
From Zion, perfect in beauty,
    God shines forth. ℟

"Gather my faithful ones before me,
    those who have made a covenant with me by
        sacrifice."
And the heavens proclaim his justice;
    for God himself is the judge. ℟

"Offer to God praise as your sacrifice
    and fulfill your vows to the Most High;
Then call upon me in time of distress;
    I will rescue you, and you shall glorify me." ℟

Alleluia. Receive and submit to the word planted in you; it can save your souls. Alleluia.

● *Let them both grow until the harvest time.* ●

A reading from
the holy Gospel according to Matthew   13: 24-30

JESUS PROPOSED to the crowds
another parable: "The reign

of God may be likened to a man who sowed good seed in his field. While everyone was asleep, his enemy came and sowed weeds through his wheat, and then made off. When the crop began to mature and yield grain, the weeds made their appearance as well. The owner's slaves came to him and said, 'Sir, did you not sow good seed in your field? Where are the weeds coming from?' He answered, 'I see an enemy's hand in this.' His slaves said to him, 'Do you want us to go out and pull them up?' 'No,' he replied, 'pull up the weeds and you might take the wheat along with them. Let them grow together until harvest; then at harvest time I will order the harvesters, first collect the weeds and bundle them up to burn, then gather the wheat into my barn.'"
The Gospel of the Lord.

PRAYER OVER THE GIFTS

    Lord,
    we honor the memory of the mother of your Son.
    May the sacrifice we share
    make of us an everlasting gift to you.
    Grant this through Christ our Lord.

COMMUNION ANTIPHON

The Almighty has done great things for me. Holy is his name. (Lk 1: 49)

PRAYER AFTER COMMUNION

    Lord,
    you give us the sacraments of eternal redemption.
    May we who honor the memory of the mother of
       your Son
    rejoice in the abundance of your grace
    and experience your unfailing help.
    We ask this through Christ our Lord.

• ————————————— •

MEDITATION OF THE DAY

The Blessed Virgin Mary,
the Weeds, and the Wheat

The crops come thronging from the ground.
The land is green with strength.
The harvests sing like confidence
In the ascetic earth.
Let there be no more patience
With your iron music, death:
Stand, continents, and wear the spring your crown!

The ox-eyed land,
The muted lakes,
The cloudy groves that praise you, Lady, with their
    blooms,
Fuse and destroy their lights
And burn them into gold for you, great Virgin,
Coining your honor in the glorious sun.

The skies speed up to meet you, and the seas
Swim you the silver of their crests.
If you delay to come, we'll see the meteors, by night,
Skimming before your way,
Lighting the time of death's dismay
In lights as lithe as animals.
And God will blaze your pathway with the incandescent
    stars.

But oh! Queen of all grace and counsel,
Cause of our joy, Oh Clement Virgin, come:
Show us those eyes as chaste as lightning,
Kinder than June and true as Scripture.
Heal with your looks the poisons of the universe,
And claim your Son's regenerate world!

FATHER THOMAS MERTON, O.C.S.O

Father Thomas Merton († 1968) was a Trappist monk and
a prolific author.

Prayer for the Evening

Vigil of the Seventeenth Sunday in Ordinary Time

Our God is a God who works wonders:
come, let us adore!

Glory to the Father, and to the Son,
and to the Holy Spirit, as it was in the beginning,
is now, and will be for ever. Amen. Alleluia!

HYMN   Meter: 87 87 D
This hymn can be sung to the tune used for
There's a Wideness in God's Mercy

Make God's deeds known to the peoples:
Tell out his exalted Name.
Praise the Lord, who has done great things;
All his works God's might proclaim.
Zion, lift your voice in singing;
For with you has come to dwell,
In your very midst the great and
Holy One of Israel.

CANTICLE   Revelation 15: 3-4

How great are God's signs, how mighty his wonders! (cf. Dn 3: 100)

Our God is a God of paradox. The mightiest of his works took place
in hiddenness: the incarnation of the Word, the defeat of death on
the cross, and the resurrection of Christ in glory. We see their power
clearly only through the eyes of faith, and yet we stake our lives on
this holy mystery of our salvation!

Mighty and wonderful are your works,
Lord God Almighty!
Righteous and true are your ways,
O King of the nations!

Who would dare refuse you honor,
or the glory due your name, O Lord?

Since you alone are holy,
all nations shall come
and worship in your presence.
Your mighty deeds are clearly seen.

___

Word of God   Hebrews 1: 2-3

I N THESE LAST DAYS, [God]
spoke to us through a son,
whom he made heir of all things and through whom he
created the universe, who is the refulgence of his glory,
the very imprint of his being, and who sustains all
things by his mighty word. When he had accomplished
purification from sins, he took his seat at the right hand
of the Majesty on high.

> *Blessed be the Lord, God of Israel,*
> *who alone works wonders.*
> (Ps 72: 18)

CANTICLE OF MARY   (Text, back cover A)
Blessed be the name of God for ever and ever, for wisdom and power
are his. (Dn 2: 20)

INTERCESSIONS

Let us pray to Jesus Christ our Savior who has conquered death by the power of the cross:

℟   Be mindful of your Church, O Lord.

Christ Jesus our Lord, stone rejected by the builders and
now made the cornerstone:
– make holy the living stones with which you build your
Temple. ℟

Christ Jesus our Lord, the faithful and true witness, first-born from the dead:
– enable your Church to bear vivid witness to you in the midst of the world. ℟

Christ Jesus our Lord, the first and the last, once dead and now alive for ever:
– bring to full maturity your life in all the baptized. ℟

Christ Jesus our Lord, lamp of God's city:
– enlighten the eyes of those who have died. ℟

Personal intentions

Our Father…

Grace be with all who love our Lord Jesus Christ in immortality. Amen. (Eph 6: 24)

MARIAN ANTIPHON (Text, page 25)

SAINTS
OF TODAY AND YESTERDAY

Holy angels, and all you beloved ones in heaven,
help me to thank my God.

BLESSED ALPHONSA MUTTATHUPANDATU
Virgin and Religious (1910-1946)

A native of India's Kerala State, Anna Muttathupandatu was raised in the eastern Catholic rite known as the Syro-Malabar rite. A Hindu friend of Anna was to recall that when on one occasion a boy prankishly pushed the two girls down against a fence Anna insisted on not seeking revenge, explaining, "If we forgive those who offend us, God will forgive our offenses." Overcoming her family's efforts to pressure her to marry, she entered a convent of Poor Clare nuns at the age of eighteen as a postulant, taking her final vows eight years later with the religious name Alphonsa. She participated in her order's teaching apostolate, but also suffered various physical ailments, of which she commented, "Let the Lord do with me what he wills… for the benefit of a world which is marching to its ruin." Sister Alphonsa saw suffering as her particular apostolate, observing, "A day without suffering is a day lost." She prayed that she might take upon herself the sufferings of others and offered her sufferings for others' intentions. Sister Alphonsa died on July 28, 1946.

> *Sacrifice is only love put into action.*
> Blessed Elizabeth of the Trinity

Word of God

for a Sunday

Luke 11: 1-13

"He will get up to give him whatever he needs because of his persistence." Nothing is clearer in the Gospels than the fact that perseverance pays. The Canaanite woman readily comes to mind, and she was not unique in pressing Christ for a healing. Christ in this Gospel and elsewhere strongly encourages this approach to God in prayer. Think of the parable of the woman and the unjust judge and also the woman who scours the house in search of the lost coin. "Great works are performed not by strength but by perseverance" (Samuel Johnson).

J. T.

■ Suggested Prayer of the Faithful ■

(Each local community should compose its own Universal Prayer, but may find inspiration in the texts proposed here.)

Let us offer our petitions to God with faith in his mercy, mindful of his promise that the one who asks will receive.

For the Church, that all members, aware of their call to holiness, may devote time each day to prayer and reflection on the truths Christ taught us in the "Our Father."

For the intentions of our Holy Father the Pope for growing unity between the churches of East and West.

That the leaders of nations may unite in a worldwide effort to provide daily bread for the hungry and starving.

That we may be open to the needs and requests of our nearest neighbors and ready to set aside thoughts of our own convenience for their sake.

For the grace of mutual forgiveness, that we may learn to overlook each other's offenses in a spirit of compassion and human solidarity.

That the Fatherhood of God may so permeate our lives and attitudes that we may come to see all people as our brothers and sisters and cherish them as such.

That the culture of life may prevail in our hearts, our families, our cities, our nation, and the entire world.

Heavenly Father, your Son has taught us to ask you for all our needs. Graciously hear our petitions, which we make in his holy name.

SUNDAY, JULY 29
Seventeenth Sunday in Ordinary Time

Prayer for the Morning

*Let everything that lives and that breathes
give praise to the Lord!*

*Glory to the Father, and to the Son,
and to the Holy Spirit, as it was in the beginning,
is now, and will be for ever. Amen. Alleluia!*

HYMN   Meter: 10 10 11 11
This hymn can be sung to the tune used for
O Worship the King

O praise ye the Lord! praise him in the height;
Rejoice in his word, ye angels of light;
Ye heavens adore him by whom ye were made,
And worship before him, in brightness arrayed.

O praise ye the Lord! thanksgiving and song
To him be outpoured all ages along:
For love in creation, for heaven restored,
For grace of salvation, O praise ye the Lord!

PSALM 150

Through Christ let us continually offer God a sacrifice of praise, that
is, the fruit of lips that confess his name. (cf. Heb 13: 15)

The Fathers of the Church speak of the eighth day of creation, the
final day which lies outside time, both Easter and Parousia. It is the
day when all things are made perfect. We keep Sunday holy by living
it as an anticipation of that glorious day.

Praise God in his holy place,
praise him in his mighty heavens.
Praise him for his powerful deeds,
praise his surpassing greatness.

O praise him with sound of trumpet,
praise him with lute and harp.
Praise him with timbrel and dance,
praise him with strings and pipes.

O praise him with resounding cymbals,
praise him with clashing of cymbals.
Let everything that lives and that breathes
give praise to the Lord. Alleluia!

Glory to the Father…

Word of God   2 Peter 3: 13-14

ACCORDING to his promise we await new heavens and a new earth in which righteousness dwells. Therefore, beloved, since you await these things, be eager to be found without spot or blemish before him, at peace.

Creation awaits with eager expectation
the revelation of the children of God!
(Rom 8: 19)

CANTICLE OF ZECHARIAH   (Text, back cover B)
God's plan for the fullness of times is to sum up all things in Christ, in heaven and on earth. (cf. Eph 1: 10)

INTERCESSIONS

God sends forth his Spirit and all things are created. Let us return our grateful praise:

℟   We praise you, O Lord, and we bless you!

You have brought your people to new life in Jesus Christ:
– grant us life to the full. ℟

You have filled the world with your presence:
– grant us the eyes of faith that we may see you in all
things. ℟

You have promised a new heaven and a new earth:
– make us eager in hope as we look forward to Christ's
return. ℟

Personal intentions

Our Father...

O God of all creation, you have set aside this day as a
memorial of the death and resurrection of your Son,
through whom all things are made new. Make this day a
foretaste of the life he has promised. Fill us with holy
longing for his return in glory. We ask this through the
same Lord Jesus Christ, who lives and reigns with you
and the Holy Spirit, one God for ever and ever. Amen.

MASS

Seventeenth Sunday in Ordinary Time

ENTRANCE ANTIPHON
God is in his holy dwelling; he will give a home to the lonely,
he gives power and strength to his people. (Ps 67: 6-7, 36)

GLORIA ———————————————————— page 226

OPENING PRAYER
God our Father and protector,
without you nothing is holy,
nothing has value.
Guide us to everlasting life
by helping us to use wisely
the blessings you have given to the world.
We ask this through our Lord Jesus Christ, your Son,
who lives and reigns with you and the Holy Spirit,
one God, for ever and ever.

God our Father,
open our eyes to see your hand at work
in the splendor of creation,
in the beauty of human life.
Touched by your hand our world is holy.
Help us to cherish the gifts that surround us,
to share your blessings with our brothers and sisters,
and to experience the joy of life in your presence.
We ask this through Christ our Lord.

● *Let not my Lord grow angry if I speak.* ●

A reading from
the Book of Genesis   18: 20-32

IN THOSE DAYS, the LORD said:
"The outcry against Sodom
and Gomorrah is so great, and their sin so grave, that
I must go down and see whether or not their actions
fully correspond to the cry against them that comes to
me. I mean to find out."

While Abraham's visitors walked on farther toward
Sodom, the LORD remained standing before Abraham.
Then Abraham drew nearer and said: "Will you sweep
away the innocent with the guilty? Suppose there were
fifty innocent people in the city; would you wipe out the
place, rather than spare it for the sake of the fifty innocent people within it? Far be it from you to do such a
thing, to make the innocent die with the guilty so that
the innocent and the guilty would be treated alike!
Should not the judge of all the world act with justice?"
The LORD replied, "If I find fifty innocent people in the
city of Sodom, I will spare the whole place for their
sake." Abraham spoke up again: "See how I am presuming to speak to my Lord, though I am but dust and

ashes! What if there are five less than fifty innocent people? Will you destroy the whole city because of those five?" He answered, "I will not destroy it, if I find forty-five there." But Abraham persisted, saying "What if only forty are found there?" He replied, "I will forbear doing it for the sake of the forty." Then Abraham said, "Let not my Lord grow impatient if I go on. What if only thirty are found there?" He replied, "I will forbear doing it if I can find but thirty there." Still Abraham went on, "Since I have thus dared to speak to my Lord, what if there are no more than twenty?" The LORD answered, "I will not destroy it, for the sake of the twenty." But he still persisted: "Please, let not my Lord grow angry if I speak up this last time. What if there are at least ten there?" He replied, "For the sake of those ten, I will not destroy it." The word of the Lord.

• PSALM 138 •

℟ (3a) **Lord, on the day I called for help, you answered me.**

I will give thanks to you, O LORD, with all my heart,
    for you have heard the words of my mouth;
    in the presence of the angels I will sing your praise;
I will worship at your holy temple
    and give thanks to your name. ℟

Because of your kindness and your truth;
    for you have made great above all things
    your name and your promise.
When I called you answered me;
    you built up strength within me. ℟

The LORD is exalted, yet the lowly he sees,
    and the proud he knows from afar.

Though I walk amid distress, you preserve me;
  against the anger of my enemies you raise your
    hand. ℟

Your right hand saves me.
  The LORD will complete what he has done for me;
your kindness, O LORD, endures forever;
  forsake not the work of your hands. ℟

● *God has brought you to life along with Christ, having forgiven us all our transgressions.* ●

A reading from
the Letter of Saint Paul to the Colossians   2: 12-14

BROTHERS AND SISTERS: You were buried with him in baptism, in which you were also raised with him through faith in the power of God, who raised him from the dead. And even when you were dead in transgressions and the uncircumcision of your flesh, he brought you to life along with him, having forgiven us all our transgressions; obliterating the bond against us, with its legal claims, which was opposed to us, he also removed it from our midst, nailing it to the cross.
The word of the Lord.

Alleluia, alleluia. You have received a Spirit of adoption, through which we cry, Abba, Father. Alleluia, alleluia.

● *Ask and you will receive.* ●

A reading from
the holy Gospel according to Luke   11: 1-13

JESUS WAS PRAYING in a certain place, and when he had finished, one of his disciples said to him, "Lord, teach us to pray just as John taught his disciples." He said to them, "When you pray, say:

Father, hallowed be your name,/ your kingdom come./ Give us each day our daily bread/ and forgive us our sins/ for we ourselves forgive everyone in debt to us,/ and do not subject us to the final test."

And he said to them, "Suppose one of you has a friend to whom he goes at midnight and says, 'Friend, lend me three loaves of bread, for a friend of mine has arrived at my house from a journey and I have nothing to offer him,' and he says in reply from within, 'Do not bother me; the door has already been locked and my children and I are already in bed. I cannot get up to give you anything.' I tell you, if he does not get up to give the visitor the loaves because of their friendship, he will get up to give him whatever he needs because of his persistence.

"And I tell you, ask and you will receive; seek and you will find; knock and the door will be opened to you. For everyone who asks, receives; and the one who seeks, finds; and to the one who knocks, the door will be opened. What father among you would hand his son a snake when he asks for a fish? Or hand him a scorpion when he asks for an egg? If you then, who are wicked, know how to give good gifts to your children, how much more will the Father in heaven give the Holy Spirit to those who ask him?"

The Gospel of the Lord.

CREDO ———————————————————— page 227

PRAYER OVER THE GIFTS

Lord,
receive these offerings
chosen from your many gifts.
May these mysteries make us holy

and lead us to eternal joy.
Grant this through Christ our Lord.

PREFACE OF SUNDAYS IN ORDINARY TIME ———— page 231

COMMUNION ANTIPHON

O bless the Lord, my soul, and remember all his kindness.
(Ps 102: 2)

Or:

Happy are those who show mercy; mercy shall be theirs.
Happy are the poor of heart, for they shall see God. (Mt 5: 7-8)

PRAYER AFTER COMMUNION

Lord,
we receive the sacrament
which celebrates the memory
of the death and resurrection of Christ your Son.
May this gift bring us closer to our eternal salvation.
We ask this through Christ our Lord.

D A Y   B Y   D A Y

Our Father

O God, how good you are to allow us to call you "our
Father"! Who am I that my Creator, my king, my sovereign
master, should allow me to call him "Father"? And not only
allow me to do so, but commands it. O God, how good you
are! How frequently I should remind myself throughout my
whole life of this most precious commandment. What gratitude, what joy, what love, and above all what confidence
it should inspire in me. And as you are my Father and my
God, how perfectly I should always hope in you. And
again – as you are so good to me – how good I ought to
be to others. It being your will to be my Father. Father to
all men. I ought unfailingly to feel like a loving brother
towards absolutely everyone, however wicked he may be.

I am filled with confusion, gratitude, trust, and unshakeable hope, a filial love for God and a fraternal love for men.

Our Father, our Father, teach me to have your name continually on my lips with Jesus, in him and through him, for it is my greatest good fortune to be able to say it.

Our Father, our Father, may I live and die saying "Our Father," and by my gratitude, love, and obedience be truly your loyal son, a son pleasing to your heart. Amen.

VENERABLE CHARLES DE FOUCAULD

Venerable Charles († 1916) was a desert hermit and the inspiration for the community known as the Little Brothers of Jesus.

Prayer for the Evening

Let us rejoice, sing praise, and give God glory!

**Glory to the Father, and to the Son,
and to the Holy Spirit, as it was in the beginning,
is now, and will be for ever. Amen. Alleluia!**

HYMN   Meter: 76 76 D

A city radiant as a bride
And bright with gold and gem,
A crystal river clear and wide,
The new Jerusalem;
A city wrought with wealth untold,
Her jeweled walls aflame
With green and amethyst and gold
And colors none can name.

A city ever new and fair,
The Lamb's eternal bride;
No suffering or grief is there
And every tear is dried.
There Christ prepares for us a place,
From sin and death restored,

And we shall stand before his face,
The ransomed of the Lord.

CANTICLE   Revelation 19: 1-7

At midnight, there was a cry, "Behold, the bridegroom! Come out to
meet him!" (Mt 25: 6)

Sunday is the day when we gather most explicitly and visibly as the
Church, the bride of Christ. Throughout the Bible, the final con-
summation of the world is seen as the profound communion of God
with all humanity. The intensity of that communion is captured in
the imagery of marriage. For that fulfillment we prepare ourselves
with anticipation and joy.

Salvation, glory, and power to our God, alleluia.
His judgments are honest and true! Alleluia, alleluia.

Sing praise to our God, all you his servants, alleluia.
All who worship him reverently, great and small!
Alleluia, alleluia.

The Lord our all-powerful God is King; alleluia.
Let us rejoice, sing praise, and give him glory!
Alleluia, alleluia.

The wedding feast of the Lamb has begun, alleluia.
And his bride is prepared to welcome him.
Alleluia, alleluia.

Word of God   Revelation 21: 9-10

ONE OF THE SEVEN ANGELS
came and said to me,
"Come here. I will show you the bride, the wife of the
Lamb." He took me in spirit to a great, high mountain
and showed me the holy city Jerusalem coming down
out of heaven from God.

Lord, you know that I love you. (Jn 21: 15)

CANTICLE OF MARY (Text, back cover A)
You shall be called "My Delight," and your land "Espoused." For the
Lord delights in you, and makes your land his spouse. (Is 62: 4)

INTERCESSIONS

God offers again and again the covenant of love.
In faith, let us pray:

℟   Hear us, O Lord!

For all those called to marriage:
– grant them a life of mutual respect, love, and fidelity
which will stand as a living sign of your abiding communion with humanity. ℟

For all those called to celibacy:
– grant them that single-hearted love for you that bears
fruit in a creative love for all people. ℟

For all those who prepare couples for marriage:
– grant them wisdom, conviction, and credibility
through their fidelity to their own life commitments. ℟

For all those who have gone before us to the wedding
feast of the Lamb:
– grant them the fullness of joy which you have
promised to your people. ℟

Personal intentions

Our Father...

*May grace, mercy, and peace be with us from God the
Father and Christ Jesus our Lord. Amen. (cf. 2 Tm 1: 2)*

MARIAN ANTIPHON (Text, page 25)

MONDAY, JULY 30
Saint Peter Chrysologus
Prayer for the Morning

Lift up your hearts! Let us lift them up to the Lord!

Glory to the Father... Alleluia!

HYMN

Meter: 76 76 D
This hymn can be sung to the tune used for
All Glory, Praise, and Honor

Light of the world, before thee
Our spirits prostrate fall;
We worship, we adore thee,
Thou Light, the life of all,
With thee is no forgetting
Of all thine hand hath made;
Thy rising hath no setting,
Thy sunshine hath no shade.

Light of the world, illumine
This darkened earth of thine,
Till everything that's human
Be filled with what's divine;
Till every tongue and nation,
From sin's dominion free,
Rise in the new creation
Which springs from love and thee.

PSALM 139   1-6, 9-12, 23-24

Let the Lord God show us what way we should take and what we
should do. (cf. Jer 42: 3)

To God, the darkest depths of the human heart are as clear as the
page of a book lying open in the sunlight. He knows us through and
through – and loves us as deeply as he knows us! Rather than hide
from him, let us put our life in the hands that fashioned us and allow
him to lead us in the path of life eternal.

O Lord, you search me and you know me,
you know my resting and my rising,
you discern my purpose from afar.
You mark when I walk or lie down,
all my ways lie open to you.

Before ever a word is on my tongue
you know it, O Lord, through and through.
Behind and before you besiege me,
your hand ever laid upon me.
Too wonderful for me, this knowledge,
too high, beyond my reach.

If I take the wings of the dawn
and dwell at the sea's furthest end,
even there your hand would lead me,
your right hand would hold me fast.

If I say: "Let the darkness hide me
and the light around me be night,"
even darkness is not dark for you
and the night is as clear as the day.

O search me, God, and know my heart.
O test me and know my thoughts.
See that I follow not the wrong path
and lead me in the path of life eternal.

Glory to the Father...

Word of God Isaiah 42: 16

I WILL LEAD THE BLIND on their journey; by paths unknown I will guide them. I will turn darkness into light before them, and make crooked ways straight. These things I do for them, and I will not forsake them.

*Straight are the paths of the Lord,
in them the just walk.* (Hos 14: 10)

CANTICLE OF ZECHARIAH (Text, back cover B)
I am the Lord, your God, who grasp your right hand; it is I who say
to you, "Fear not, I will help you." (Is 41: 13)

INTERCESSIONS

God searches us and knows us. Let us lift up to him our
prayers, saying:

℟ In your love, remember us.

Our ways lie open to you, O Lord:
– make your ways our own. ℟

Our words are known to you before we speak, O Lord:
– make each word a work of kindness done in your
name. ℟

You will not forsake us, O Lord:
– keep us from forsaking you. ℟

You stir your Church to life by the power of your word:
– send your people eloquent preachers after the example
of Saint Peter Chrysologus. ℟

Personal intentions

Our Father...

O God our Father, you sent your only Son, our Lord
Jesus Christ, to be our way, our truth, and our life.
At this morning hour, we lift our hearts to you in prayer
and ask that you will guide us through this day according
to your will, through the same Christ our Lord. Amen.

MASS

Monday of the Seventeenth Week of the Year

PETER CHRYSOLOGUS *Optional memorial*

● *Saint Peter was born about the year 380 in Imola,
Emilia, and there entered the priesthood. He was elect-*

ed bishop of Ravenna in 424 and instructed his flock by his learned sermons and writings. He died around the year 450. ●

ENTRANCE ANTIPHON

The mouth of the just man utters wisdom, and his tongue speaks what is right; the law of his God is in his heart. (Ps 36: 30-31)

OPENING PRAYER

Father,
you made Peter Chrysologus
an outstanding preacher of your incarnate Word.
May the prayers of Saint Peter help us to cherish
the mystery of our salvation
and make its meaning clear in our love for others.
Grant this through our Lord Jesus Christ, your Son,
who lives and reigns with you and the Holy Spirit,
one God, for ever and ever.

● *This people has committed a grave sin, making themselves gods of gold.* ●

A reading from
the Book of Exodus   32: 15-24, 30-34

MOSES TURNED and came down the mountain with the two tablets of the commandments in his hands, tablets that were written on both sides, front and back; tablets that were made by God, having inscriptions on them that were engraved by God himself. Now, when Joshua heard the noise of the people shouting, he said to Moses, "That sounds like a battle in the camp." But Moses answered, "It does not sound like cries of victory, nor does it sound like cries of defeat; the sounds that I hear are cries of revelry." As he drew near the camp, he saw the calf and the dancing. With that, Moses' wrath flared up, so that he threw the tablets down and broke them on the base of the mountain. Taking the calf they had made, he fused it in the fire and then ground it down to powder, which he scattered on the water and made the Israelites drink.

Moses asked Aaron, "What did this people ever do to you that you should lead them into so grave a sin?" Aaron replied, "Let not my lord be angry. You know well enough how prone the people are to evil. They said to me, 'Make us a god to be our leader; as for the man Moses who brought us out of the land of Egypt, we do not know what has happened to him.' So I told them, 'Let anyone who has gold jewelry take it off.' They gave it to me, and I threw it into the fire, and this calf came out."

On the next day Moses said to the people, "You have committed a grave sin. I will go up to the Lord, then; perhaps I may be able to make atonement for your sin." So Moses went back to the Lord and said, "Ah, this people has indeed committed a grave sin in making a god of gold for themselves! If you would only forgive their sin! If you will not, then strike me out of the book that you have written." The Lord answered, "Him only who has sinned against me will I strike out of my book. Now, go and lead the people whither I have told you. My angel will go before you. When it is time for me to punish, I will punish them for their sin."
The word of the Lord.

━━━━━━ • PSALM 106 • ━━━━━━

℟ (1) **Give thanks to the Lord for he is good.**

Or: Alleluia.

They made a calf in Horeb
    and adored a molten image;
They exchanged their glory
    for the image of a grass-eating bullock. ℟

They forgot the God who had saved them,
  who had done great deeds in Egypt,
Wondrous deeds in the land of Ham,
  terrible things at the Red Sea. ℟

Then he spoke of exterminating them,
  but Moses, his chosen one,
Withstood him in the breach
  to turn back his destructive wrath. ℟

Alleluia. The Father gave us birth by his message of truth, that we might be as the first fruits of his creation. Alleluia.

  ● *When the seed grows it is the biggest shrub of all and the birds of the air come and nest in its branches.* ●

A reading from
the holy Gospel according to Matthew   13: 31-35

JESUS PROPOSED TO THE CROWDS another parable: "The reign of God is like a mustard seed which someone took and sowed in his field. It is the smallest seed of all, yet when full-grown it is the largest of plants. It becomes so big a shrub that the birds of the sky come and build their nests in its branches."

He offered them still another image: "The reign of God is like yeast which a woman took and kneaded into three measures of flour. Eventually the whole mass of dough began to rise." All these lessons Jesus taught the crowds in the form of parables. He spoke to them in parables only, to fulfill what had been said through the prophet:

"I will open my mouth in parables,/ I will announce what has lain hidden since the creation of the world."
The Gospel of the Lord.

Prayer over the gifts

>   Lord,
>   accept our sacrifice on this feast of Saint Peter
>   Chrysologus,
>   and following his example
>   may we give you our praise
>   and offer you all we have.
>   Grant this in the name of Jesus the Lord.

Communion antiphon

The Lord has put his faithful servant in charge of his household, to give them their share of bread at the proper time. (Lk 12: 42)

Prayer after communion

>   God our Father,
>   Christ the living bread renews us.
>   Let Christ our teacher instruct us
>   that on this feast of Saint Peter Chrysologus
>   we may learn your truth
>   and practice it in love.
>   We ask this through Christ our Lord.

MEDITATION OF THE DAY

The Mustard Seed and the Church

Christ became all things in order to restore all men through himself. Christ as man received the grain of mustard seed, that is, Christ as man received that kingdom of God which he as God had always possessed. He cast the seed into his garden, that is, into his spouse, the Church. He is often mindful of this garden in the Canticle of Canticles, when he speaks of "a garden enclosed." The Church is the garden, spread through her worship over all the world by the plow of the Gospel. She is a garden enclosed by the goads of her discipline, and cleared of all rank weeds by the labor of the apostles. She is a garden beautiful to see because of the young trees of the faithful, the lilies of the virgins, the roses of the martyrs, the verdure of the confessors. She is fragrant with unfailing flowers.

Accordingly, Christ cast this grain of mustard seed into his garden, that is, because of the promise of his kingdom. The seed had its roots in the patriarchs, was born in the prophets, and grew in the apostles. In the Church it became a great tree, and through the gifts it produced numerous branches.

SAINT PETER CHRYSOLOGUS

Saint Peter Chrysologus († 450) was the archbishop of Ravenna, Italy, and is a Doctor of the Church.

Prayer for the Evening

Give thanks to the Lord for he is good;
for his love endures for ever!

Glory to the Father, and to the Son,
and to the Holy Spirit, as it was in the beginning,
is now, and will be for ever. Amen. Alleluia!

HYMN
Meter: LM
This hymn can be sung to the tune used for
Around the Throne a Glorious Band

O Dayspring of the long sought day,
Cold, cold the prison where we lay
Until you broke the gates of sin
To free the weary ones within.

O Dawn awaited more than dawn,
Deep, deep the pit where we had gone
Until through death you did descend
To put all exile to an end.

O God, still hid in glory bright,
We yearn in praise for morning's light;
We sing of what we long to see:
Your Face, O holy One in Three.

PSALM 107   1-3, 10-16

He has sent me to proclaim liberty to captives, to let the oppressed go free. (cf. Lk 4: 18)

The notion that one gains freedom by rebelling against God has been a popular illusion since Eden. The paradox of the Gospel is that we are set free from the chains of our own making by choosing to yoke ourselves to Christ, who bursts our bonds by his own death and resurrection.

"**O** give thanks to the Lord for he is good;
for his love endures for ever."

Let them say this, the Lord's redeemed,
whom he redeemed from the hand of the foe
and gathered from far-off lands,
from east and west, north and south.

Some lay in darkness and in gloom,
prisoners in misery and chains,
having defied the words of God
and spurned the counsels of the Most High.
He crushed their spirit with toil;
they stumbled; there was no one to help.

Then they cried to the Lord in their need
and he rescued them from their distress.
He led them forth from darkness and gloom
and broke their chains to pieces.

Let them thank the Lord for his goodness,
for the wonders he does for men:
for he bursts the gates of bronze
and shatters the iron bars.

Glory to the Father…

Word of God   Matthew 11: 28-30

COME TO ME, all you who
labor and are burdened,

and I will give you rest. Take my yoke upon you and learn from me, for I am meek and humble of heart; and you will find rest for yourselves. For my yoke is easy, and my burden light.

Where the Spirit of the Lord is, there is freedom.
(2 Cor 3: 17)

CANTICLE OF MARY   (Text, back cover A)
He has sent me to proclaim liberty to the captives and release to the prisoners. (Is 61: 1)

INTERCESSIONS

For freedom Christ set us free. (Gal 5: 1)
In grateful trust, let us pray to him:

℟   We cry to you, O Lord, in our need.

For those who are in prison,
– that they may learn the way to true freedom. ℟

For those who are entrapped in addiction,
– that they may find the road to recovery. ℟

For those who live in defiance of your word,
– that they may discover the freedom of the Gospel. ℟

For those who have been sent to minister in your name
to all who are captive in body or spirit,
– that they may be rewarded. ℟

Personal intentions

Our Father…

To the one who is able to keep us from stumbling and to present us unblemished and exultant, in the presence of his glory, to the only God, our savior, through Jesus Christ our Lord be glory, majesty, power, and authority from ages past, now, and for ages to come. Amen. (cf. Jude 1: 24-25)

MARIAN ANTIPHON   (Text, page 25)

Saints
OF TODAY AND YESTERDAY

Behold me, O my Lord and God, before this altar,
on which you reside night and day.

Blessed Simon of Lipnicza
Priest and Religious († 1482)

As a young man, Simon, a student in Poland's University of Cracow, had preserved his purity through devotion to the Blessed Virgin Mary. Upon hearing the preaching of the Franciscan Saint John Capistrano, he was inspired to join the Franciscan Friars Minor. Ordained a priest, he converted many with his sermons that habitually ended with his asking the congregation to pronounce the name of Jesus three times in an effort to inculcate devotion to the Holy Name. His preaching was also characterized by his clear explanations of the Scriptures. As a priest his continued Marian devotion took the form of several hours spent daily in prayer to the Blessed Virgin, including the Office of Our Lady and the rosary. After returning from a pilgrimage to the Holy Land, he resumed his labors in Cracow where he was later made provincial of his order. When in 1482 the plague struck his city, he ministered to the dying victims until he himself contracted the fatal illness.

In the most Blessed Sacrament we can converse at pleasure with Jesus, we can open our hearts to him, we can lay our wants before him, and we can ask him for his graces.
Saint Alphonsus Liguori

TUESDAY, JULY 31
Saint Ignatius of Loyola

Prayer for the Morning

Come, let us seek God with all our hearts.

Glory to the Father, and to the Son,
and to the Holy Spirit, as it was in the beginning,
is now, and will be for ever. Amen. Alleluia!

HYMN   Meter: LM
This hymn can be sung to the tune used for
Creator of the Stars of Night

I love you, O my Lord most high,
For first your love has captured me;
I seek no other liberty:
Bound by your love, I shall be free.

May memory no thought suggest
But shall to your pure glory tend,
May understanding find no rest,
Except in you, its only end.

All mine is yours: say but the word,
Say what you will, it shall be done;
I know your love, most gracious Lord,
I know you seek my good alone.

Apart from you, nothing can be,
So grant me this, my only wish,
To love you, Lord, eternally,
You give me all in giving this.

PSALM 119   17-24

I will put my law within them, and I will write it on their hearts;
and I will be their God, and they shall be my people. (Jer 31: 33)

Following Christ in obedience to God's will discerned in prayer was central to Saint Ignatius' spirituality. The law of the new covenant is an expression of God's love for us. It prescribes peace, justice, and love in place of the violence, oppression, and alienation we tend to create when we fail to listen to God's voice speaking in the depths of our heart.

Bless your servant and I shall live
and obey your word.
Open my eyes that I may see
the wonders of your law.

I am a pilgrim on the earth;
show me your commands.
My soul is ever consumed
as I long for your decrees.

You threaten the proud, the accursed,
who turn from your commands.
Relieve me from scorn and contempt
for I do your will.

Though princes sit plotting against me
I ponder on your rulings.
Your will is my delight;
your statutes are my counsellors.

Glory to the Father…

Word of God   Deuteronomy 30: 11-14

THIS COMMAND WHICH I en-
join on you today is not too
mysterious and remote for you. It is not up in the sky,
that you should say, 'Who will go up in the sky to get it
for us and tell us of it, that we may carry it out?' Nor is
it across the sea, that you should say, 'Who will cross
the sea to get it for us and tell us of it, that we may carry
it out?' No, it is something very near to you, already in

your mouths and in your hearts; you have only to carry it out.

Take to heart these words which I enjoin on you today.
(Dt 6: 6)

CANTICLE OF ZECHARIAH   (Text, back cover B)
Come to me heedfully, listen, that you may have life. (Is 55: 3)

INTERCESSIONS

To God who directs all our ways toward the coming of his kingdom, we pray through the intercession of Saint Ignatius:

℟   Your word is a lamp for our steps.

Guide us, O Lord, in the way of your Word,
– that today we may follow where you lead us. ℟

Guide us, O Lord, in the way of your truth,
– that today we may choose wisely among the many ideas the media present to us. ℟

Guide us, O Lord, in the way of your love,
– that today we may treat those we meet as you have treated us. ℟

Personal intentions

Our Father…

O Lord our God, you poured forth into your Church a spirit of renewal in prayer and life through the work of Saint Ignatius and the Society of Jesus. Grant us the spirit of discernment so that we may hear the still, small voice of your Word speaking in the depths of our heart, and, hearing, may obey. We ask this through our Lord Jesus Christ your Son, who lives and reigns with you and the Holy Spirit, one God for ever and ever. Amen.

MASS

Tuesday of the Seventeenth Week of the Year

IGNATIUS OF LOYOLA   *Memorial*

● *Saint Ignatius was born in 1491 in Loyola, Cantabria. He spent his early years at court and as a soldier. Later he was converted to God and undertook theological studies in Paris where he attracted his first followers. Afterwards in Rome he joined them together as the first members of the Society of Jesus. He exercised a most fruitful apostolate both by his written works and in the training of his disciples who won great praise for their renewal of the Church. He died in Rome in 1556.* ●

ENTRANCE ANTIPHON

At the name of Jesus every knee must bend, in heaven, on earth, and under the earth; every tongue should proclaim to the glory of God the Father: Jesus Christ is Lord. (Phil 2: 10-11)

OPENING PRAYER

Father,
you gave Saint Ignatius of Loyola to your Church
to bring greater glory to your name.
May we follow his example on earth
and share the crown of life in heaven.
We ask this through our Lord Jesus Christ, your Son,
who lives and reigns with you and the Holy Spirit,
one God, for ever and ever.

● *The Lord God spoke to Moses face to face.* ●

A reading from
the Book of Exodus   33: 7-11; 34: 5-9, 28

THE TENT, which was called
the meeting tent, Moses

used to pitch at some distance away, outside the camp. Anyone who wished to consult the Lord would go to this meeting tent outside the camp. Whenever Moses went out to the tent, the people would all rise and stand at the entrance of their own tents, watching Moses until he entered the tent. As Moses entered the tent, the column of cloud would come down and stand at its entrance while the Lord spoke with Moses. On seeing the column of cloud stand at the entrance of the tent, all the people would rise and worship at the entrance of their own tents. The Lord used to speak to Moses face to face, as one man speaks to another. Moses would then return to the camp, but his young assistant, Joshua, son of Nun, would not move out of the tent.

Moses invoked the name of the Lord who stood with him there and proclaimed his name, "Lord." Thus the Lord passed before him and cried out, "The Lord, the Lord, a merciful and gracious God, slow to anger and rich in kindness and fidelity, continuing his kindness for a thousand generations, and forgiving wickedness and crime and sin; yet not declaring the guilty guiltless, but punishing children and grandchildren to the third and fourth generation for their fathers' wickedness!" Moses at once bowed down to the ground in worship. Then he said, "If I find favor with you, O Lord, do come along in our company. This is indeed a stiff-necked people; yet pardon our wickedness and sins, and receive us as your own."

So Moses stayed there with the Lord for forty days and forty nights, without eating any food or drinking any water, and he wrote on the tablets the words of the covenant, the ten commandments.

The word of the Lord.

—— • PSALM 103 • ——

℟ (8) **The Lord is kind and merciful.**

The Lord secures justice
  and the rights of all the oppressed.
He has made known his ways to Moses,
  and his deeds to the children of Israel. ℟

Merciful and gracious is the Lord,
  slow to anger and abounding in kindness.
He will not always chide,
  nor does he keep his wrath forever. ℟

Not according to our sins does he deal with us,
  nor does he requite us according to our crimes.
For as the heavens are high above the earth,
  so surpassing is his kindness toward those who fear
    him. ℟

As far as the east is from the west,
  so far has he put our transgressions from us.
As a father has compassion on his children,
  so the Lord has compassion on those who fear
    him. ℟

Alleluia. Teach me your paths, my God, and lead me in
your truth. Alleluia.

  ● *Just as the weeds are gathered up and burnt in the
  fire, so it will be at the end of time.* ●

**A reading from
the holy Gospel according to Matthew**   13: 35-43

JESUS DISMISSED THE CROWDS
and went home. His disciples
came to him with the request, "Explain to us the parable

of the weeds in the field." He said in answer: "The farmer sowing good seed is the Son of Man; the field is the world, the good seed the citizens of the kingdom. The weeds are the followers of the evil one and the enemy who sowed them is the devil. The harvest is the end of the world, while the harvesters are the angels. Just as weeds are collected and burned, so it will be at the end of the world. The Son of Man will dispatch his angels to collect from his kingdom all who draw others to apostasy, and all evildoers. The angels will hurl them into the fiery furnace where they will wail and grind their teeth. Then the saints will shine like the sun in their Father's kingdom. Let everyone heed what he hears!"

The Gospel of the Lord.

PRAYER OVER THE GIFTS

Lord God,
be pleased with the gifts we present to you
at this celebration in honor of Saint Ignatius.
Make us truly holy by this Eucharist
which you give us as the source of all holiness.
We ask this in the name of Jesus the Lord.

COMMUNION ANTIPHON

I have come to bring fire to the earth. How I wish it were already blazing! (Lk 12: 49)

PRAYER AFTER COMMUNION

Lord,
may the sacrifice of thanksgiving which we have offered
on the feast of Saint Ignatius
lead us to the eternal praise of your glory.
Grant this through Christ our Lord.

MEDITATION OF THE DAY

The Weeds the Enemy Sows

Regarding the first part, the general procedure of the enemy with those who love God our Lord and are beginning to serve him is to bring in hindrances and obstacles. This is the first of the weapons with which he tries to inflict wounds. Thus, "How are you going to live your whole life in such great penance, deprived of relatives, friends, and possessions, in such a lonely life, without even some slight respite? You can be saved in other ways without such great risks." He has us believe that as a result of the hardships he sets before us we are to live a life longer and more drawn-out than ever a human being lived; he does not get us to think about the abundant comforts and consolations normally given by the Lord if the new servants of the Lord shatter these difficulties by choosing to desire to suffer with their Creator and Lord.

Then the enemy tries with the second weapon, that is boasting or vainglory, giving a person to understand that there is much goodness or holiness within them, and setting them in a higher place than they deserve....

If you look properly you will clearly understand that [your] desires of serving Christ our Lord are not from you, but given by the Lord, and then you will say, "The Lord gives me increased desires of serving him, the Lord himself!" By making his gift known you are giving praise to him, and your exultation is in fact in him and not in yourself, since you are not attributing that grace to yourself.

SAINT IGNATIUS OF LOYOLA

Saint Ignatius of Loyola († 1556) was the founder of the Society of Jesus.

Prayer for the Evening

Let us praise the Lord in all his saints!

Glory to the Father, and to the Son,
and to the Holy Spirit, as it was in the beginning,
is now, and will be for ever. Amen. Alleluia!

HYMN   Meter: 87 87 87

Christ is made the sure foundation,
Christ the head and corner-stone,
Chosen of the Lord, and precious,
Binding all the Church in one;
Holy Zion's help for ever,
And her confidence alone.

All that dedicated city,
Dearly loved of God on high,
In exultant jubilation
Pours perpetual melody;
God the One in Three adoring
In glad hymns eternally.

PSALM *127*

Every house is founded by someone, but the founder of all is God.
(Heb 3: 4)

At God's bidding and with God's help, Saint Ignatius founded a
religious order of immense influence and peopled it with many
spiritual sons. All of us are given a spiritual "house" to build, to live
in, and to hand on to future generations: what will yours look like?

If the Lord does not build the house,
in vain do its builders labor;
if the Lord does not watch over the city,
in vain does the watchman keep vigil.

In vain is your earlier rising,
your going later to rest,
you who toil for the bread you eat:
when he pours gifts on his beloved while they slumber.

Truly sons are a gift from the Lord,
a blessing, the fruit of the womb.
Indeed the sons of youth
are like arrows in the hand of a warrior.

O the happiness of the man
who has filled his quiver with these arrows!
He will have no cause for shame
when he disputes with his foes in the gateways.

Glory to the Father…

Word of God   1 Corinthians 3: 10-13

ACCORDING TO THE GRACE of
God given to me, like a wise
master builder I laid a foundation, and another is building upon it. But each one must be careful how he builds
upon it, for no one can lay a foundation other than the
one that is there, namely, Jesus Christ.

Christ Jesus is the cornerstone.

CANTICLE OF MARY   (Text, back cover A)
We know that if our earthly dwelling, a tent, should be destroyed, we
have a building from God, a dwelling not made with hands, eternal
in heaven. (2 Cor 5: 1)

INTERCESSIONS

The Scriptures paint a portrait of God as designer and
builder of a home for all peoples, and of Jesus as
carpenter. Through the intercession of Saint Ignatius of
Loyola, let us pray:

℟   Build up your house, O Lord.

You have called us to encourage one another and build one another up:
– make us skilled laborers in the art of mutual support. ℟

You have granted us different gifts for the upbuilding of your Body, the Church, in love:
– give us generous hearts for the works of mutual service. ℟

You have gone before us to prepare a place for us among the many dwellings that make up your Father's house:
– keep us strong in hope and fidelity as we await your return in glory. ℟

You have given us a vision of the great city to come:
– bring our dead to dwell with you in glory. ℟

Personal intentions

Our Father…

May the all-powerful God protect us from all evil and bring us to life everlasting! Amen.

MARIAN ANTIPHON   (Text, page 25)

SAINTS
OF TODAY AND YESTERDAY

You have redeemed us, O Lord, in your blood.

BLESSED MARY OF SAINT EUPHRASIA PELLETIER
Virgin and Religious (1796-1868)

Born in Vendée, France, Rose Virginie Pelletier at the age of eighteen entered a congregation devoted to the care of fallen women and girls, that of Our Lady of Charity of the Refuge. She took the religious name Mary of Saint Euphrasia. Inspired with particular fervor to fulfill the congregation's fourth vow to work for the salvation of souls, she humbly and patiently overcame opposition to centralize the governance of the congregation which now was given a new name – the Institute of Our Lady of Charity of the Good Shepherd – with Mother Euphrasia as the first superior general. Working to spread the institute around the world, she told her sisters, "I do not wish any longer to be called French. I am Italian, English, German, Spanish; I am American, African, Indian; every country is my own where there are souls to be saved." She saw knowledge of the faith through the learning of the catechism as integral to the moral reformation of fallen girls. As for her own spiritual life, she said of the Eucharist, "Holy Communion is my very life."

*What are we in this world for,
if not to love God and help to save souls?*
Blessed Mary of Saint Euphrasia Pelletier

ACKNOWLEDGMENTS

The English translation of the Order of Mass, opening prayers, prayers over the gifts, prayers after communion, prefaces, and antiphons from *The Roman Missal* © 1973, International Committee on English in the Liturgy, Inc. (ICEL); excerpts from the English translation of *The Liturgy of the Hours* © 1974, ICEL.

Mass readings for Sundays and solemnities, Copyright © 1970, 1997, 1998, Confraternity of Christian Doctrine, Inc., Washington, D.C. Mass readings for weekdays, Copyright © 1970 Confraternity of Christian Doctrine, Inc., Washington, D.C.

Readings for morning and evening prayers from the *New American Bible* © 1970, Confraternity of Christian Doctrine, Inc., Washington, D.C. All rights reserved. No part of this work may be reproduced or transmitted in any form or by any means, electronic or mechanical, including photo-copying, recording or by any information storage and retrieval system, without permission in writing from the copyright owner.

Psalm Texts (except Psalm 95) for morning and evening prayers from *The Psalms: A New Translation* © 1963 by The Grail, England.

The English translation of some psalm responses, some alleluia and Gospel verses, and the Lenten Gospel Acclamations, some summaries, and the titles and conclusion of the readings, from the *Lectionary for Mass* © 1968, 1981, 1997, International Committee on English in the Liturgy, Inc., Washington, D.C. All rights reserved.

The poetic English translation of the sequences of the Roman Missal are taken from the *Roman Missal* approved by the National Conference of Catholic Bishops of the United States © 1964, by the National Catholic Welfare Conference, Inc. All rights reserved.

Excerpted from *Table Blessings: Mealtime Prayers Throughout the Year* by Brother Victor-Antoine d'Avila-Latourrette. © 1994 by Ave Maria Press, P.O. Box 248, Notre Dame, Indiana, 46556, USA. Used with permission.

A Prayerbook of Favorite Litanies, compiled by Fr. Albert J. Hebert, s.m. © 1985, Tan Books and Publishers, Rockford, IL.

For the Fruits of This Creation, text: 84 84 88 84, by Fred Pratt Green. © 1970, Hope Publishing Company, Carol Stream, IL 60188. All rights reserved. Used by permission.

Marthe Robin, The Cross and the Joy, by Raymond Peyret. © 1983, Alba House, New York. Used with permission.

The formatting of some texts may be altered in keeping with guidelines required by the NCCB/USCC.

FIRST WORDS	© INFORMATION	PAGE
O Dayspring...	Genevieve Glen, OSB, b. 1945. © 1998, Benedictine Nuns, Abbey of St. Walburga, Virginia Dale, CO 80536-8942. Used with permission.	409
O God, our help...	Isaac Watts, 1674-1748. Public domain.	30
O love of God...	Horatius Bonar, 1861, slightly alt. Public domain.	272
O Mother of almighty...	© Stanbrook Abbey, Callow End, Worcester WR2 4TD. Used by permission.	104
O my soul...	Adap. Hymns Ancient and Modern, 1861. Public domain.	92, 253
O praise ye the Lord...	Henry Williams Baker, 1821-1877. Public domain.	391
O Son of God...	Anna Hope, 1889-1941, alt. 1978. Agent: Board of Publications, The Lutheran Church in America.	261
O Splendor, Glory...	Blessed by your sacrifice. Jeanne Frolick, SFCC. © 1979, 1982, OCP Publications.	67
Our God is love...	Thomas Cotterill, 1779-1823, alt. Public domain.	283
Praise the Lord...	Anonymous; Foundling Hospital Collection, 1796; Edward Osler, 1798-1863. Public domain.	34
Rejoice, the Lord...	Charles Wesley, 1707-1788. Public domain.	201
Rejoice, you righteous...	Isaac Watts, 1674-1748, slightly alt. Public domain.	330
Remember, Lord...	Henry Williams Baker, 1861. Public domain.	148
See, the streams...	Glorious things of thee are spoken; John Newton, 1779. Public domain.	294
Sing we of the blessed...	Text: George B. Timms. From English Praise. © Oxford University Press. Used by permission. All rights reserved.	298
Tall stands the Tree...	Genevieve Glen, OSB, b. 1945. © 2000, Benedictine Nuns, Abbey of St. Walburga, Virginia Dale, CO 80536-8942. Used with permission.	130
Thanks be to God...	Cornelius Becker, 1561-1604; tr. by Daniel G. Reuning, b. 1935. © 1972 by GIA Publications, Inc., Chicago, Illinois. All rights reserved. Used with permission.	265
The pilgrim church...	Words: Timothy Dudley-Smith. © 1993 by Hope Publishing Co., Carol Stream, IL 60188. All rights reserved. Used by permission.	213
The rocks would shout...	Text: Thomas H. Troeger. From Borrowed Light. © 1994, Oxford University Press, Inc. Used by permission. All rights reserved.	352
The works of the Lord...	Words: Christopher Idle. © 1982, Jubilate Hymns Ltd. Admin. by Hope Publishing Co., Carol Stream, IL 60188. All rights reserved. Used by permission.	334
This world, my God...	Hamish Swanston. © 1971, Faber Music Ltd.	220
Upon the heights...	Genevieve Glen, OSB, b. 1945. © 1999, Benedictine Nuns, Abbey of St. Walburga, Virginia Dale, CO 80536-8942. Used with permission.	209
We plow the fields...	Matthias Claudius, 1740-1815; tr. by Jane Montgomery Campbell, 1817-1878. Public domain.	53
We sing for all...	Words: Carl P. Daw, Jr. © 1994 by Hope Publishing Co., Carol Stream, IL 60188. All rights reserved. Used by permission.	171
We walk by faith...	Henry Alford, 1810-1871, alt. Public domain.	64, 276
When from bondage...	Text: Delores Dufner, OSB. © 1984, 1988, 1996 by the Sisters of St. Benedict, 104 Chapel Lane, St. Joseph, MN 56374-0220. Used by permission.	341
When God restored...	Isaac Watts, 1674-1748. Public domain.	367
When Thomas first...	O filii et filiae; Jean Tisserand, b. 1494; tr. by John M. Neale, 1818-1866, alt. Public domain.	57
Word of God...	James Quinn, SJ. © 1969, James Quinn, SJ. Geoffrey Chapman, Continuum.	320

MAGNIFICAT®

Publisher: **Pierre-Marie Dumont**

Editor-in-Chief: **Peter John Cameron**, O.P.

Senior Editor: **Romanus Cessario**, O.P.

Editor for Daily Offices: **Sr. Genevieve Glen**, O.S.B.

Contributors: **James Turro, Michael Morris**, O.P.,
Cardinal Bernard Law, Sr. Mary Timothea Elliott, R.S.M., **James Monti,
Sr. Mary Thomas Noble**, O.P., **and Sr. Mary Lucy Chmura**, O.P.

Assistant to the Editorial Staff: **Violaine Seydoux**

Assistant to the Editor: **Catherine Kolpak**

Administrative Assistant: **Jeanne Shanahan**

Managing Editor: **Frédérique Chatain**

First Assistant: **Julia Schmidt** Assistant: **Diaga Seck**

Cover and Inset: **Solange Bosdevesy**

Proofreaders: **Janet Chevrier, Sr. Myriam-Therese O'Hanrahan**, C.P.,
and Sr. Mary Paul Thomas Maertz, O.P.

LETTERS TO THE EDITOR: MAGNIFICAT – Dunwoodie
201 Seminary Avenue, Yonkers, New York 10704-1896
CUSTOMER SERVICE Tel.: **1-800-317-6689 or 1-301-853-6600**

MAGNIFICAT (ISSN 1521-5172) is published monthly with an additional Holy
Week issue in the spring and a Christmas issue in December by MAGNIFICAT
USA LLC, 751 East Gude Drive, Rockville MD 20850-1356. Periodicals
Postage Paid at Rockville, Maryland, and at additional mailing offices.
Pierre-Marie Dumont: Manager; Philippe Thiout: Financial Officer. The
annual subscription rate is US $39.95; single-copy price is US $5.95.
Circulation records are maintained at FULFILLMENT MANAGEMENT, 751 East
Gude Drive, Rockville MD 20850-1356. POSTMASTER: send address
changes to MAGNIFICAT, PO Box 91, Spencerville MD 20868-9978. Original
Concept: P.-M. Dumont. MAGNIFICAT, copyright 2001 by MAGNIFICAT USA
LLC. Printed in France by MAULDE ET RENOU.
In the United States, the title MAGNIFICAT is used with the kind permission of
MAGNIFICAT® *A Ministry To Catholic Women*.
Published with the approval of the Committee on the Liturgy, National
Conference of Catholic Bishops. Published with ecclesiastical permission.

CONTENTS JULY 2001 / VOL. 3, No. 5

The Meeting

Illustration: *The Meeting of Joachim and Anne at the Golden Gate.* 1306. Part of a fresco cycle by Giotto in the Scrovegni (Arena) Chapel, Padua, Italy.
Text: Michael Morris, O.P.

*I*t is a rare sight in Christian art, a husband and wife kissing. The meeting of Joachim and Anne at the Golden Gate of Jerusalem is a scene of extreme rejoicing for it is intimately connected to the birth of the Virgin Mary, destined in time to be the

Mother of God. But the story which is depicted in this episode with such happiness and affection actually had its beginning in sorrow and distress.

The Gospels tell us about the birth of Jesus, but say nothing about the birth and infancy of Mary. For that, artists had to turn to the ancient and apocryphal text called The Protoevangelium of James. In that document it tells the story of a rich man named Joachim who was a pious Jew. He wanted to give a great offering to the Temple of Jerusalem but was forbidden to do so because he and his wife Anne had produced no offspring, a sign to the Jews of God's disfavor. Joachim was filled with sadness and wandered straight away into the wilderness where he pitched his tent and fasted and prayed for forty days and forty nights. Back at their home, Anne too lamented the situation. Her husband was gone and she shared in his shame. Even her maidservant mocked her saying, "The Lord God has shut up your womb, to give you no fruit in Israel."

But Anne did not wallow in her sadness. She took off her mourning garments, washed her hair and put on her wedding gown. Thus adorned, she wandered into her garden to contemplate and pray. Looking at a laurel tree she saw a nest of sparrows. She looked at her fountain where a school of fish swam about. She looked at the trees laden with fruit. With all these signs of life surrounding her, she pondered how it might be that she could praise the Lord as did all these bountiful wonders of nature.

Then suddenly an angel of the Lord appeared to her and said, "Anne, Anne, the Lord has heard your prayer. You shall conceive and bear, and your offspring shall be spoken of in the whole world." Exulting at this message of divine blessing, Anne promised that whether her child be male or female, she would offer it as a gift to the Lord, to serve him all the days of its life. An angel also appeared to Joachim in the wilderness to announce the good news, whereupon he rejoiced and ordered his herdsmen to gather ten lambs without blemish as an offering to the Lord, twelve calves as an offering to the priests and elders, and a hundred baby goats as a festal sharing with the people. In the meantime, two messengers ran ahead to the city of Jerusalem to announce to Anne that her husband was returning with his flocks. She waited for him at the gate of the city. When she saw him she ran toward him, and embraced him.

And then they kissed.

In Giotto's dramatic rendition of this meeting the robes of the two figures flow together. Joachim extends a protective arm around his wife, and Anne cradles her husband's head in her hands. The kiss fuses their two faces, and at the same time their haloes con-join.

Even though the story continues saying that Joachim then "rested" that first day back home with his wife, the celebrated kiss became an artistic device that would be a symbolic visual attempt to explain the sublime mystery of the Immaculate Conception. It is as if it were a spirit-filled procreative kiss between husband and wife that produced an offspring free from the stain of Original Sin. How Mary was conceived was debated for centuries by theologians. That she was conceived immaculately free from Original Sin by virtue of her destiny to be Christ's mother was proclaimed dogma by Pope Pius IX in the nineteenth century. It had long been a theological concept cherished by the Franciscan Order, with whom Giotto was attached as a lay member.

And why the Golden Gate? The story does not name the city gate at which Anne anxiously awaited her husband. But the Jews have always believed that the Messiah would come to Jerusalem through that entrance known as the Golden Gate. The artist has painted the arch in the color gold. Prophecy and fulfillment are imbedded in the picture. Here the grandmother and grandfather of the Messiah

© G.Dagli Orti - Paris

embrace with marital affection as a party of smiling ladies looks on. Perhaps they are some of Anne's more faithful and sympathetic servants. But the woman in black who wears no smile, who turns away, could she be the servant who ridiculed Anne? Or is she perhaps a figurative omen of their daughter, who will experience much happiness as the mother of the Lord but will also experience many sorrows as the "Mater Dolorosa," a woman whose heart will be pierced with sadness?

Become part
of the growing world-wide
Magnificat family!

IN THE
UNITED STATES

 **ave over $31**
off the cover price

1 year: 14 issues for only $39.95

❏ **YES!** enter my one year subscription
to MAGNIFICAT (14 issues) for only $39.95.
I save 44% off the cover price.

 ave over $72
off the cover price

2 years: 28 issues for only $69.95

❏ **YES!** enter my two year subscription
to MAGNIFICAT (28 issues) for only $69.95.
I save 51% off the cover price.

IN OTHER
COUNTRIES

❏ **YES! enter my one year subscription to MAGNIFICAT
(14 issues) for ....***

INTERNATIONAL RATES:
CANADA: C$69
EUROPE: EURO 56 OR US $59
REST OF THE WORLD: US $64

* Euro payments are accepted from residents of the European Community only.
All others payments must be made in US currency, except Canada.

ORDER CARD

Name: _____

Address: _____

_____

City: _____

State: _____

Zip: _____

Phone number: _____

M E T H O D   O F   P A Y M E N T

❏   Check enclosed   ❏ Please bill me

❏   Visa   or   ❏ Master Card

Card N°: _____

Exp. date: _____

Signature: _____

INTERNET: www.magnificat.net

ADDRESS THIS ORDER CARD AND YOUR PAYMENT TO
MAGNIFICAT
PO BOX 91
SPENCERVILLE MD 20868-9978
Tel.: (301) 853-6600

**Subscription requests received 5 weeks prior
to the first of the month are treated for said month.**

PM 102